AUSSIE
INSULTS

GREAT AUSSIE INSULTS

BILL WANNAN

VIKING O'NEIL

Viking O'Neil
Penguin Books Australia Ltd
487 Maroondah Highway, PO Box 257
Ringwood, Victoria 3134, Australia

First published by John Currey, O'Neil Publishers Pty Ltd 1982
This paperback edition published by Penguin Books Australia Ltd 1987
Copyright © This collection: Bill Wannan, 1982

Produced by Viking O'Neil
56 Claremont Street, South Yarra, Victoria 3141, Australia
A division of Penguin Books Australia Ltd

Designed and set in Australia
Printed and bound in Singapore through Bookbuilders Ltd

National Library of Australia
Cataloguing-in-Publication data

Great Aussie insults.

  Includes index.
  ISBN 0 670 90043 5.

  1. Invective. 2. Australian wit and humour. I. Wannan,
  Bill, 1915-   . II. Title: The great Australian book
  of insults.

A827'.008

FOR THOSE WHO READ PREFACES

An injury, as the Earl of Chesterfield (1694–1773) observed, is much sooner forgotten than an insult; in other words, the hurt we suffer to our persons or property is rarely as long lasting or as deep seated as the hurt to our pride, prestige, credibility or honour. And yet such is the perversity of most of us that we can take pleasure, of a kind, in the insults, ridicule and invective that are hurled at others with whom we are not directly associated. Who has not enjoyed, at some time or other, the kind of literary criticism which leaves an author in shreds—Pope slaying his poetaster contemporaries, and Macaulay hopping into poor old Bowdler, for instance; or A. D. Hope annihilating the young Max Harris; or, for that matter, an older Max Harris himself dismissing a former Victorian Premier, Sir Henry Bolte, with a few contempt-uous sentences? Who has not been secretly delighted, if he is honest with himself, by the indignities of parliamentary abuse, or the kind of cheap but effective vituperation (so often used by Sir Robert Menzies) with which a political candidate has put down an opposition voice at an election meeting? It is not my purpose to explain such attitudes; that is for the psychologist. I merely emphasise the sadistic pleasure principle underlying our feelings towards the abuse suffered by others, especially those of whom we know nothing, or for whom we have little sympathy.

I must qualify this observation, however, by pointing out that the majority of us rationalise our sense of guilt in watching a fellow creature being verbally assaulted. We tend to feel that there is probably some justification for the invective or abuse. It is only when we know with certainty that an innocent person is being subjected to vituperation, or that the author of an insult is a person not to be trusted to speak the truth (John Norton, the newspaper proprietor, here comes to mind), that our sense of justice is likely to be outraged.

The idea of this anthology first suggested itself to me following the publication in the Australian Press many years ago of a defence of a former Prime Minister, John Grey Gorton, by his wife Bettina, against attacks being made on his leadership by Mr Edward St John, then a Liberal Party back-bencher in the House of Representatives. The admirable First Lady used a time-honoured and legitimate defence weapon — versified invective. In this instance she paraphrased some couplets by the English poet, Sir William Watson. This was followed by verse in similar vein, published in the *Australian* (March 27, 1969), exposing Mr Gorton to equally deadly attack. (See Section 3: CONFOUND THEIR POLITICS!) The rare character and flavour of this kind of public invective, nowadays, caused me to look further into the matter of how people — well-known, little-known, and anonymous — in the Australian context, have vented their anger, irritation, spleen, choler, envy, indignation and malice throughout our history. Some of the results of my researches will be found in the pages that follow. They include famous insults and ridicule as well as samplings of invective and abuse that will be unfamiliar to many readers. Most of the examples given will throw, I think, as much (and sometimes more) light on the author of the invective as on the victim.

Perhaps I should make it clear to the reader that as he surveys this field of wounded egos and apparently shattered reputations he is in the presence largely of opinions, and not necessarily of facts or truths. It is important to make this distinction, because, although there's much wisdom in the old adage, 'sticks and stones will break my bones, but names will never hurt me', particularly if one is thick-skinned, nevertheless words can, as Lord Chesterfield noted, often have a superior power to maim or destroy; and words in print tend to have an authority which can easily be equated with truth. Furthermore, the victims paraded in this book have not, in most cases, been given the right of reply. They are spread-eagled like a naturalist's specimens for all to see. It follows, therefore, that the reader should not necessarily be swayed by the opinions expressed before making some inquiries of his own.

Such an anthology as this could easily be expanded beyond tolerable proportions. I have excluded, because of space considerations, some excellent material such as the heated public exchanges between those two rivals whose names are inseparably linked in the Australian consciousness — Hume and Hovell; and I have done no more than touch upon the unpleasant relationship between two other famous explorers, Mitchell and Sturt — the enmity being largely on Mitchell's side. Again, I have omitted some well-known insults (for example, Arthur A. Calwell's 'Two Wongs don't make a white') because I did not feel that they could stand except in their wider contexts. Finally, I have included a considerable number of blasts and broadsides fired at impersonal targets such as warmongering, the clergy, morality, imperialism, foreign migrants, politicians in general, Australian localities and regions, and so on. This kind of invective, because it is not concerned with named individuals, frequently proves less ephemeral in its interest and more serious in its implications than the kind already mentioned.

In most extracts, particularly those from media sources, the original punctuation, and in some cases spelling, have been retained.

I hope that the contents of this book will entertain; and that it will serve as a small reminder that the forts of folly fall not to the battering-rams of brute force but to the thistledown of reason.

Bill Wannan

EDITOR'S NOTE

The Great Australian Book of Insults first appeared in 1973 under the title *With Malice Aforethought*. However, the present edition has been expanded to twice its original size and brought up to date, and is virtually a new book.

I am deeply indebted to Helen Duffy, whose delvings and researches have unearthed a considerable amount of the fresh material and most recent insults assembled for your delectation.

B.W.

CONTENTS

1

ROYALTY REBUKED

Queen Victoria and Some Others

John Norton

ON KING GEORGE IV

Whatever his faults, and they were many, George IV, King of England from 1820 to 1830, scarcely deserved the shower of vitriol which John Norton poured upon his reputation. A master of blistering, alliterative invective, Norton (1858–1916) often over-reached himself in his attempts to expose some alleged villainy. He was especially hostile towards the British monarchy. Norton became a proprietor of Sydney *Truth* and other publications. He was active in the political life of New South Wales.

[George IV] was the biggest blasphemer, the greatest liar, the foulest adulterer, the most infamous swindler and impudent turf blackleg or 'welsher' that the world has ever seen. He was a bigamist, a wife-beater and a madman with prolonged lucid intervals.

A Wordless Insult

NO LOYAL ADDRESS

From Michael Cannon's *Who's Master? Who's Man?* (1971).

The scene was Sydney, 12.30 p.m. on the pleasant spring afternoon of 16 November 1837. The news of Victoria's accession to the throne had reached this remote corner of the world only a few days before. The sheriff, Thomas Macquoid, refused to call together a meeting of colonists in order to send a Loyal Address to Her Majesty. The last time he summoned a public meeting, a mob of 'nut-browns'—the sun-bronzed convicts of England who had completed their sentences in the colony—had attended in a group. When their leader shouted 'Let fly', reported the *Sydney Herald*, many of them broke wind simultaneously 'with a crack as if they came from the spontaneous explosion of three or four hundred bottles of ginger beer', followed by 'such a stench as fairly obliged the Sheriff to vacate the chair'.

John Norton

ON PRINCE ALFRED, DUKE OF EDINBURGH

Alfred Ernest Albert, Duke of Edinburgh (1844–1900), was the second son and fourth child of Queen Victoria. His visit to Australia in 1868–69 was marked by several scandalous and sensational incidents. See Cyril Pearl's biography of 'Orion' Horne, *Always Morning* (1960).

. . . one of the most prurient-minded, lecherous-living, brothel-bilking, tradesmen-tricking rascals that ever ran amok.

.   .   .

He left this colony amid the howls of the harlots whom he bilked and the lamentations of the poor washerwomen whom he had refused to pay for the disagreeable task of washing his doubly dirty linen. Traced and tracked to New Zealand, he was, under threats of detention and legal process, compelled to pay for his dirty living and settle some of his tradesmen's bills.

The Melbourne *Age*

PRINCE ALFRED: 'PLEASURE WITH PARSIMONY'

Quoted by Cyril Pearl in *Always Morning* (1960).

It is no libel to say that the prince is at once fond of pleasure and fond of money . . . If the object of [his voyage to Australia] was to enable the Prince to combine pleasure with parsimony, then never were better means devised for the accompaniment of a purpose.

The Sydney *Bulletin*

MORE BLISS!

The cry of 'Australia for the Australians', and expressions of support for a Republic of Australia, were widely and clearly heard during the 1880s and 1890s. The Sydney *Bulletin* (founded in 1880) and the Sydney *Truth* encouraged the voicing of these senti-

3

ments. Public attacks on Queen Victoria and her family, like those by Henry Lawson, Francis Adams and Victor Daley, were part of this upsurge of republican feeling. It quickly faded away with the inauguration of the Commonwealth of Australia in 1901. From the Sydney *Bulletin* (1886).

> *Her Royal Highness, Princess Beatrice,*
> *has given birth to a son. Her Royal High-*
> *ness and the little Royal Highness are be-*
> *lieved to be doing well.*

Another hungry mouth to feed,
Another hand to clutch the greed;
One little god of clay the more,
For Tory toadies to adore;
Clap your hands and jump for joy —
Beety's got a baby boy!

Never shall the darling soil
Royal hands with honest toil;
Never shall that happy kid
Fairly earn an honest 'quid';
Other hands will skill employ
In keeping Beety's baby boy.

Plentiful as grains of sand
Are princelets in that happy land
Where the starving cry for bread,
Getting but a stone instead;
Troubles such as those annoy
Beety and her baby boy.

Outcasts (whom the Lord forgive!)
Die that better folks may live;
Weary women work and weep
While princes guzzle, gorge, and sleep;
That fact won't the peace destroy
Of Beety and her baby boy.

Blessed thing is noble birth!
Nobler far than simple worth.
Tennyson has changed, you know,
Since he said it wasn't so —
His feeble pen he may employ
To butter Beety's baby boy.

4

Mothers, with your babes at breast,
Read, mark, inwardly digest:
Teach those babes, when older grown,
That this babe's better than your own —
That millions to this life are born
For tens to hold in royal scorn;

Ay, teach your pets to 'know their place',
And lisp 'Your Highness', or 'Your Grace';
Let them pray, poor little dears,
That we may have Colonial Peers.
Meanwhile the tidings sweet enjoy,
That Beety's got a baby boy.

Francis Adams

TO QUEEN VICTORIA IN ENGLAND
(An Address on her Jubilee Year)

Scottish-descended Francis Adams (1862–1893) spent only five years in Australia,
most of them in Queensland; but during that time he published some dozen volumes
of verse, fiction and essays. A Socialist, and a great admirer of Karl Marx, Adams
expressed in his powerful poetry a hatred of the shams and hypocrisy that bedevilled
man's social relationships. His *Poetical Works* (1887) and *Songs of the Army of the Night*
(1888) contain the essence of his radical thought.
   Queen Victoria's Jubilee was celebrated on June 21, 1887.

Madam, you have done well! Let others with praise unholy,
    speech addressed to a woman who never breathed upon
        earth,
daub you over with lies or deafen your ears with folly,
    I will praise you alone for your actual imminent worth.
Madam, you have done well! Fifty years unforgotten
    pass since we saw you first, a maiden simple and pure,
Now when every robber landlord, capitalist rotten,
    hated oppressors, praise you — Madam, we are less sure!
Never once as a foe, open foe, to the popular power,
    as nobler kings and queens, have you faced us, fearless
        and bold.
No, but in backstairs fashion, in the stealthy twilight hour,

you have struggled and struck and stabbed, you have
   bartered and bought and sold!
Melbourne, the listless liar, the gentleman blood-beslavered,
   Disraeli, the faithless priest of a cynical faith out-worn—
these were dear to your heart, these were the men you
   favoured.
   Those whom the People loved were fooled and flouted
   and torn!

Never in one true cause, for your people's sake and the
   light's sake,
   did you strike one honest blow, did you speak one noble
   word.
No, but you took your place, for the sake of wrong and the
   night's sake,
   ever with blear-eyed wealth, with the greasy respectable
   herd.
Not as some robber king, with a resolute minister slave to
   you,
   did you swagger with force against us to satisfy your
   greed.
No, but you hoarded and hid what your loyal people gave
   to you,
   golden sweat of their toil, to keep you a queen indeed!

Pure at least was your bed? Pure your court?—We know not.
   Were the white sepulchres pure? Gather men thorns from
   grapes?
Your sons and your blameless spouse's, *certes*, as Galahads
   show not.
   Round you gather a crowd of bloated hypocrite shapes!
Never, sure, did one woman produce in such sixes and
   dozens
   such intellectual *canaille* as this that springs from you;
sons, daughters, grandchildren, with uncles, aunts and
   cousins,
   not a man or woman among them—a wretched crew!

Good, you were good, we say. You had no wit to be evil.
   Your purity shines serene over Floras mangled and dead.
You wasted not our substance in splendour, in riot or revel—

you quietly sat in the shade and grew fat on our wealth
    instead.
Madam, you have done well! To you, we say, has been given
    a wit past the wit of women, a supercomputable worth.
Of you we can say, if not 'of such are the Kingdom of
        Heaven',
    of such (alas for us!), of such are the Kingdom of Earth!

Henry Lawson

THE ENGLISH QUEEN
A Birthday Ode

Henry Lawson (1867–1922) published a number of anti-monarchial verses. 'The
English Queen' appeared in *Truth* (May 22, 1892), and 'When the Duke of Clarence
Died' was printed in *Truth* (January 31, 1892). Excerpts only are given here. The full
texts will be found in Colin Roderick (Ed.) *Henry Lawson: Collected Verse* (Vol. I,
1967).

There's an ordinary woman whom the English call 'the
        Queen':
They keep her in a palace, and they worship her, I ween;
She's served as one to whom is owed a nation's gratitude;
(May angels keep the sainted sire of her angelic brood!)
The people must be blind, I think, or else they're very green,
To keep that dull old woman whom the English call 'the
        Queen',
    Whom the English call 'the Queen',
    Whom the English call 'the Queen'—
That ordinary woman whom the English call 'the Queen'.

The Queen has reigned for fifty years, for fifty years and
    five,
And scarcely done a kindly turn to anyone alive;
It can be said, and it is said, and it is said in scorn,
That the poor are starved the same as on the day when she
    was born.
Yet she is praised and worshipped more than God has ever
    been—

That ordinary woman whom the English call 'the Queen',
  Whom the English call 'the Queen',
  Whom the English call 'the Queen' —
That cold and selfish woman whom the English call
    'the Queen'.

The Queen has lived for seventy years, for seventy years
    and three;
And few have lived a flatter life, more useless life than she;
She never said a clever thing or wrote a clever line,
She never did a noble deed, in coming times to shine;
And yet we read, and still we read, in every magazine,
The praises of that woman whom the English call 'the Queen',
  Whom the English call 'the Queen',
  Whom the English call 'the Queen' —
That dull and brainless woman whom the English call 'the
    Queen'.

         .   .   .

She lived a 'virtuous life', 'tis true, but then there's nothing in
The useless life of one who ne'er had heart enough to sin.
She's lived a blameless life, they say — she thinks it not a crime
To take her thousands while the poor are starving half the
    time.
And when they blow the final trump, we rather think Faustine
Will stand as good a show as she whom English call 'the
    Queen'.
  Whom the English call 'the Queen',
  Whom the English call 'the Queen' —
That pure and selfish woman whom the English call 'the
    Queen'.

The Prince of Wales is worshipped next (it is a funny thing)
For he will be the loafer whom the fools will call 'the King'.
They keep the children of 'the Queen', and they are not a few;
The children of 'the Queen' and all her children's children
    too.
The little great-grandchild is great because the nation's green
And Grandmama's the person whom the English call 'the
    Queen',

Whom the English call 'the Queen',
Whom the English call 'the Queen' —
The dull, yet gilded dummy whom the English call 'the
    Queen'.

And yearly, on the Queen's birthday they praise her and
    rejoice,
And even far across the sea is heard the toady's voice.
They gammon Christianity, and go to church and pray,
Yet thrust HER in the sight of God, an idol of to-day.
And she is praised and worshipped more than God has ever
    been —
That ordinary woman whom the English call 'the Queen',
Whom the English call 'the Queen',
Whom the English call 'the Queen' —
The selfish, callous woman whom the English call 'the
    Queen'.

Henry Lawson

WHEN THE DUKE OF CLARENCE DIED

Albert Victor, Duke of Clarence (1864–1892) was the eldest son of the Prince of
Wales, later Edward VII.

Let us sing in tear-choked numbers how the Duke of
    Clarence went,
Just to make a royal sorrow rather more pre-eminent.
Ladies sighed and sobbed and drivelled — toadies spoke with
    bated breath,
And the banners floating half-mast made a mockery of death,
And they said Australia sorrowed for the Prince's death —
    they lied!
She had done with kings and princes ere the Duke of
    Clarence died.

.   .   .

Ignoble living — splendid dead! behold the pomp of royal
    woe!
Lo, the funeral! battle-hero never yet was buried so.
Who and what was he? What has he done to benefit mankind?

9

Has he nought to show Saint Peter save a royal race behind?
Who is worthy? Who is noble? God! shall gold alone decide?
Better men like dogs were buried ere the Duke of Clarence
    died.

.   .   .

Thrones of earth and earthly rulers soon shall all be swept
    aside,
And 'twere better for his comfort that the Duke of Clarence
    died.

John Norton

NEMESIS: THE DEATH OF THE DUKE OF CLARENCE

John Norton wrote the following lines in January, 1892. He accused the Duke of
seducing Lydia Marton, a Gaiety girl, who had killed herself three months before.
Quoted by Cyril Pearl in *Wild Men of Sydney* (1958).

[The Duke of Clarence] was nothing better than a mentally
feeble and morally vicious young man whose chief aim in life
seemed to be to bring into fashion an absurdly high collar,
with enormous cuffs to match, which he had invented as a
means of hiding his defects from the vulgar . . .

The lecherous lascivious son of a loose and lustful sire cast his
weak eyes on the sparsely draped chorus girl . . . The blood of
Lydia Marton is on his shrivelled soul and though he makes
his peace with God, hell is its eternal abiding place.

Victor Daley

A TREAT FOR THE LONDON POOR

Although he is probably best-known for several tender lyrics, Victor Daley (1858–1905)
wrote a number of powerful satires and sardonic verses, using the pen-name 'Creeve
Roe'. See Muir Holburn and Marjorie Pizer, *Creeve Roe: Poetry by Victor Daley* (1947).

From St Paul's Cathedral the return journey will be by way of
Cheapside, London Bridge, the Borough, St George's Circus,

Westminster Bridge and back to the Palace. The poorer classes on the south side of the water will thus have an opportunity of seeing their Sovereign and witnessing the day's spectacle.

— Melbourne *Argus*

They will troop in loyal thousands from the putrid purlieus
    where
Foul Disease and Crime and Famine have their pestilential
    lair;
They will crawl from foetid alley, they will creep from
    courts obscene,
When they hear the joyous tidings of the passing of their
    Queen.
    She has reigned — aloft, sublime —
    Sixty years — let joy-bells chime!
And these God-forgotten wretches were her subjects all the
    time!

They are hungry; they are ragged; they are gaunt and
    hollow-eyed;
But their frowsy bosoms palpitate with fine old British pride;
And they'll belt their rags in tighter, and they'll hoarsely cry
    'Hooray!'
When their good Queen's circus passes on Sexagenary Day.
    O the thunder of the drums,
    And the cry of 'Here she comes!'
Will be better than a breakfast to the natives of the slums.

Sixty years their gracious Queen has reigned a-holding up
    the sky,
And a-bringing round the seasons, hot and cold, and wet
    and dry;
And in all that time she's never done a deed deserving
    gaol —
So let joy-bells ring out madly and Delirium prevail!
    Oh her Poor will blessings pour
    On their Queen whom they adore;
When she blinks her puffy eyes at them they'll hunger never
    more.

John Norton

PORTRAIT OF QUEEN VICTORIA

... this flabby, fat, and flatulent looking scion and successor of the most ignoble line of Royal Georges.

John Smith

ON QUEEN VICTORIA

John Smith, a political agitator in Queensland, was jailed for nine months in 1894 for uttering the following words.
See Cyril Pearl, *Wild Men of Sydney* (1958).

Half the workers of Great Britain are starving. At the same time we are paying half a million a year to the sauerkrauted old brute, the Queen. If I had my way, I'd blow her sky-high.

John Norton

ON THE PUBLIC REVERENCE PAID TO ROYALTY

Cyril Pearl, in *Wild Men of Sydney* (1958), points out that in 1896 the statue of Prince Albert (now in Macquarie Street, Sydney) stood in close proximity to that of Queen Victoria in Queen's Square.

[Norton deplored the fact that it was, in the eyes of 'nice' people, a social offence and a political crime] to hesitate to grovel at the foot of the throne, and to refuse to lick the dust off the biggest of the two big toes of the podgy-figured, sulky-faced little German woman whose ugly statue at the top of King Street sagaciously keeps one eye on the Mint while with the other she ogles the still uglier statue of Albert the Good a few paces across the road, in the garb and posture that is suggestive neither of decency in attire, nor decorum in attitude ...

12

John Norton

QUEEN VICTORIA'S BROOD

Her chief claim to the remembrance of posterity will be that she has been the means of afflicting the English people with a most prolific brood of pestiferous German pauper pensioners, who comprise some of the most physically and morally scabby specimens of the human genus extant . . .

John Norton

ON THE FUTURE EDWARD VII

The future King of England is one of the most unmitigated scoundrels and foul-living rascals which the dirty Guelphic breed has produced. He is the chum of card-sharpers and horse jockeys; the consort of ballet-girls and the houris of the demi-monde.

John Norton

ON THE LATE EDWARD VII

The good old chap who has just been buried at Windsor will not be long missed or much mourned . . .

As a King he was not bad; indeed as Kings go, he was the best we ever had, or are likely to get, out of what has been described as 'a darned bad lot'. Personally, Edward was a most pleasing person; but mentally, he was a mediocrity, and morally no better than he ought to have been.

A. D. Hope

THE PLEASURE OF PRINCES

A. D. Hope (1907–) is one of Australia's greatest modern poets. His devastating use of satire 'evokes the spirit of the finest seventeenth and eighteenth century ironists'.

The following satiric verses paint a far from rosy portrait of royalty.
From A. D. Hope, *Collected Poems 1930–1970* (1972).

What pleasures have great princes? These: to know
Themselves reputed mad with pride or power;
To speak few words—few words and short bring low
This ancient house, that city with flame devour;

To make old men, their father's enemies,
Drunk on the vintage of the former age;
To have great painters show their mistresses
Naked to the succeeding time; engage

The cunning of able, treacherous ministers
To serve, despite themselves, the cause they hate,
And leave a prosperous kingdom to their heirs
Nursed by the caterpillars of the state;

To keep their spies in good men's hearts; to read
The malice of the wise, and act betimes;
To hear the Grand Remonstrances of greed,
Led by the pure; cheat justice of her crimes;

To beget worthless sons and, being old,
By starlight climb the battlements, and while
The pacing sentry hugs himself for cold,
Keep vigil like a lover, muse and smile,

And think, to see from the grim castle steep
The midnight city below rejoice and shine:
'There my great demon grumbles in his sleep
And dreams of his destruction, and of mine.'

A. D. Hope

THE KINGS

These satirical verses from Hope's *Collected Poems 1930–1970* (1972) present a portrait
of a parasitic monarchy, a kind of life-devouring sponge.

The lion in deserts royally takes his prey;
Gaunt crags cast back the hunting eagle's scream.
The King of Parasites, delicate, white and blind,

Ruling his world of fable even as they,
Dreams out his greedy and imperious dream
Immortal in the bellies of mankind.

In a rich bath of pre-digested soup,
Warm in the pulsing bowel, safely shut
From the bright ambient horror of sun and air,
His slender segments ripening loop by loop,
Broods the voluptuous monarch of the gut,
The Tapeworm, the prodigious Solitaire.

Alone among the royal beasts of prey
He takes no partner, no imperial mate
Seeks his embrace and bears his clamorous brood;
Within himself, in soft and passionate play,
Two sexes in their vigour celebrate
The raptures of helminthine solitude.

From the barbed crown that hooks him to his host,
The limbless ribbon, fecund, flat and wet,
Sways as the stream's delicious juices move;
And, as the ripe joints rupture and are lost,
Quivers in the prolonged, delirious jet
And spasm of unremitting acts of love.

And Nature no less prodigal in birth
In savage profusion spreads his royal sway:
Herds are his nurseries till the mouths of men,
At public feasts, or the domestic hearth,
Or by the hands of children at their play,
Transmit his line to human flesh again.

The former times, as emblems of an age,
Graved the gier-eagle's pride, the lion's great heart,
Leviathan sporting in the perilous sea;
Pictured on History's or the Muse's page,
All knew the King, the Hero, set apart
To stand up stiff against calamity,

Breed courage amid a broken nation's groans,
Cherish the will in men about to die,
To chasten with just rule a barbarous tribe
And guard, at last, the earth that kept his bones.

And still the Muse, who does not flatter or lie,
Finds for our age a symbol to describe

The secret life of Technocratic Man,
Abject desire, base fear that shape his law,
His idols of the cave, the mart, the sty —
No lion at bay for a beleaguered clan,
No eagle with the serpent in his claw,
Nor dragon soter with his searing eye,

But the great, greedy, parasitic worm,
Sucking the life of nations from within,
Blind and degenerate, snug in excrement.
'Behold your dream!' she says. 'View here the form
And mirror of Time, the Shape you trusted in
While your world crumbled and my heavens were rent.'

David Campbell

THE AUSTRALIAN DREAM

David Campbell (1915–1979) was a writer of fine, lyrical, and more recently, satirical
poetry. The following poem, 'The Australian Dream', although hardly rating as an
insult, does provide the reader with an amusing piece of irreverence which gently
holds royalty up for ridicule. As such it seems worthy of inclusion.
From Chris Wallace-Crabbe (Ed.) *The Golden Apples of the Sun* (1980).

The doorbell buzzed. It was past three o'clock.
The steeple of Saint-Andrew's weathercock
Cried silently to darkness, and my head
Was bronze with claret as I rolled from bed
To ricochet from furniture. Light! Light
Blinded the stairs, the hatstand sprang upright,
I fumbled with the lock, and on the porch
Stood the Royal Family with a wavering torch.
'We hope,' the Queen said, 'we do not intrude.
The pubs were full, most of our subjects rude.
We came before our time. It seems the Queen's
Command brings only, "Tell the dead marines!"
We've come to you.' I must admit I'd half
Expected just this visit. With a laugh
That put them at their ease, I bowed my head.

'Your Majesty is most welcome here,' I said.
'My home is yours. There is a little bed
Downstairs, a boiler-room, might suit the Duke.'
He thanked me gravely for it and he took
Himself off with a wave. 'Then the Queen Mother?
She'd best bed down with you. There is no other
But my wide bed. I'll curl up in a chair.'
The Queen looked thoughtful. She brushed out her hair
And folded up *The Garter* on a pouf.
'Distress was the first commoner, and as proof
That queens bow to the times,' she said, 'we three
Shall share the double bed. Please follow me.'

I waited for the ladies to undress—
A sense of fitness, even in distress,
Is always with me. They had tucked away
Their state robes in the lowboy; gold crowns lay
Upon the bedside tables; ropes of pearls
Lassoed the plastic lampshade; their soft curls
Were spread out on the pillows and they smiled.

'Hop in,' said the Queen Mother. In I piled
Between them to lie like a stick of wood.
I couldn't find a thing to say. My blood
Beat, but like rollers at the ebb of tide.
'I hope your Majesties sleep well,' I lied.
A hand touched mine and the Queen said, 'I am
Most grateful to you, Jock. Please call me Ma'am.'

The *Australian*

THE SILVER JUBILEE OF
QUEEN ELIZABETH II

Australian columnist, Charles Wright, had this to say on the 1977 Silver Jubilee
celebrations in England.
Quoted in Bill Hornadge, *The Australian Slanguage* (1980).

This Silver Jubilee has certainly fired and inspired the
British, as ever a nation of shopkeepers. Having failed to sell
Concorde, they are now flogging the Queen for all she is
worth.

Copyright Ranan Lurie
From the Melbourne *Age* (August 5, 1981)

18

RHUBARB ROYALTY

Max Harris, poet and journalist, espouses the republican cause and makes a virulent attack on the royal wedding (July 29, 1981) in this extract from an article entitled 'Rhubarb Royalty'.
From the *Australian* (July 25, 1981).

The Royal Wedding is an interesting occasion because it has demonstrated that the British hoopla, combined with a desperate media froth-up of the nuptial ceremonials, hasn't worked.

. . . The reason for Australia's interest languishing behind that of Germany, Luxembourg, or Outer Mongolia is partly due to the inevitable de-mythologising of the monarchy.

. . . Charlie Prince projects an image of an untutored RAF mechanic who's been given the job of going around declaring ball-bearing factories open. Lady Di winsomely displays the harmless insipidity of a good pre-kindergarten play supervisor. The magic has assuredly gone out of the royal ménage.

OF PRINCE PHILIP

This comment on the Duke of Edinburgh from Nobel prize winner Patrick White, in his latest book, a self-portrait called *Flaws in the Glass* (1981), was quoted in the Melbourne *Herald* (October 13, 1981).

. . . he more than ever a Glucksburg bully apeing the English in his tweedy hacking jacket.

2

'DREST IN A LITTLE BRIEF AUTHORITY'

Governors, Administrators, and Other Public People

Convict Ballad

ON LAW ENFORCERS

Quoted in Bill Wannan, *The Australian* (1954).

And some dark night when everything
Is silent in the town,
I'll kill the tyrants one and all
And shoot the floggers down.
I'll give the law a little shock—
Remember what I say,
They'll yet regret they sent Jim Jones
In chains to Botany Bay.

Governor Hunter

ON JOHN MACARTHUR

John Macarthur (1767–1834), one of the largest and most powerful landholders in early New South Wales, achieved undying fame as the chief founder of the Australian wool industry. His clashes with the governors of New South Wales in his time, notably the naval governors, Arthur Phillip, John Hunter, Philip Gidley King, William Bligh, became notorious. Macarthur was the master-mind of the New South Wales Corps' insurrection—the Rum Rebellion—against Bligh in 1808.

The following extracts are from a despatch by Governor Hunter to the Duke of Portland, Secretary of State for Home Affairs, in London.

Before I had been long in the country I had cause to remark that scarcely anything short of the full power of the Governor wou'd be consider'd by this person as sufficient for conducting the dutys of his office.

.   .   .

I shall add further, my Lord, that the sacred character of our Savior, were he to appear in this colony in its present state, would not be secure from the dark attack of those whose private views he might oppose in favor of the public interest. There are people here who would most readily prepare for His sacred head another crown of thorns, and erect another cross for His second crucifixion; and none I am persuaded more so than the person of whom I have complained.

22

Governor King

JOHN MACARTHUR: 'THIS PERTURBATOR'

From a despatch by Captain Philip Gidley King to the Colonial Office in London.

If the records of this colony, now in your office, are examined, you will find his name very conspicuous. Many and many instances of his diabolical spirit had shown itself before Gov'r Phillip left this colony, and since, altho' in many instances he has been the master worker of the puppetts he has set in motion. So sensibly wounded were Gov'r Hunter's feelings previous to his leaving this colony that he was obliged to call this perturbator to a private account, which he declined. The injuries Col'l Paterson received from him have been such as to compel him to that resource; and I can assure you, sir, that nothing but the inevitable confusion and ruin the colony would have fallen into by any accident happening to me has prevented my sacrificing duty and the publick welfare to resenting the injuries I have received . . .

If Captain Macarthur returns here in any official character it should be that of Governor, as one half of the colony already belongs to him, and it will not be long before he gets the other half.

Free Settlers' Memorial

JOHN MACARTHUR: 'THE SCOURGE OF THIS COLONY'

In April, 1808, during the period of the Rum Rebellion, a large body of free settlers of New South Wales called on Major George Johnston, who was in charge of the rebel administration, to remove John Macarthur from the post of Secretary of the Colony. Part of their Memorial declared:

We believe that, under colour of discharging the duty of the Office, the said John Macarthur has violated the law, violated public faith, and trampled on the most sacred and constitutional rights of British subjects . . . We believe John Macarthur has been the scourge of this Colony by fomenting quarrels between H.M.'s Officers, Servants and Subjects; his monopoly and extortion have been highly injurious to the Inhabitants of every description.

George Caley

ON GOVERNOR KING: 'I WOULD AS SOON FACE A WILD BEAST AS FACE HIM'

Captain Philip Gidley King (1758–1808) was the third governor of New South Wales, his administration lasting from September 1800 to August 1806. George Caley, whose detraction of the governor follows, was sent to New South Wales by Sir Joseph Banks to collect botanical specimens. The detraction was contained in a letter from Caley to Banks. See J. E. B. Currey's edition of Caley's *Reflections on the Colony of New South Wales* (1966).

Nothing is more tedious than waiting at his door for hours as if one is going to ask for charity. The loss of such time is valuable to me for I value my credit. I assure you I trouble him as little as I can help . . . but to tell you the Truth at once, I would as soon face a wild beast as face him, as then I should be at liberty to repel an attack and which I prefer rather than stand and be jeered and bullied, for such is the treatment I have often met with. The office of a Governor must and ought to be respected, yet I consider such language beneath the dignity of one in such a situation . . .

Sir Thomas Mitchell

GOVERNOR DARLING: 'MY PERSONAL ENEMY'

Sir Ralph Darling (1775–1858) was Lieutenant-Governor of New South Wales from 1825 to 1831. Strictly authoritarian, Darling's regime inspired the antagonism of such noted publicists and liberal reformers as Edward Smith Hall and the young William Charles Wentworth. One cannot but sympathise with Darling, however, in his efforts to cope with the overbearing personality of the explorer and Surveyor-General, Sir Thomas Mitchell. The following is from a letter from Mitchell to R. W. Hay, Permanent Under-Secretary at the Colonial Office, written in March, 1831.

It is impossible to respect a Governor who, conscious of an officer's services and his perseverance in the performance of his duties still would persecute him even to the prejudice of the public service . . . There is no species of injustice worse than that of robbing him, whose chief object is fame, of that reward he seeks by years of unusual exertion in the performance of his duty . . . The Governor at first ill-advised (as I suppose) has at length become my personal enemy.

Governor Gipps

WILLIAM CHARLES WENTWORTH'S 'JOBBERY AND CORRUPTION'

Sometimes referred to as 'The Australian Patriot' and 'The Father of Australian Liberties', William Charles Wentworth (1790–1872) fought to win representative government, trial by jury, and other democratic institutions for the people. In his later years he, as a wealthy landowner, came to represent the forces of conservatism and reaction.

Wentworth's attempt, on behalf of a small syndicate, to purchase the greater part of the South Island of New Zealand from a number of Maori chiefs, for a few hundred pounds, stirred the then Governor of New South Wales, Sir George Gipps, to declare at a meeting of the Legislative Council in Sydney:

Talk of corruption! Talk of jobbery! Why, if all the corruption which has defiled England since the expulsion of the Stuarts were gathered in one heap, it would not make such a sum as this. If all the jobs which have been done since the days of Sir Robert Walpole were collected, they would not equal that one which Mr Wentworth asked me to lend a hand in perpetrating. That is to say: of making him a grant of ten million acres at the rate of one hundred acres for a farthing. The Land Company of New Zealand has been said to be a job: one million acres at eighteenpence an acre; but it vanishes into nothing as compared with that of Mr Wentworth.

Anon

LINES ADDRESSED TO SIR GEORGE GIPPS

Sir George Gipps (1791–1847) was governor of New South Wales from 1838 to 1846. A man of liberal outlook, who instituted a number of land reforms and championed the rights of the Aboriginal people, Gipps incurred the enmity of many of the most powerful landholders. The ensuing diatribe, from the *Atlas*, a Sydney journal of Gipp's time, is quoted in *The Squatting Age in Australia, 1835–1847* (1935) by Stephen Henry Roberts.

Such, oh such, art thou, oh! Gipps!
Never resting, ever toiling,
Ne'er repenting, ever sinning—
Meddling still, and still embroiling,
Fighting oft but never winning.
Ah! the flaws of head and heart,

Making up the thing thou art;
Tinsel reason, boorish wit,
Still to graze but scarce to hit.
Shallow judgement, flippant style,
Artless art and guileless guile,
Which had given thee note and vogue
As a smartish pedagogue,
Or had raised thee from the dark,
As a pettish kind of clerk!

The Sydney *Atlas*

ON THE DEPARTURE OF GOVERNOR GIPPS

On the eve of his departure from Sydney in 1846, Sir George Gipps was assailed by a final burst of invective from his arch-enemies of the *Atlas*:

This day is one likely to be memorable in the annals of New South Wales — for it is the day on which His Excellency Sir George Gipps leaves our shores for ever. After eight long years of despotism and mis-government, the incubus that sat so heavy on us is removed, and we can breathe freely once more. We have often said, and what is more, have often proved, that Sir George Gipps is not only the worst Governor we have ever had, but the worst that could possibly have been selected — and that assertion we now deliberately, but not maliciously, nor sorrowfully, repeat!

Mrs Alexander Maconochie

JOHN MONTAGU: 'THAT SNAKE IN THE GRASS'

John Montagu, related by marriage to Governor Sir George Arthur of Van Diemen's Land, was appointed Colonial Secretary of that colony in 1834, and continued in the post until dismissed by Arthur's successor, Sir John Franklin. The following extract is from a letter written by Mrs Maconochie, wife of Captain Alexander Maconochie of Van Diemen's Land, to Sir George Black. It is quoted by Frances J. Woodward in *Portrait of Jane*, a biography of Lady Jane Franklin (1951).

You will probably meet our deadly enemy Capt. Montagu — that snake in the grass, sleek, smooth, and slippery, a specimen of our Genus homo well worthy of the attention of the naturalist . . . — like many noxious animals he has the power of soothing and fanning his victims to sleep, never attacking openly or boldly . . . But from close and repeated examination, it is found he possesses *invisible* tentacula, which come from many quarters, puncturing, and injuring the victim, gradually destroying and undermining its character . . .

John Montagu

CONCERNING LADY JANE FRANKLIN

A high-spirited, vigorous-minded woman, Lady Jane Franklin tended, perhaps, to be a little too protective of the interests of her husband, Sir John Franklin, Governor of Van Diemen's Land. Sir John, having incurred the enmity of the Colonial Secretary, John Montagu, did what he could to expose the machinations of that subtle and secretive civil servant; and his wife, Lady Jane, proved a powerful ally. Montagu, in a letter to the former Governor, Sir George Arthur, made clear his own fears concerning the lady.

. . . a more troublesome, interfering woman I never saw — puffed up with the love of Fame and the desire of acquiring a name by doing what no one else does and she and Sir John are totally regardless how much public money is spent.

.   .   .

I can never go into Government House again as Mr Montagu — nor can I allow my wife to enter the doors while she remains there.

Lady Jane Franklin

ON CAPTAIN MATTHEW FORSTER
AND HIS PARTY

Captain Matthew Forster was Chief Police Magistrate and head of the Convict Establishment in Van Diemen's Land during the administration of Governor Arthur, and his successor, Governor Franklin. Lady Franklin, in a letter to her sister, Mrs Simpkinson, written at New Norfolk on January 1, 1842, commented disgustedly on one of the principal factions ranged against her husband, Sir John Franklin:

Mr Forster and his party are unworthy of his [Sir John

Franklin's] confidence, are dishonest, base minded, selfish and unfeeling men, without principle, without scruple, and almost without shame, where their personal passions and interests are concerned.

The *Van Diemen's Land Chronicle*

ON SIR JOHN FRANKLIN

The administration of Sir John Franklin (1786–1847), one of the ablest of the Australian governors, who succeeded Sir George Arthur in Van Diemen's Land in January, 1837, lasted until August, 1843. Sir John fell foul of an entrenched colonial bureaucracy, led by the Colonial Secretary, John Montagu. See Kathleen Fitzpatrick, *Sir John Franklin in Tasmania* (1949).

As the Lieutenant-Governor of this Colony, Sir John Franklin has long outlived respect. His policy has been only distinguished by its time-serving expediency.

.   .   .

No man ever made more violent efforts to gain popularity than Sir John Franklin, not only at the expense of the dignity of his station, but at the sacrifice of his publicly proclaimed sentiments. Ever since His Excellency's arrival in this Colony, the government has been made to depend, not as governments are usually made to do — on fixed principles and laws, but upon, first, the desire to conciliate all elements; second, upon caprice and intrigue, and the undermining of every public officer who has not a taste for 'carousels' of tea, muffins and lectures.

Robert Lowe

A SATIRE ON THE GLADSTONE COLONY

Robert Lowe (1811–1892) lived in Australia from 1842 to 1850, being active in journalism and politics. He had a further political career in England, where he entered the House of Commons. He was created Viscount Sherbrooke in 1880. His poems, including a number of satires, were collected in *Poems of a Life* (1885). Lowe's 'A Satire on the Gladstone Colony' is one of two sets of verses on the ignominious attempt by Colonel George Barney to create a new settlement for convict expirees at Port Curtis, on the site where Gladstone, northern Queensland, now stands. W. E.

Gladstone, the Colonial Secretary, instructed that the settlement be established; and in January, 1847, Colonel Barney, in charge of his party of more than eighty intending settlers, left Sydney for that purpose. The steamer carrying the immigrants was grounded on a shoal at Port Curtis. Fearing that the vessel was in danger of capsizing, Barney made sure that his wife and children were safely landed before attending to his other duties. The settlement scheme, which Barney did little to promote, had been ill-conceived; and when the colonel returned to Sydney in May, 1847, he learned that Lord Grey, who had succeeded Gladstone in the post of Colonial Secretary, had ordered that the project be abandoned.

See Brian Elliott and Adrian Mitchell, *Bards in the Wilderness* (1970).

Here Barney landed—memorable spot,
Which Mitchell never from the map shall blot—
Leaving his steamer stranded on a bank,
Regardless if the sailors swam or sank.
Obeying Nature's most esteemed command—
Self-preservation—here did Barney stand.
What did he there? The venerable man!
He came an embryo city's birth to plan;
Wiser than Solomon, when first he traced
Tadmor and Balbec, cities of the waste.
For six long hours he did the search pursue—
For six long hours—and then he thirsty grew;
Back to the rescued steamer did he steer,
Drew the loud cork and quaffed the foaming beer;
Then ate his dinner with tremendous gust
And with champagne relieved his throat adust;
Fished for his brother flatfish from the stern,
And thus, victorious, did to Sydney turn!

Weep not, my Barney! tremble not, my Brown!
Nor dread abatement of your high renown;
What though the Commissariat growl to pay
Your steamer's hire at thirty pounds a day;
What though your city on the northern shore
Remain as much a phantom as before;
Though people ask you for their *quo a quid*,
And say: ''Twas ever thus that Barney did.
Thus did he build a quay beneath the tide—
Thus scoop a basin where no ship can ride—
Thus carry roads on lowlands and o'er highlands—
Thus spoil our harbour—thus blow up our islands.'

Weep not, my friends! Who knows, or who can tell
How well yourselves he served, and us, how well?
Oh! had some fever with its breath of flame
Blighted heroic Barney's stalwart frame;
Or had some savage, ignorant and dull,
Spiked the electric battery of his skull,
Then had our cup of woe indeed been full.
But now, let envy howl, let faction groan,
Yet, Barney! yet we have thee all our own.
Critics may cavil, governors may chafe,
We've lost a thousand pounds—but Barney's safe!

Anon

THE TRAPS

Ditty of the mid-nineteenth century quoted in Bill Wannan, *My Kind of Country* (1967).

Oh, the traps, the dirty traps;
Kick the traps when e'er you're able;
At the traps, the nasty traps;
Kick the traps right under the table.

G. T. W. Boyes

ON GOVERNOR EARDLEY-WILMOT

Sir John Eardley-Wilmot (1783–1847) was Governor of Tasmania from 1843 to 1846. G. T. W. Boyes, Tasmanian Government Auditor, thus summed up his impressions of this governor:

I have never heard such a collection of inconsistencies and unconnected matter rattled through in my life before. He skims the surface of his subject, just picking up the light rubbish swimming on the top. He does not appear to me to have the capacity for going deeper or making himself master of the facts of the case—judgement, prudent reserve, discretion, are qualities to which he seems an utter stranger . . . In short it is hardly possible to imagine a person so utterly disqualified by an absence of all the elements of wisdom for a Governor.

30

The Melbourne *Age*

GOVERNOR SIR CHARLES HOTHAM: 'ACTS OF TYRANNY, TREACHERY'

A contemporary view of Hotham is forthrightly expressed in this extract from a Melbourne *Age* editorial.

We have often thought that Sir Charles Hotham was sent here [to Victoria] by destiny to precipitate the advent of our national independence. At all events, if acts of tyranny, treachery, repudiation and faithlessness, on the part of a ruler have any tendency to make people disloyal and rebellious, his Excellency is taking the most effectual plan to cut short his own career, and attain the distinction of being the last Downing Street Governor whose presence cursed the colony of Victoria . . .

In character, and even in physiognomy, Sir Charles Hotham finds his prototype in Charles I; and he seems disposed to repeat here the policy which brought that wretched monarch to the scaffold.

Charles Thatcher

THE PRIVATE DESPATCH OF CAPTAIN BUMBLE
of the 40th, stationed at Ballarat, to His Excellency Sir Charles Hotham

Charles Thatcher (1831–1878), the self-styled 'Colonial Minstrel', composed and sang many topical songs concerned with the life of Victorian goldfields during the 1850s and early 1860s. These were mostly sardonic ditties and appealed to the prospectors and diggers who heard them sung by Thatcher in Bendigo or Ballarat. One of the best is certainly 'The Private Despatch of Captain Bumble', a send-up of the 'gallant' officers who, on Governor Sir Charles Hotham's instructions, led their soldiers against rebellious diggers at Ballarat in December, 1854.

Tune—Jeremiah

Don't talk about Sebastopol,
    The Russian war is flat now;
Just listen to despatches
    Just come from Ballarat, now.

Our noble Governor, Sir Charles,
　　And where is there a better,
Has permitted us to publish
　　Captain Bumble's private letter.

He writes thus to His Excellency:
　　'Myself and Major Stiggins
Got our brave fellows all equipped
　　And started for the diggins.
Our band struck up God Save the Queen,
　　Into cheers our men were bursting,
And every gallant soldier was
　　For glorious action thirsting.

'Our first attack was on two drays,
　　Which we saw in the distance,
But the enemy surrendered
　　After just a slight resistance.
We were disappointed in our search
　　Of these two wretched traitors,
For instead of seizing powder
　　It was loaded with potatoes.

'We marched but were obliged to halt
　　On behalf of Sergeant Trunnions,
Who was unable to proceed
　　On account of having bunions;
We stationed pickets all around
　　To give us timely warning,
And there we bivouacked and slept
　　Till nine the following morning.

'At length into the diggings
　　Footsore our men did tramp there,
And we took up our position
　　Within the Government Camp there.
Provisions were served out to all,
　　And my very soul it tickles
To contemplate their charges
　　On the cold boiled beef and pickles.

'We watched at night, but all was still;
    For glory we were yearning,
And we fired upon a tent in which
    A candle was seen burning.
We killed a woman and a child,
    Though 'twas not our intention:
But that slight mistakes sometimes occur
    Of course I needn't mention.

'At length in earnest was the strife;
    While buried in their slumbers,
We made a bold and desperate charge
    And cut them down in numbers.
Our gallant fellows fought like bricks,
    The rebels were defeated,
And then by hundreds off they ran
    And to the bush retreated.

'Thus all is quiet, and I now
    Subscribe myself your humble,
Devoted servant of the Crown,
    Frederick Augustus Bumble.'

Postscript
'Pray send us up some good cheroots,
    And anything that's handy,
And by all means, pray don't forget
    We're nearly out of brandy.'

Anon

JOHN GILBERT (BUSHRANGER)

The notorious accomplice of the outlaw Ben Hall, Johnny Gilbert, is the subject of
this parody of 'John Gilpin'. The parodist's aim was to draw attention to the ineptness
of parliament and police in New South Wales, in the early 1860s, in their measures to
capture Gilbert and his bushranger associates. From A. B. Paterson's collection, *Old
Bush Songs* (1905).

Air: Four and Twenty Blackbirds

John Gilbert was a bushranger of terrible renown,
For sticking lots of people up and shooting others down.

33

John Gilbert said unto his pals, 'Although they make a bobbery
About our tricks, we've never done a tip-top thing in robbery.

'We have all of us a fancy for experiments in pillage,
Yet never have we seized a town, or even sacked a village.'
John Gilbert said unto his mates, 'Though partners we have been
In all rascality, yet we no festal day have seen.'

John Gilbert said he thought he saw no obstacle to hinder a
Piratical descent upon the town of Canowindra.
So into Canowindra rode Gilbert and his men,
And all the Canowindra folk subsided there and then.

The Canowindra populace cried 'Here's a lot of strangers!!!'
But immediately recovered when they found they were bushrangers.
And Johnny Gilbert said to them, 'You need not be afraid:
We are only old companions whom bushrangers you have made.'

And Johnny Gilbert said, said he, 'We never hurt a hair
Of men who bravely recognize that we are just all there.'
The New South Welshmen said at once, not making any fuss,
That Johnny Gilbert, after all, was 'just but one of us.'

So Johnny Gilbert took the town (including public houses),
And treated all the 'cockatoos' and shouted for their spouses.
And Miss O'Flanagan performed in manner quite gintailly
Upon the grand pianner for the bushranger O'Meally.

And every stranger passing by they took, and when they got him
They robbed him of his money and occasionally shot him.
And Johnny's enigmatic feat admits of this solution,
That bushranging in New South Wales is a favoured institution.

So Johnny Gilbert ne'er allows an anxious thought to fetch him,
For well he knows the Government don't really want to ketch him;

And if such practices should be to New South Welshmen
    dear,
With not the least demurring word ought we to interfere.

Ned Kelly

ON SUPERINTENDENT BROOK SMITH

There's bush humour of a sardonic kind in outlaw Kelly's contemptuous reference to
Brook Smith, a superintendent in the Victoria Police, in the letter Ned dictated at
Jerilderie (NSW) during the Kelly gang's visit there in 1879. In this excerpt, and in
those following, the original spelling and punctuation have been retained.

I would like to know who put that article that reminds me of
a poodle dog half clipped in the lion fashion, called Brook
E. Smith, Superintendent of Police he knows as much about
commanding Police as Captain Standish [the Victorian Police
Commissioner] does about mustering mosquitoes and boiling
them down for their fat on the back blocks of the Lachlan.

Ned Kelly

THE VICTORIA POLICE:
'A PARCEL OF ARMED CURS'

From the outlaw Ned Kelly's so-called 'Jerilderie Letter', 1879.

The Queen must surely be proud of such heroic men as the
Police and Irish soldiers as It takes eight or eleven of the
biggest mud crushers in Melbourne to take one poor little
half starved larrakin to a watchhouse. I have seen as many as
eleven, big and ugly enough to lift Mount Macedon out of a
crab hole more like the species of a baboon or Guerilla than
a man actually come into a court house and swear they could
not arrest one eight stone larrakin and then armed with
battens and niddies without some civilians assistance and
some of them going to the hospital from the effects of hits
from the fists of the larrakin and the Magistrate would send
the poor little larrakin into a dungeon for being a better man
than such a parcel of armed curs.

Ned Kelly

MORE ON THE VICTORIA POLICE

Also from the 'Jerilderie Letter'.

I have been wronged and my mother and four or five men
lagged innocent and is my brothers and sisters and my
mother not to be pitied also who has no alternative only to
put up with the brutal and cowardly conduct of a parcel of
big ugly fat-necked wombat headed big bellied magpie
legged narrow hipped splay-footed sons of Irish Bailiffs or
english landlords which is better known as officers of Justice
or Victorian Police who some calls honest gentlemen but I
would know what business an honest man would have in the
Police as it is an old saying it takes a rogue to catch a rogue
and a man that knows nothing about roguery would never
enter the force.

Francis Adams

DUBLIN AT DAWN

In 'Dublin at Dawn' Francis Adams scathingly summed up his feelings about British
policy in Ireland, at the time of the Phoenix Park murders in Dublin. Lord Frederick
Cavendish, Chief Secretary for Ireland, and Thomas Henry Burke, Under-Secretary
for Ireland, were assassinated by members of an Irish secret society in Phoenix Park
on May 6, 1882.

In the chill grey summer dawn-light
   we pass through the empty streets;
the rattling wheels are all silent;
   no friend his fellow greets.

Here and there, at the corners,
   a man in a great-coat stands;
a bayonet hangs by his side, and
   a rifle is in his hands.

This is a conquered city;
   it speaks of war not peace;
and that's one of the English soldiers
   the English call 'police'.

You see, at the present moment
    that noble country of mine   [England]
is boiling with indignation
    at the memory of a 'crime'.

In a part of the Phoenix Park where
    the children romped and ran,
an Irish ruffian met his doom,
    and an English gentleman.

For a hundred and over a hundred
    years on the country side
men and women and children
    have slaved and starved and died,

that those who slaved and starved them
    might spend their earnings then,
and the Irish ruffians have a 'good time',
    and the English gentlemen.

And that's why at the present moment
    that noble country of mine
is boiling with indignation
    at the memory of a 'crime'.

For the Irish ruffians (they tell me),
    and it looks as if 'twere true,
and the English gentlemen are so scarce
    we could not spare those two!

And that's why the Irish love us,
    and there is not war but peace—
And that's one of the English soldiers,
    the English call 'police'.

George Higinbotham
ON LORD LYVEDEN

Judge Higinbotham (1826–1892), who became Chief Justice of Victoria in 1886, was in all ways a remarkable man. Randolph Bedford eulogised his greatness in that readable book, *Naught to Thirty-three* (1944). Higinbotham's wit is evidenced by this comment on Lord Lyveden, quoted by Vance Palmer in *National Portraits* (1940):

Lord Lyveden is a new nobleman. He formerly, under the name of Mr Vernon Smith—which, it is believed, he very painfully endured—was Under-Secretary of State for the Colonies. I remember it was said to be the ambition of Mr Vernon Smith to change his patronymic. I believe that any person who has either seen or heard Mr Vernon Smith will not be curious to learn the opinion of Lord Lyveden on any subject of human interest.

Paris Nesbitt, Q.C.

ON GOVERNOR SIR ARCHIBALD WEIGALL
AND
PREMIER MR BARWELL

Keith Dunstan, in *Sports* (1973), describes the vigorous campaign carried out by Paris Nesbitt, Q.C., against coursing with live hares, which reached a peak of popularity during the 1880s. Nesbitt's wrath was aimed at the Governor of South Australia, Sir Archibald Weigall, who was 'a man of little intrinsic interest or importance' and the Premier, Mr Barwell, who was 'a man of pitiable insignificance'.

[Governor Sir Archibald Weigall was] the man who was not man enough to promise not to attend any more coursing matches.

.   .   .   .

I am told by one who has been to a coursing match that the attendance comprises the very dregs and scum of the community; bookmakers, Governors, members of Parliament, and the like.

The Sydney *Bulletin*

'A NICE LOT OF CHUCKLE-HEADS'

From the Sydney *Bulletin* (1889).

A nice lot of chuckle-heads are getting into the Victorian police. At Box Hill (Melb.), last week two active and intelligent officers were called to a boarding-house where one of the lodgers had been threatening mischief with a revolver. They found the lodger lying on his bed with a revolver in his hand, and came to the official conclusion that he was sleeping it off, yer Honor. They shook the lodger up a bit, and told him to come out of that; but the stupid fellow lay there on the bed, just like a log of wood. Then they hoisted him into a chair, and Constable Jones put the handcuffs on. 'Walk down to the police-station like a man,' said the mimbers av the foorce. But the lodger neither spoke nor moved, so they put him on a stretcher and carried him down to the police-station. Not a limb had the lodger stirred. 'He must be bastly dronk,' says the foorce. About this time the proprietor of the boarding-house arrived, and kept on trying to wake up the prisoner, until it appeared that he was getting rather cold and stiff. The poor fellow was dead, in point of fact. There were a few bullets in his body, and he had been as dead as Lazarus all the time. Then they took the handcuffs off the corpse and laid it out, and thought they never knew such a bad case of insulting behaviour.

John Norton

OF ALDERMAN WATERHOUSE

From Cyril Pearl, *Wild Men of Sydney* (1958).

I invented the word [wowser] myself . . . I first gave it public utterance in the City Council [in 1899], when I applied it to Alderman Waterhouse, whom I referred to as the white, woolly, weary, watery, word-wasting wowser from Waverley.

John Norton

ON GOVERNOR-GENERAL THE EARL OF DUDLEY AND OTHERS

John Norton wrote scathingly on the alleged adultery of the Earl of Dudley, who was Governor-General from 1908 to 1911.
Quoted in Cyril Pearl, *Wild Men of Sydney* (1958).

The capitals are clamant with circumstantial charges of your alleged concupiscent capers.

... When Sir Charles Augustus Fitzroy was here as 'Governor-General of all H.M. Possessions' ... he comported himself in pretty much the same pornic fashion as you are alleged to have been doing of late ... He was a lecher, a 'roué', a drunkard—a veritable bipedal pig, fit only to habit with pigs in the sty.

... Then too there was Governor Carrington, 'Champagne Charlie' ... under [his] regime, Government House in Sydney became a rendezvous for the demi-mondaine and demi-reps—a kind of assignation house ...

Governor-General Sir William Slim

SIR WILLIAM SLIM VERSUS HOTEL DRINKERS

Sir William Slim was Governor-General from 1953 to 1959.
Quoted from Fred Daly, *From Curtin to Kerr* (1977).

When Sir William went into a hotel bar in North Queensland he addressed a drinker who had not shaved for some days and was fat and bloated with more paunch outside his trousers than inside. Slim said he knew he had made a mistake the minute he spoke to him. Slim said, 'Good day, will you have a drink?' The drinker replied, 'Ain't you Slim, the Governor-General? Well, I don't hold with your mob.' 'Well,' said Slim, 'having a good look at you I don't hold with you either. Have a drink.'

.   .   .

On another occasion Slim walked into a hotel with his numerous medals prominently displayed on his expansive chest. A drinker looked at him and said, 'Jesus Christ!' 'No,' he replied, 'Slim, Governor-General.'

Randolph Stow

THE UTOPIA OF LORD MAYOR HOWARD

Randolph Stow (1935–   ) is a poet and novelist from Western Australia.

From Douglas Stewart (Ed.) *Poetry in Australia* (Vol. II, Modern Australian Verse, 1964).

Lord Mayor Howard . . . said that the trees on the corner had grown so tall that they had lost their attraction. Neat rose gardens would be much more attractive.

—The *West Australian*

His delicate fingers, moving among the roses,
became a symbol. His words, a battle-cry.
'Nothing shall be taller than Lord Mayor Howard
but insurance buildings.'

A fanatical army, wild with Cromwellian zeal,
laid waste Kings Park, denuded Darlington.
Guerillas of Pemberton fried alive in their forests,
as mile on mile, that the giant unattractive karri
had once encumbered, fell thrall to triumphant Peace.

And not Peace alone, but also Dame Edith Helen,
Comtesse Vandal, and even a brand new strain:
Mrs Lord Mayor Howard.

Only you and I, my subversive and admirable brethren,
did not join in the celebrations. A malicious rumour
that some of us had been seen to spit on roses
obliged us to fly the land.

On Kerguelen, New Amsterdam, and such friendly islands
pitching our tents, and on each one planting one karri,
under the name of Yggdrasil we worshipped them.
—Tenderly, humbly, as became the last plants on earth
that were taller than Lord Mayor Howard.

And although the news of our ruthless persecution
of every breed of rose caused shudders in Guildford,
and although our faith, known as anti-Rosaceanism,
was condemned in the United Nations and *The Times*,

the remembrance of our trees so sighs in their sleep
that the immigrants have been more than we can handle.
And in truth, we half expect to see Lord Mayor Howard.

41

Sir Robert Menzies

ON BUREAUCRATS

A comment made by Sir Robert in 1946 and quoted in Ray Robinson, *The Wit of Sir Robert Menzies* (1966).

One thing about bureaucrats is that they never swallow their young. Leave them alone and you'll find them increasing every year.

Sir Robert Menzies

ON EXPERTS

From Ray Robinson, *The Wit of Sir Robert Menzies* (1966).

Expert advice is the very devil. You want at least 100 experts, then conduct a Gallup Poll among them—then think out the answer for yourself.

Anon

COPPERS

Melbourne school-yard rhyme from the 1970s.
From *Cinderella Dressed in Yella* (1978) and quoted in Bill Hornadge, *The Australian Slanguage* (1980).

We hate you coppers
Oh yes we do,
We hate you coppers
And that is true,
When you're near us
We spew,
Oh coppers, we hate you.

Colin Thiele

BIRD IN THE CLASSROOM

Colin Thiele, born in South Australia in 1920, is a poet and novelist who has done

much writing for radio and television. His teaching experiences undoubtedly evoked the following lines on the boring schoolmaster.
From C. Copeman, J. Gibson, D. Murdoch (Eds.) *As Large As Alone* (1971).

The students drowsed and drowned
In the teacher's ponderous monotone—
Limp bodies looping in the wordy heat,
Melted and run together, desks and flesh as one,
Swooning and swimming in a sea of drone.

Each one asleep, swayed and vaguely drifted
With lidding eyes and lolling, weighted heads,
Was caught on heavy waves and dimly lifted,
Sunk slowly, ears ringing, in the syrup of his sound,
Or borne from the room on a heaving wilderness of beds.

And then, on a sudden, a bird's cool voice
Punched out song. Crisp and spare
On the startled air,
Beak-beamed
or idly tossed,
Each note gleamed
Like a bead of frost.

A bird's cool voice from a neighbour tree
With five clear calls—mere grains of sound
Rare and neat
Repeated twice . . .
But they sprang the heat
Like drops of ice.

Ears cocked, before the comment ran
Fading and chuckling where a wattle stirred,
The students wondered how they could have heard
Such dreary monotones from man,
Such wisdom from a bird.

Vincent Buckley

SECRET POLICEMAN

Born in Victoria in 1925, Professor Vincent Buckley is currently with the English Department at Melbourne University.

43

From Frank Ritchie (Ed.) *Ends and Beginnings* (1972).

Pledge me: I had the hangman for a father
And for my mother the immortal state;
My playground was the yard beside the lime-pit,
My play-songs the after-cries of hate.

Admire me: I fill these shining boots,
I am soul expanded to a uniform:
A hired world glitters at my senses,
The smell of blood keeps my blood-stream warm.

Pity me: from a world ruddy with flame
I am tugged in dreams to the first cave again,
And in that humid soil and atmosphere
Lie down each night beside the murdered men.

The dead eyes point the way I go,
The dead hands presage me in air.
I run on shifting pavements, by fired walls
Falling, and weighted lamp-posts everywhere.

Sir Paul Hasluck

OF DEVELOPMENT 'EXPERTS'

This observation by the then Governor-General of Australia, Sir Paul Hasluck, was quoted in the Melbourne *Age* (May 22, 1973).

They sit around, in what some people call a think tank, opening their mouths at each other like goldfish and being just about as useful.

THE WRITING ON THE WALL

This slogan was painted in large white letters on the brick wall of a Melbourne railway viaduct in late 1975. Sir John Kerr, Governor-General in 1975, wrote his name into history when he sacked the Whitlam Labor Government. Ron Barassi is famous in Melbourne as a footballer who became the ardent, very one-eyed coach of the North Melbourne team.

HAVING SIR JOHN KERR FOR GOVERNOR-GENERAL IS LIKE HAVING RON BARASSI FOR UMPIRE

From *A Decade of Pickering* (1980)

Patrick White

OF SIR JOHN KERR

Australian author, Patrick White, made this comment on Sir John Kerr in a book
Flaws in the Glass (1981).
See the Melbourne *Herald* (October 13, 1981) and the Melbourne *Age* (October 17,
1981).

The Governor-General struck me as being harmless enough:
an amiable, rorty, old, farting Falstaff . . . When I first met
him he was already a florid figure whose suits had difficulty
in containing him, his hair white and fluffy like a wig in one
of those amateur productions of *The Rivals*.

    . . . as time passed and history unfolded, I was made more
conscious of the voice: it had a tinny, common edge.

Lee Knowles

BAILIFF

Lee Knowles is a Western Australian poet. The verse quoted is an extract only from
his poem 'Bailiff'.
See A. Choate, B. Y. York (Eds.) *Summerland* (1979).

Bailiffs have ears down to their knees,
the print of their hands is a rubber stamp,
they devour money jars, furniture, children.
Their knocking is heavily rehearsed.

Noel Hawken

PLEBEIAN PLANNERS

From an article, 'The sorry saga of *Vault*', in the Melbourne *Herald* (July 22, 1981).

Melbourne decided to have a nice plaza. Year after year the
project was no more than a series of greedy-to-moronic
bungles. Then a design was accepted. It was hailed en masse
by people who spent not a moment in wondering how the
devil it would look and operate when finished.

    The massively costly concept was pushed ahead on the
say-so of councillors whose qualifications for such decisions
could be written on the point, let alone the head, of a pin.

John Ford

OF CIVIL SERVANTS

Author John Ford's words were quoted in the Melbourne *Age* (August 22, 1981).

The civil servant's idea of a perfect world is where the Minister okays everything that passes across his desk. They regard Canberra as a ship's engine room where they are the engineers.

Bumper Sticker

PUBLIC SERVANTS

Quoted in the *Herald* (August 28, 1981).

Sleep with a public servant — he needs the exercise.

Professor Chipman

MANY STATE TEACHERS FAILURES

Professor Lauchlan Chipman, professor of philosophy at the University of Wollongong, severely attacked teachers' training, their educational standards and philosophies, when he spoke at a Melbourne conference of educational administrators on September 3, 1981.
Quoted in the Melbourne *Age* (September 4, 1981).

Australia's State schools are filled with teachers from the bottom of the barrel . . . [There has been] mass hiring of educational failures . . . It is difficult to exaggerate just how bad some of these teachers are. Many are incapable of spontaneously generating a grammatically well-formed sentence . . .

Secondary school teachers, especially in Government schools, represent most of the worst, and few of the best, of the output of the universities.

Often being nearer university failures themselves — indeed, in some cases they graduated from colleges of advanced education because they were not good enough to enter any of the universities to which their pupils aspire — they have

47

an impudent contempt for the most successful.

Fact, discipline, academic, structure, form and even learn are negative words, while approach, discover, feel, experience, impression and change are words of approbation.

The very idea that there are facts worth knowing (other than facts about the rape of our resources by multi-nationals and greedy businessmen, and the dependence of our corrupt economy upon the exploitation of working-class women, Aborigines and migrants) is regarded with scorn.

. . . Infantile philosophical nihilism smugly affirmed by philosophically illiterate teachers spreads like wildfire in the bureaucratically frustrated and classically alienated giant State teaching services.

Bill Hayden

ON THE GOVERNOR-GENERAL

Quoted in the Melbourne *Age* (November 14, 1981).

The Governor-General should be put in his proper place—as a ceremonial figure on leave from *The Merry Widow*.

3

'CONFOUND THEIR POLITICS!'

Politicians, Parties, Parliament

Charles Harpur

ON WILLIAM CHARLES WENTWORTH

The contrast between William Charles Wentworth's liberal and reformist political attitudes as a young man, when he and Robert Wardell established the influential newspaper, the *Australian*, and his reactionary role as the mouthpiece of the great landowners in his later political life, struck many of his contemporaries as an indication of the depth of his betrayal of the popular cause. One of those who deplored this 'apostasy' was Charles Harpur (1813–1868), a poet of radical views with a pronounced aptitude for satire. The first of the two verses here offered is from a long satirical work by Harpur, 'The Temple of Infamy'; the latter was one of a series of *Sonnets Dedicated to Senators* appearing in the Sydney *Weekly Register* during 1845. See J. Normington-Rawling's *Charles Harpur* (1962).

His state is that, so infamously sad,
When Talent hath through selfishness run mad.
In his well-masked displays of by-gone years,
With democratic wrath he tore the ears
Of Sydney's groundlings, being then
Thwarted and snubbed by Darling's party-men!
But now behold him in his native hue,
The bullying, bellowing champion of the Few!
Patriot!—he who hath nor sense nor heed
Of public ends beyond his *own* mere need!
Whose country's ruin, to his public fear,
Means only this—the loss of Windermere!

Charles Harpur

IS WENTWORTH A PATRIOT?

A patriot is one who has no aims
    Dividual from the Public Good! whose heart
    Is of his country's a fraternal part!
Whose interest on that country's altar flames!
A Patriot is one who has no Self,
    Dividual from his people!—tell me then,
    Is Wentworth such, amongst Australia's men?
Where's Hampden's wisdom, Marvell's scorn of pelf?
What though a Faction's magnates, when they're mellow,
    Trumpet him forth—'a Patriot!' What, though all

The 'brandy-faced', when they behold him, bellow
'A Patriot!' Yet, however loud he bawl
About his country, 'twere as fit to call
Maize dumpling gold, because forsooth—'tis yellow.

Charles Harpur

ON SIR CHARLES COWPER

Sir Charles Cowper (1807–1875) was prominent in the politics of New South Wales, forming five Ministries during the period from 1856 to 1870. Political opponents nicknamed him 'Slippery Charlie'.

. . . when flies shall have sufficient ken
To comprehend a mountain's magnitude,
Thou shalt be fit to legislate for men
As well as sheep—but, Cowper, not till then.

Alfred Deakin

ON SIR HENRY PARKES

Sir Henry Parkes (1815–1896), an artisan emigrant from England, was in the forefront of many democratic struggles, following his arrival in Australia in 1839. Five times Premier of New South Wales, he was an ardent advocate of the federation of the Australian colonies. Alfred Deakin, elected to the Victorian Parliament in 1879, when only twenty-two years of age, also fought for the federation of Australia; and he became the second Prime Minister of the Commonwealth.

He had always in his mind's eye his own portrait as that of a great man, and constantly adjusted himself to it.

Sir Henry Parkes

TO G. D. CLARK

G. D. Clark was Member for Balmain in the New South Wales Legislative Assembly, in the early 1890s. Parkes, whose aspirates were always a problem to him, addressed himself thus to Clark during a debate in the Assembly:

Ho, the honourable member for Balmain, who for once—and, of course, quite by haccident—has made a sensible hob-servation.

John Haynes

ON NINIAN MELVILLE

Ninian Melville, son of an undertaker, and himself an undertaker by trade, became the Member for Northumberland in the New South Wales Legislative Assembly during the 1880s. The following anecdote is given in E. H. Collis's *Lost Years* (1948).

In 1891 rumours became rife that Ninian Melville was to be made either Minister for Lands or Minister for Mines in the Cabinet which Premier Dibbs was then in the process of forming. At the time, John Haynes, who had been co-founder with J. F. Archibald of the Sydney *Bulletin* and was now the Member for Mudgee, was violently opposed to Melville's political views and contemptuous of his parliamentary standing. Rising in the Assembly, Haynes said scornfully: 'What nonsense is it to talk of making the honourable member for Northumberland the Minister for Mines! He may be a good Chairman of Committees, but what on earth does he know about mining? The only shaft he ever sank was a dead man's grave. The only gold he ever took was from a dead man's mouth. It would be ridiculous to make him Minister for Mines. On the other hand, he might do as Minister for Lands, because he has probably settled more people on the land than any other member of the House.'

Henry Kendall

THE SONG OF NINIAN MELVILLE

In this savage satire, first published in 1880, Henry Kendall (1839–1882) attempted to pour ridicule on the career of Ninian Melville, who entered the New South Wales Legislative Assembly in the year in which Kendall's verse was written. Before entering politics Melville had worked in his father's undertaking business.

Sing the song of noisy Ninny—hang the Muses—spit it out!
(Tuneful Nine ye needn't help me—poet knows his way
     about!)
Sling me here a penny whistle—look alive, and let me slip
Into Ninny like a father—Ninny with the nimble lip.
Mister Melville, straight descendant from Professor
     Huxley's ape,

Started life as mute for daddy—pulling faces, sporting
   crape;
But, alas, he didn't like it—lots of work and little pay!
Nature whispered, 'You're a windbag—play your cards
   another way.'

Mister Melville picked the hint up—pitched the coffin 'biz'
   to pot:
Paid his bills, or didn't pay them—doesn't matter now a
   jot!—
Twigging how the bread was buttered, he commenced a
   'waiting game';
Pulled the strings upon the quiet—no one 'tumbled' to his
   aim.
Paine, he purchased, Strauss, he borrowed—read a page or
   two of each:
Posed before his father's porkers—made to them his maiden
   speech.
Then he spluttered, '*Ninny has it*! Nin will keep himself in
   clothes,
Like that gutter Tully, Bradlaugh, leading noodles by the
   nose!'

In the fly-blown village pothouse, where a dribbling bag of
   beer
Passes for a human being, Nin commenced his new career—
Talked about the 'Christian swindle'—cut the Bible into
   bits—
Shook his fist at Mark and Matthew—gave the twelve
   Apostles fits:
Slipped into the priests and parsons—hammered at the
   British Court—
Boozy boobies were astonished: lubbers of the Lambton sort!
Yards of ear were cocked to listen—yards of mouth began to
   shout,
'*Here's a cove as is long-headed—Ninny knows his way about!*'

Mister Melville was delighted—game in hand was paying
   well!
Fools and coin don't hang together—Nin became a howling
   swell!

Took to 'stumping' on the Racecourse—cut the old debating
    club:
Wouldn't do for mighty Ninny now to mount a local tub!
Thornton's Column was his platform: here our orator began
Hitting at the yellow heathen—cracking up the 'working
    man'—
Spitting out at Immigration: roaring, like a worried bull,
At the lucre made on tallow—at the profit raised on wool!

Said our Ninny to our Ninny, 'I have not the slightest doubt
Soaping down the "'orny-'anded" is the safest "bizness" out!
Little work for spanking wages—this is just the thing they
    like,
So I'll prop the eight hours swindle—be the boss in every
    strike.
In the end, I'll pull a pot off—what I'm at is bound to take:
Ninny sees a bit before him—Ninny's eyes are wide-awake!
When the boobies make me member, Parkes, of course, will
    offer tip—
I will take the first fat billet—then my frouzy friends may
    rip!'

So it came to pass that Melville—*Mister* Melville, I should
    say—
Dodged about with deputations, half a dozen times a day!
Started strikes and bossed the strikers—damned employers,
    every one,
On the Column—off the Column—in the shanty—in the
    sun!
'Down with masters—up with wages! keep the "pigtail" out
    of this!'
This is what our Ninny shouted—game, you see, of hit or
    miss!
World, of course, is full of noodles—some who bray at
    Wallsend sent
Thing we know to be a windbag bounding into Parliament!
Common story, this of Ninny! many fellows of his breed
Prowl about to bone the guinea, up to dirty tricks indeed!
Haven't now the time to tan them; but, by Jove, I'd like to
    tan

Back of that immense impostor that they call the 'working
    man'!
Drag upon our just employers—sponger on a worn-out
    wife—
Boozing in some alley pothouse every evening of his life!
Type he is of Nin's supporters: tot him up and tot him down,
He would back old Nick tomorrow for the sake of half a
    crown!

House with high, august traditions—Chamber where the
    voice of Lowe,
And the lordly words of Wentworth sounded thirty years
    ago—
Halls familiar to our fathers, where, in days exalted, rang
All the tones of all the feeling which ennobled Bland and
    Lang—
We in ashes—we in sackcloth, sorrow for the insult cast
By a crowd of bitter boobies on the grandeur of your past!
Take again your penny whistle—boy, it is no good to me:
Last invention is a bladder with the title of M.P.!

Brunton Stephens

THE GENTLE ANARCHIST

One stanza only of Brunton Stephens's 'The Gentle Anarchist' is given here. From
Selected Poems of Brunton Stephens (1925).

    I am a gentle Anarchist,
        I couldn't kick a dog,
    Nor ever would for sport assist
        To pelt the helpless frog.
    I'd shoot a czar, or wreck a train,
        Blow Parliament sky-high,
    But none could call me inhumane;
        I wouldn't hurt a fly.
        I wouldn't hurt a fly,
        And why indeed should I?
          It has neither land nor pelf
          That I covet for myself,
        Then wherefore should I hurt a fly?

'Dryblower' (E. G. Murphy)

THE BURDEN

Sir George Houston Reid (1845–1918) was Premier of New South Wales in the years
from 1894 to 1899, and was Prime Minister of Australia, as leader of the Free Trade
party, during 1904–5. The cream of 'Dryblower' Murphy's jest lies in the fact that
Reid was a man of enormous physical bulk—a fact which sometimes led his political
opponents to underestimate his energy and his nimbleness of mind.

The Perth express came panting up,
    'Twas clearly overloaded;
The steam was pouring from its stack
As slowly up the gleaming track
    The iron horse was goaded.

Thick flew the clouds of Collie smoke
    As on the rattler steamed;
From off the fireman's toiling form,
Like raindrops in a summer storm,
    The perspiration streamed.

'This yacker,' said the sooty slave,
    Amid the noisy puffing,
'From any man that feeds a fire,
Unless he's made of (crimson) wire,
    Would knock the (scarlet) stuffing.'

At last they lumbered in and stopped—
    The train had reached Kalgoorlie;
'We've been delayed upon the road,'
Explained the guard; 'a heavier load
    Was never carried, surely.'

They 'ran' the train to find the cause,
    At last that cause they dug up.
'No wonder,' said the engineer,
'With all the weight they've stowed in here
    The train was hard to lug up.'

He pointed to a sleeping car,
    With weight 'twas close capsizing,
'You're right,' the anxious S.M. said,
'If there were found a load of lead
    It wouldn't be surprising.'

The carriage door they tried to force,
 The weight inside had jammed it;
But never budged an inch that door
Though guard and stationmaster swore,
 And all the porters d——d it.

At last the door was battered down,
 The toilers shrank affrighted,
The springs unburdened, upward flew,
The car no longer sat askew,
 As G. H. Reid alighted.

W. P. ('Paddy') Crick

ON 'GEORGIE' REID

'Paddy' Crick, a member of the New South Wales Legislative Assembly during the
1890s, and part proprietor of John Norton's Sydney *Truth* for some time, was a
political bully-boy. The following extract from the N.S.W. Parliamentary Debates
(August 28, 1894) is quoted in H. V. Evatt's *Australian Labour Leader* (1945).

Crick: 'During the whole term of the last Parliament he was
 regarded as a man destined by God and formed by nature
 to fill the position of corner man in a Christy minstrel
 show. When did he take upon himself to speak seriously
 and throw out from his empty skull—'
Mr Speaker: 'The hon. member is not in order in making
 reflections of this kind.'
Crick: 'Then I will say that the hon. and learned gentleman
 has a full skull, though I will not say what it is made of.'

Victor Daley

OF SIR GEORGE REID

From Daley's 'Federation Convention Vignettes', in *Victor Daley* (Australian Poets
series, 1963).

A sophist-statesman, ever-grey,
 Whose brow no cares corrode;
He loves the shady, crooked way,
 And hates the plain, straight road.

W. P. Crick

ON MR HINDLE

From Cyril Pearl, *Wild Men of Sydney* (1958).

When Mr Hindle, the member for Newtown, told the worshippers of the Primitive Methodist Church that 'Parliament contained some notorious drunken blackguards and licentious brutes', Crick, who boasted that he was 'a confirmed boozer' at sixteen, considered it necessary to uphold the honour of the drunks and the lechers from the floor of the House:

'It may be that the honourable member for Newtown—a human mullet—has poured into his carcass as much grog as would make any other man drunk. But it may be that he has not the necessary mental structure to be affected by alcohol... [And as for Mr Hindle's mention of licentious brutes] If he has not sinned in that particular direction it may be no fault of his. There are certain people connected with the harem of the Sultan of Turkey who could not sin in that direction.'

Sir George Reid

SIR GEORGE REID VERSUS INTERJECTORS

Irate Woman (at an election meeting in Parramatta, NSW): 'If you were my husband I'd give you a dose of poison.'
Reid: 'Madam, if I were your husband I'd take it.'

.   .   .

Reid (gazing contemptuously at an egg of venerable vintage, hurled by a heckler, which had scored a direct hit below his chin): 'Another of my opponent's arguments—rotten, of course.'

.   .   .

Reid (addressing a public gathering on his Government's record of achievement): '. . . and when at last the time comes for me to die—'
Interjector (gazing at Sir George's huge bulk on the platform): 'The fat'll be in the fire then, won't it, Georgie?'

W. P. Crick

SIR HENRY

'Paddy' Crick, one-time Member for West Macquarie in the Legislative Assembly of New South Wales, thus fulminated against Sir Henry Parkes:

Like that foul fiend of our race—the abortionist—who would outrage nature and prevent our material birth, this mental Mokanna exuded his most malignant maledictions to stifle my political birth . . . Parkes possesses the mental attributes of snakes and monkeys.

Sir Henry Parkes

TO W. N. WILLIS

William Nicholas Willis was active in the politics of New South Wales in the last decade of the 19th century. He represented the Bourke constituency in the Legislative Assembly. Willis became involved in Land Office scandals.

Ho! the honourable member for Bourke, who is believed to have committed every crime in the calendar—hexcept the one we could so easily have forgiven him—suicide.

John Norton

BADLY-BEHAVED BALDY BLACK

George Black was sub-editor of the Sydney *Bulletin* from 1889 to 1891, a pioneer of the New South Wales Labor party, and a member of the Legislative Assembly for West Sydney during the 1890s. Black had arrived in Sydney in 1873 and had set up house with a Mrs Duggan, whom he had enticed away from her husband during the voyage to Australia. After eighteen years and twelve children Black left Mrs Duggan in 1891, and was often seen in the company of another married woman, whom he presented as his sister-in-law at various social and political functions. John Norton became politically opposed to Black and tried to force him out of parliament. See Cyril Pearl, *Wild Men of Sydney* (1958).

That black-hearted bawdy blackguard and barbarous brutal benedict 'Baldy Black' who had befooled, befouled and betrayed women, should be banned and blackballed from brotherhood until he behaves himself better.

[Black retaliated in the *Australian Workman*, which he was

then editing.] Who would pay sixpence to see the wild beasts at the Zoo when it was possible to see John Norton eat at the Metropolitan for nothing?

W. A. Horn

THE PARLIAMENTARY BORE

William Austin Horn (1841–1922) was a Member of the South Australian House of Assembly from 1887 to 1893. In 1894 he led an exploring party into Central Australia. The following verse, entitled 'The Squatter's Dream', was included by Horn in a volume, *Bush Echoes*, which he published in 1901.

I had a dream not long ago,
    I don't know when or where;
I dreamed that once again I bowed
    Before the Speaker's chair.

The Members seemed the very same
    I'd known long years before;
Oh! what an age since I had seen
    A Parliamentary Bore.

Some Members aired their special fads
    In Egotistic phrase,
As clucking hens will oft-times chant
    Their *Egg-otistic* lays.

.   .   .

I heard a Member pregnant with
    An Anti-Squatting speech,
A glass of water on his desk,
    A pile of notes in reach.

Those dull and dreary platitudes,
    I knew I'd heard before.
Ah, yes! it was my ancient friend
    So redolent of straw.

The same old hot and feverish haste
    To catch the Speaker's eye,
The same old pre-historic word,
    That ill-used pronoun, I.

The Speaker's eye when once 'twas caught,
    That Member would retain
And speak as long as breath would last:
    Then rest—and speak again.

He lost the letter H at times,
    That old Aeolian Bore,
But still he kept the average up,
    And sometimes rather more.

For every H one word did lose,
    Some other would annex,
His quantities were very false,
    Unknown as those of X.

The less he knew the more he talked--
    I heard the Speaker snore--
The more he talked the less he said,
    That wind-begotten Bore.

.   .   .

His mountain seemed to labour
    With that old historic mouse:
The parturition seemed to shake
    The ceiling of the House.

The Speaker tried to stop him
    By a ruling that he gave:
He might as well have tried to stop
    Atlantic's tidal wave.

'Twixt diaphragm and necktie now
    An H got tightly jammed,
I really thought I heard him say
    The Speaker might be [damned.]

The Treasurer had fainted
    And the Premier loudly sighed,
The Speaker called out 'ORDER!'
    And the Members called 'DIVIDE!'

He suddenly was stricken dumb,
    No further sound he gave,

But still his tongue kept wagging
Though as silent as the grave.

It wagged until I had to fling
A 'Hansard' at his head,
But still it went on wagging
Although—the man was dead.

Victor Daley

THE DOVE

First printed in 1902, 'The Dove' expresses Daley's opposition to the Boer War. At
the time Joseph Chamberlain (1836–1914) was Britain's Minister for Trade in the
Gladstone Ministry.
From *Creeve Roe: Poetry by Victor Daley* (1947), edited by Muir Holburn and Marjorie
Pizer.

Within his office, smiling,
    Sat *Joseph Chamberlain*,
But all the screws of Birmingham
    Were working in his brain.

The heart within his bosom
    Was as a millstone hard;
His eye was cold and cruel,
    His face was frozen lard.

He had the map of Africa
    Upon his table spread:
He took a brush, and with the same
    He painted it blood-red.

He heard no moan of widows,
    But only the hurrah
Of charging lines and squadrons
    And 'Rule Britannia'.

A white dove to his window
    With branch of olive sped—
He took a ruler in his hand,
    And struck the white dove dead.

John Norton

SIR JOSEPH CARRUTHERS: 'PRESS-PUFFED NINCOMPOOP'

Sir Joseph Hector Carruthers was a prominent politician in New South Wales at the turn of the century. Minister for Lands in the Reid Government, and Treasurer (1898–99), he became Premier of New South Wales in 1904.

Joseph Hector, you are a hidebound humbug and a high-faluting hypocrite . . . I always did regard you as a press-puffed nincompoop and a parson-boosted humbug . . . While your past connubial conduct makes you the concupiscent compeer of some of those pornographic pulpiteers who have taken you under their pious parsonical protection.

W. P. ('Paddy') Crick

TO JOHN NORTON

'Paddy' Crick's invective against Norton frequently reached greater heights than this. The reader should not, under any circumstances, fail to experience the full flavour of the political low-life of Sydney in the late 19th century through the fascinating pages of Cyril Pearl's *Wild Men of Sydney* (1958).

. . . You are a _____ criminal from the top of your head to the soles of your feet. I have fixed it all for you and will have you lumbered tonight. You are the two ends of a scoundrel!

Richard Denis Meagher

TO JOHN NORTON

Meagher, a political associate of 'Paddy' Crick in late 19th century Sydney, mastered the alliterative sound and heady virulence of Nortonian invective. Charged with horse-whipping Norton in a Sydney street, Meagher followed up this attack with a verbal assault from which the following is extracted:

You scaly scurvy contemptible viper . . . you scaly, scrofulous bit of carrion . . .

63

Gilbert Probyn Smith

ON JOHN NORTON:
'BLASPHEMOUS WRETCH'

Cyril Pearl, in his *Wild Men of Sydney*, described Gilbert Probyn Smith as 'an eccentric Sydney journalist', son of an Indian army officer. He was frequently engaged as a court interpreter. For a time he conducted a paper, the *Australian Police News* ('Sensational, Fearless and Spicy'). He had done some freelance work for Norton's *Truth*, and knew a great deal about Norton's public and private life. Smith, in 1899, published a ten-page pamphlet entitled 'Open Letter to Mr John Norton, &c.', and this document was distributed while Norton was campaigning as candidate for the Northumberland electorate. It read in part:

. . . after having proved yourself the most indecent person in the colony, after wallowing in the mire of your filth, after the breath of your body had sent a sirocco of blasphemy and filthy language through the House of Parliament . . . you actually asked the women in the constituency . . . to pray to Almighty God to secure your return! Blasphemous wretch! The appeal of John Norton, seducer, violater, destroyer of home and family, guilt-laden, scrofulous-tongued filthily loathsome viper, asking good women to pray to the Architect of the Universe, Almighty God, to return such a wretch as you.

No decent woman dares to go to your office but you insult her . . . No tramp or larrikin can approach you for dirty, filthy language . . . Many a time your language has been driven down your blackguard mouth by a good blow. Surrounded by a cohort of criminals for a bodyguard, always carrying a revolver, you think you are a hero . . . I have seen you thrown out of hotels because your language was so obscene and blasphemous.

John Norton

FROM AN 'OPEN LETTER' TO
EDMUND BARTON, PRIME MINISTER OF THE
COMMONWEALTH, CONCERNING HIS
DISGUSTING DRINKING HABITS'

For sheer scurrility it would be difficult to find the equal of Norton's 'Open Letter to

64

Edmund Barton'. Sir Edmund Barton (1849–1920) fought for the federation of the Australian colonies and became the first Prime Minister of the new Commonwealth in 1901. He was widely known by the sobriquet 'Australia's Noblest Son'.

. . . permit me to premise that, in view of your hopes of seeing me in perdition having been blighted, I am going to give you the opportunity of revenge by sending me to prison—if you can. I intend telling something of the truth about you and your doings here in Melbourne in your dual capacity of 'Australia's Noblest Son' and 'First Federal Premier of Australia'. What I have to say is, if possible, worse than anything I have yet spoken and printed about you. I have already categorically charged you with political poltroonery as a politician, professional dishonour as a Cabinet Minister, and personal dishonesty as a citizen. The capacity and digestive power of your moral stomach seem even more abnormal than that of your physical 'corporation'. You have 'stomached' these outrageous charges, reiterated in the press and on the platform, with the same complacency with which you would swallow an elephantine repast, and wind up with a gargantuan guzzle. To these charges I now add another, and in view of the onerous responsibilities of the position you hold, a much more serious charge than any I have yet brought against you. Hitherto I have been content to depict you merely as a genial but withal gluttonous guzzler and gorger. *I now charge you with being not only a disgusting drunkard, but also a most decidedly dangerous one from a public point of view.* This is an accusation which no decent citizen could ignore; much less can a public man in your position be permitted to brush it aside as a matter of no serious concern, either to you or the public. Either it is true or false. If true, you ought to be compelled, with as little scandal as possible, to retire into private life; if false, you ought to prosecute me and get me sent to prison. You know whether you are a drunkard or not. Beware, of the attitude you assume in this matter. The public, acting on the popular maxim 'Silence gives consent', will condemn you should you not seek to clear your character of this serious charge in a Court of Law.

Henry E. Boote

WILLIAM ARTHUR HOLMAN:
'HYPOCRITICAL THROUGH AND THROUGH'

William Holman (1871–1934) was prominent in Australian politics during much of
his adult life. He and William Morris Hughes played a vital part in the founding and
rise to power of the Australian Labor Party. He was a staunch conscriptionist during
World War I. See H. V. Evatt, *Australian Labour Leader* (1945). Henry E. Boote (1868–
1949) was for many years editor of the *Australian Worker*. The extract below is from
the issue of December 20, 1917.

Quite recently you breathed an unctuous hope that absolute
freedom of discussion would be permitted on the platform
and in the press. I was completely taken in by your perfervid
advocacy of a free press. I waited upon you to secure your
help in this connection.

I understand that you addressed a meeting of the Institute
of Journalists on the subject. They were not aware then, nor
was I, that, only a few months before, you had formulated *a
scheme for the gagging of the press* more drastic than anything
in existence anywhere on earth.

But we know you now, William Holman, thanks to the
discovery of your confidential 'Memo. on Recruiting'.

We know that your public utterances are *hypocritical through
and through*. We know that in secrecy you were planning, not
only to throttle the papers—especially those opposed to
your Government—but to victimise tens of thousands of
young men by taking their means of livelihood from them,
and lashing them with the knotted whip of hunger into
fighting for well-fed eligibles in nice soft billets, like yourself.

The Sydney *Worker*

WILLIAM ARTHUR HOLMAN

These excerpts from articles in the Sydney *Worker* are from the issues of August 26,
1893 and December 9, 1893.

. . . judged from the Holman standard, the crucifixion of
Christ, the poisoning of Socrates, the massacre of the

Huguenots in France, and every other act of legislative infamy ever perpetrated was right.

.   .   .

Murmur the name of the new economic Messiah in subdued and holy accents—down on your faces in mother dust, groundlings! W. A. Holman—most eminent of iconoclasts. Hail, Holman, hail! Seer of the great new dawn. . .

The Sydney *Labor Daily*

WILLIAM ARTHUR HOLMAN: 'THIS MELLIFLUOUS GENTLEMAN WITH THE PRONOUNCED WAR KINK'

From the Sydney *Labor Daily* (December 9, 1931).

The Labor renegade and 'Alias' party candidate for Martin, tunefully announces at his meetings that he would disfranchise all unionists who had partaken in an unauthorised strike—and he informs all and sundry that a current of fresh air is needed to blow through union offices generally. Mr Holman's prescription for a deodorant need not be taken seriously, coming from the source it does. But in reply it might be stated that no decent democrat would handle, even with fumigated tongs, this mellifluous gentleman with the pronounced war kink, who is always posturing in the mask of democracy.

J. K. McDougall

WILLIAM MORRIS HUGHES: PUBLIC CENSOR

William Morris Hughes (1864–1952), popularly known as 'Billy' and 'The Little Digger', was four times Prime Minister of Australia between the years 1914 and 1923. During World War I, as a leading conscriptionist, Hughes was expelled from the Australian Labor Party which he had helped to establish; and for the remainder of

67

his political life he devoted his considerable energies to conservative platforms and policies.

> We must not hit with trenchant wit
> A profiteer or parson,
> Or, Hughes will hale us off to jail
> For felony and arson.
> We must not doubt or write about
> A crooked politician,
> For 'tis a crime, worse any time,
> Than murder and sedition.

William Arthur Holman

MR HUGHES

Quoted in the Sydney *Daily Telegraph* (January 11, 1918).

I have long known Mr Hughes as a man whose pledged word is absolutely worthless.

The Brisbane *Truth*

OUR BILLY

This couplet on 'Billy' Hughes was penned in 1916.

> Our Billy's talk is just like bottled stout,
> You draw the cork and only froth comes out.

William Morris Hughes

DEAKIN AND JUDAS

Alfred Deakin (1856–1919) entered the Victorian Parliament in 1879. He became Attorney-General in the first Commonwealth Parliament, and formed the second Commonwealth Ministry (1903–4). The attack on Deakin by Hughes, which follows, occurred during the Commonwealth parliamentary debates in May, 1909. See W. Farmer Whyte, *William Morris Hughes* (1957).

The Honourable Member abandoned the finer resources of political assassination and resorted to the bludgeon of the cannibal. Having perhaps exhausted all the possibilities of that fine art, or desiring to exhibit his versatility in his execrable profession, he came out and bludgeoned us in the open light of day. It was then that I heard from this side of the House some mention of Judas. I do not agree with that; it is not fair — to Judas, for whom there is this to be said, that he did not gag the man whom he betrayed, nor did he fail to hang himself afterwards!

William Morris Hughes

SILENCE

Here's another attack by Hughes on the then Attorney-General, Alfred Deakin. It was quoted by Edward Beeby in John Thompson's *On Lips of Living Men* (1962).

[Hughes] was a brilliant debater, brilliant in repartee. And one of his best retorts was given in the first Commonwealth Parliament. Hughes, as a Labor member, was making a most ferocious attack on some of Deakin's policies, and one statement brought Deakin to his feet with the cry, 'I deny it! I deny it!' There was dead silence in the House. Hughes stood in his place with his hand to his ear, and the silence lasted so long that the Speaker asked whether the Honourable Member had finished his remarks. Then Hughes looked round at the House and looked at the Speaker and said, 'Oh no, Mr Speaker, I was just waiting for the cock to crow.'

William Morris Hughes

ON KING O'MALLEY

Born in the United States in 1862, King O'Malley became active in Australian politics from 1896. He was elected to the House of Representatives in 1901. O'Malley played an important part in the founding of the Commonwealth Bank (1911) and with the establishment of the Federal Capital at Canberra.

It is lamentable that he was not coeval with the Creator at the making of the Universe, because I feel convinced that he could have given Him a great many hints.

John Norton

ON WINSTON CHURCHILL

. . . a witless wild ass . . . a bulgy-eyed, frothy-mouthed, loose-tongued, leather-lunged, British-Yankee half-breed . . . a demi-demented decadent . . . the blatant, mad-brained bounder . . . this sibilating shyster.

Sir Earle Page

ON THE SCULLIN FEDERAL GOVERNMENT

The Federal Labor Government of James Henry Scullin was in office from Octobe 1929 to January 1932, a period marked by grave economic depression.

. . . the most futile, bankrupt, discredited, fatuous Govern ment the world has ever seen.

'Eddie' Ward

THE LYONS FEDERAL GOVERNMENT

On October 3, 1935, during a debate on the war in Ethiopia in the House of Representatives, Edward John Ward, a Labor member, attacked the Ministry of Joseph Aloysius Lyons in the following terms. Lyons, as head of the United Australia Party, led two Commonwealth Ministries between 1932 and 1939.

You are a lot of imperialist jingoes . . . None of you would be eligible for war yourselves. You are all mentally deficient.

Arthur A. Calwell

COMMUNISM

Arthur Augustus Calwell (1896–1973) entered the House of Representatives in 1940 as a Labor member; was Minister for Immigration (1945–49) and Leader of the Parliamentary Labor Party (1960–67).

Pathological exhibits . . . human scum . . . paranoics, degenerates, morons, bludgers . . . pack of dingoes . . . industrial outlaws and political lepers . . . ratbags. If these people went to Russia, Stalin wouldn't even use them for manure.

71

Sir Arthur Fadden

'ARTIE' FADDEN VERSUS INTERJECTORS

Sir Arthur Fadden was described by Fred Daly in *From Curtin to Kerr* (1977) as 'sharp-witted with a fund of jokes' and 'a very effective speaker, particularly on the public platform'. He was Leader of the Australian Country Party (1941–1958) and Commonwealth Treasurer (1949–1958).

Fadden: 'Look, my friend, I work when you are asleep.'
Interjector: 'Of course you do. You're a bloody burglar.'

. . .

Fadden (to a constant interjector at a meeting): 'Look, my friend. When I was a boy, I ill-treated a donkey and my dear Mother said, "Artie, that donkey will come back and haunt you." She was right. You've turned up tonight.'

Sir Robert Menzies

ON 'EDDIE' WARD

Edward John Ward (1899–1963), popularly known as 'Eddie', started work as a labourer; and became Labor M.H.R. for East Sydney in 1931. He held ministerial posts in the Curtin and Chifley Governments, in the years from 1941 to 1949. The following attack by Robert Gordon Menzies, then Leader of the Opposition in the House of Representatives, took place during a debate on the war situation, in February 1944.

Menzies: 'I do not propose to endeavour to bandy words with the Minister for Transport and External Territories. He has the foulest tongue that has ever been unleashed in this House.'
The Speaker: 'Order! Such remarks do not improve the situation.'
Menzies: 'I do not propose to improve it. Nor do I propose to enter into a hopeless competition with a man with such a mastery of the argot of the gutter. All I can do is to express my very great regret that in this year of grace a Minister should be able so to conduct himself in the presence of the Leader of his Government and continue to be a Minister.'

'Eddie' Ward

ON SIR ROBERT MENZIES

Fred Daly in *From Curtin to Kerr* (1977), recounts Ward's counter-attack on Menzies after the dialogue in the House, quoted above.

. . . this posturing individual with the scowl of a Mussolini, the bombast of a Hitler and the physical proportions of Goering . . . this military genius who a high military officer in this country said would have had a brilliant military career had it not been for the outbreak of the last war.

Frank Forde

ON SIR ROBERT MENZIES

When [Sir] Robert Menzies founded the Liberal Party in December 1944, Labor's acting Prime Minister, Mr Frank Forde, was filled with scorn. See B. Muir, *Bolte From Bamganie* (1973).

Mr Menzies is trying to resuscitate a corpse while making a vain endeavour to hoodwink the people into believing that a new democratic party is being formed. Nobody will be fooled by his political manoeuvres. The Leader of the Opposition has such a divisive record in politics that he is the last man to lead successfully for any length of time any political party. Like the boy on the football field who cannot get all his own way, he is liable to grab the ball and run home.

William Morris Hughes

ON SIR ROBERT MENZIES

Quoted in Fred Daly, *From Curtin to Kerr* (1977).

Menzies could not lead a flock of homing pigeons.

.   .   .

Mr Menzies deplores self-seeking, whispering campaigns and petty intrigues. He passionately urges the need for unity but is himself the great self-seeker, the man behind the scenes in

73

every intrigue, the fountainhead of every whispering campaign, the destroyer of unity. His demands for courageous leadership, which of course mean leadership by himself, is an eye-opener. Courage and Mr Menzies—never was courage so ill-matched since man came upon earth.

Archie Cameron

ON 'EDDIE' WARD

,

Archie Cameron became MHR for Barker in South Australia in 1934 and was Speaker of the House of Representatives during the early 'fifties.
Quoted in Fred Daly, *From Curtin to Kerr* (1977).

I have a strong suspicion that when all of us come before the Archangel Gabriel, when the trumpet sounds and we are called upon to give an account of our doings, the Minister for External Territories [Mr Ward] will produce a copy of the Bill of Rights, plead parliamentary privilege and thus be the only one among us who will escape the consequences of his deeds.

Ben Chifley

TO A CONSTITUENT

Ben Chifley was Labor Prime Minister from 1945 to 1949. The following anecdote is related by Fred Daly in *From Curtin to Kerr* (1977).

Chifley told the story of interviewing his constituents in a country town when a woman barged in over those waiting and proceeded at great length to demand that he have her husband released from the Army. Two things about her annoyed Chifley: that she had barged in and that he could not get a word in. To end the conversation she hit the table and said, 'He only enlisted to get away from me.' Chifley said he could not resist replying, 'And I don't bloody well blame him.'

Les Haylen

ON J. T. LANG

In *From Curtin to Kerr* (1977), Fred Daly states that between 1946 and 1949 J. T. Lang, former Labor Premier of New South Wales, was the Chifley Government's most bitter opponent in parliament. On March 15, 1949, Labor member Les Haylen bitterly attacked Lang in the House:

I admit that I am a comparatively new member of the Parliamentary Labor Party but the honourable member must admit that he is old and shrivelled in villainy . . . his attack is unwarranted and childish. He is not a man. He is a simulacrum, the image of a man who has been forced on the people of this country. He is the greatest phoney Australia has known.

Sir Robert G. Menzies

SIR ROBERT MENZIES VERSUS INTERJECTORS

Robert Gordon Menzies (1894–1978) was Prime Minister of Australia between the years 1939 and 1941, and again, for a record term, from 1949 to 1966.

Woman Interjector (at an election meeting at Williamstown, Vic.): 'I wouldn't vote for you if you were the Archangel Gabriel.'
Menzies: 'If I were the Archangel Gabriel, madam, I'm afraid you wouldn't be in my electorate.'

. . .

Menzies (to a woman heckler at Brighton Town Hall, Vic.): 'Madam, I have no objection to your speaking in this hall provided you either do so some other night or that you pay half the cost of the hiring of it tonight.'

. . .

Heckler (at an Oakleigh, Vic., election meeting): 'Wotcha gunna do about 'ousing?'
Menzies: 'Put an "h" in front of it.'

. . .

Menzies (to an interjector at a Melbourne University meeting): 'No Government has ever promoted education as I have. After listening to you, I can understand what vast amounts will still have to be spent.'

. . .

Menzies (to an interjector in Tasmania): 'I did not come here to be insulted by the sons of convicts.'

. . .

Menzies (to a member who asked a long and involved question on petrol and oil): 'If I was a bowser I'd answer you.'
Member: 'You're no bowser. You're a tanker.'

E. J. Ward

'EDDIE' WARD VERSUS 'BOB' MENZIES

Ward (in the House of Representatives, to R. G. Menzies, on the latter's return from one of his regular trips overseas): 'I desire to welcome the Right Honourable gentleman on one of his rare visits to Australia.'

. . .

Ward (at an election rally, to an interjector, during the Prime Ministership of Menzies): 'As false as the dye the Prime Minister uses on his eyebrows.'

. . .

Ward (during a debate in the House of Representatives on a Bill to outlaw the Communist Party of Australia, in June, 1950): 'I have never attempted to address the House in a drunken state, like you are.'
Menzies: '. . . a characteristic lying and dirty remark.'

Sir Robert Menzies

TO ARCHIE CAMERON

Quoted in Fred Daly, *From Curtin to Kerr* (1977).

Menzies: 'Archie, I do not suffer fools gladly.'
Cameron: 'It might be news to you to know that bloody fools
have a lot of trouble putting up with you too.'

Tom Dougherty

B. A. SANTAMARIA'S 'FIFTH COLUMN'

Bartholomew Augustine Santamaria (1915–   ), a prominent Roman Catholic layman
living in Melbourne, became president of a largely Catholic-oriented organisation,
the National Civic Council, in 1957. He has exercised a strong influence on Australian
political trends. The late Mr Tom Dougherty, General Secretary of the Australian
Workers' Union, abused Mr Santamaria in the *Australian Worker* (October 20, 1954).
Quoted in Tom Truman's *Catholic Action and Politics* (1960).

. . . Mr Santamaria has been for some considerable time
organising and leading a Fifth Column to undermine and
destroy the authority of the Federal Executive and the
Federal Conference of the Australian Labor Party in regard
to A.L.P. policy . . .
That, from a man who says he is not interested in politics!
A man who is not a member of the Australian Labor Party; a
man who has not openly come out and attacked the Australian Labor Party . . . but, who using the cloak and stiletto
method, desires through his followers to substitute his own
policy in the place of Labor's policy.

Dr Herbert Vere Evatt

'SMEAR AND SLANDER, SLANDER
AND SMEAR'

Mr Laurie Short, Federal Secretary of the Ironworkers' Union, was quoted in the
Adelaide *Advertiser* (October 7, 1954) as saying of Dr H. V. Evatt, then Leader of the
Australian Labor Party, and Leader of the Opposition in the House of Representatives: 'Dr Evatt is a millstone round the Labor Party's neck. It will never win an
election with him as leader . . . He is receiving lavish support from the Communist
newspapers. They are absolutely delighted at his stand, and are calling for full
support for him. The resources of the Communist Party are obviously behind him
and are being mobilised in a desperate campaign to bolster up Dr Evatt . . . His only
friends are Communists and pro-Communists.' Dr Evatt's public reply to this

77

statement, which also appeared in the Adelaide *Advertiser*, is quoted in Tom Truman, *Catholic Action and Politics* (1960).

Mr Short's insinuation that I have ever taken action to assist Communism is wickedly false, and he knows it. But his long tradition in Communist-Trotskyite techniques qualifies him to indulge in McCarthyite smearing, of which he is so ardent an exponent.

His frequent pro-Menzies statements have been injurious to Labor . . .

Mr Short proves out of his own mouth his readiness at all times to utter the big lie of McCarthyism — that is, 'smear and slander, slander and smear'.

Dr Herbert Vere Evatt

EVATT VERSUS WILLIAM CHARLES WENTWORTH

Evatt and Wentworth constantly clashed over unity tickets in Victorian union elections. The following dialogue is related by Fred Daly in *From Curtin to Kerr* (1977).

Evatt: 'I don't know what is happening in Victoria.'

Wentworth: 'Well, if you don't know what is happening in Victoria you are like a pianist in a brothel, you do not know what is happening upstairs.'

Evatt: 'I suggest that the honorable member get back to the haunts he knows so well.'

Jim Killen

ON GOUGH WHITLAM

Gough Whitlam was Deputy Leader of the Opposition (1960–1967), Leader of the Opposition from 1967 to 1972 and Prime Minister of Australia from 1972 to 1975. Quoted by Fred Daly in *From Curtin to Kerr* (1977).

. . . I am bound to say of the Deputy Leader of the Opposition, Mr Whitlam, that as he sat down this evening I reached the firm conclusion that he would be the most perfect product of pomposity ever to emerge out of upper middle class society and fasten himself leech-like onto the egalitarian movement.

B. A. Breen

O'FLAHERTY IS ASKED TO BE
POLITICALLY ACTIVE

This poem is number seven in a series of ten, collectively titled 'Fragments of O'Flaherty'. See B. A. Breen, *Behind My Eyes* (1968).

Thump drums for them? Not
on your bloody! Why should I
put my hand to the bum of some
loose-mouthed mediocrity and
push?
  To build a better world.
Listen to them — better
beer for the men and pills for
the ladies and gin-dipped
dummies maybe for babies more
money for
education, farmers, public shit-houses and
  politicians. Hell
and they expect me
to spit into their trumpets.

Bettina Gorton

COMMENT ON CURRENT AFFAIRS

Edward Henry St John (1916–   ), while a Liberal Party member of the House of Representatives, was openly critical of the leadership of the then Prime Minister, John Grey Gorton. Mrs Gorton defended her husband, and attacked Mr St John, in the rhyme which follows, a copy of which appeared in the newspaper, the *Australian* (March 25, 1969). Mrs Gorton's verse is a paraphrase of Sir William Watson's poem, 'The Woman with the Serpent's Tongue'. See also, W. M. Cameron's 'Slighting the Worthiest', a defence of Mr St John, in this anthology.

He is not old, he is not young,
The Member with the serpent's tongue.
The haggard cheek, the hungering eye,
The poisoned words that wildly fly,
The famished face, the fevered hand —
Who slights the worthiest in the land,
Sneers at the just, condemns the brave,
And blackens goodness in its grave.

From *A Decade of Pickering* (1980)

W. M. Cameron

SLIGHTING THE WORTHIEST
(With apologies to both William Watson and Bettina Gorton)

In the March 27, 1969 issue of the *Australian*, Mr W. M. Cameron of Rodd Point (NSW), Vice-President of the Ex-Service Human Rights Association, replied to Bettina Gorton's attack on E. H. St John (q.v.) with this counter-blast against the then Prime Minister, John Grey Gorton:

> He is not old, he is not young,
> The Leader with the ready tongue,
> The unctuous smile, the steely eye,
> The platitudes that often fly.
> The vacuous face, the hearty hand—
> Who slights the worthiest in our land,
> Sneers at the 'nuts', condemns the brave,
> And conscripts youth for a foreign grave.

George Moss

ON SIR HENRY BOLTE

Sir Henry Edward Bolte (1908–) became Premier of Victoria in 1955, and retired from that office in 1972. Mr George Moss, while leader of the Victorian Country Party, was quoted in the Melbourne *Age* (March 8, 1969) as saying:

I even doubt the Premier's ability to handle the petty cash box at a hot-dog stand at the local Sunday school picnic.

Sir Henry Bolte

BOLTEISMS

The Melbourne *Age* (July 12, 1972) quoted some of the more famous statements made by Sir Henry Bolte during his career as Premier of Victoria (1955–1972). Here are several of the more trenchant ones:

On Striking Railwaymen

They can march up and down until they're bloody well foot-sore. (February, 1969)

On a Moratorium March in Melbourne

A complete flop packed by juveniles. (September, 1970)

On Demonstrating Teachers in the Parliamentary Gallery

Go back to school — you're not teachers, you're rabble . . .
larrikins, louts. This is the longest day some of them have
ever worked. (November 19, 1970)

On Censorship

It's a lot of bloody nonsense, this permissiveness. (August 22,
1970)

On a Senate Select Committee

They always see the tram after it hits them. (June, 1970)

Max Harris

'EXQUISITE INANITY'

From Max Harris, 'Darkness at Mascot', an article in the *Australian* (May 31, 1969).

. . . the exquisite inanity of Sir Henry Bolte, luxuriating
before an international Press audience in London, and
declaring that he 'wouldn't walk across the road' to see some
of the more prestigious (if permissive) productions of London
theatre, and that New South Wales had 'considerably
weakened morals' as against Victoria's.

Sir Henry climaxed this public demonstration of towering
intellect by informing the British they would soon see the
error of their ways and reintroduce the hangman in the style
of good old Victoria, Australia.

Oh my God. The shuddering embarrassment of it.

Don Dunstan

TO A LIBERAL GOVERNMENT MEMBER

From Bill Hornadge, *The Australian Slanguage* (1980).

Don Dunstan, then South Australian Opposition Leader, 1970, during a debate on the Dartmouth Dam site, said of a Government member that on this issue he had taken more stands than were described in the 'Kama Sutra' and 'some of them even more difficult'.

Senator R. J. D. Turnbull

WILLIAM McMAHON: 'HE HAS BEEN A DISASTER'

Dr Turnbull, an independent Tasmanian senator, referred in the course of a public statement (July, 1972) to the performance of the then Prime Minister, William McMahon. He said, *inter alia*:

. . . This then brings us to the present Prime Minister, who obtained his office solely by a vote of charity from the former Prime Minister, and since then has thought of nothing else but to keep himself in office, rather than the welfare of Australia. Any questions requiring decisions he always defers, and, in fact, the only decisions he has made have been those forced on him by the Country Party or the Democratic Labor Party. He has done not one thing for the benefit of Australia in over a year of office.

This may, of course, account for his lack of credibility in Parliament, where in any other sphere it would be said that he lied to Parliament, when he made statements which he could not confirm. He would state that he had written letters to various people and afterwards, when pressed, would have to come to the conclusion that perhaps he only thought he had written them. A typical reaction of the tired or senile mind.

As an example of McMahon's lucidity may I quote his remarks in Singapore? Referring to the Straits of Malacca, he said, 'Our attitude is a clear one: as yet we have not made up our mind definitely as to what our policy should be.'

There is nothing wrong of course with his physical fitness, and having won the award of Father of the Year last year, he is going on to greater triumphs by being this year enthroned

Thanks, Malcolm. And now farewell!

From *A Decade of Pickering* (1980)

84

as The Oldest Father of the Year—anything to win an election.

I have not heard of anyone who does not agree that McMahon has been a dismal failure—all agree he has been a disaster. And there is no greater danger to any country than when it is led by a universally confirmed failure who still believes he is the greatest. In the interests of Australia this man must go. Fortunately I have heard the first bit of real political sanity from reliable Liberal sources—that if the Liberals *do* win the election they are going to get rid of McMahon.

Mr Jones

OF WILLIAM McMAHON

A Bill to extend the two-airline system until 1982 was typical of Government 'hand-outs' for its friends, Labor's shadow Transport Minister Mr Jones said in Parliament on October 25, 1972.
From a report in the Melbourne *Age* (October 26, 1972).

It is typical of what happened with Jetair, which was a putrid, blatant act of corruption by a crooked Prime Minister . . .

It was the putrid act of a Prime Minister who would have no difficulty sleeping on a corkscrew.

Clyde Packer

ON THE McMAHON GOVERNMENT

After the victory for the Federal Labor Party in 1972, Mr Clyde Packer, a Liberal MLC in the New South Wales Parliament, made the following comment during a luncheon speech, December 4, 1972.
Reported in the Melbourne *Herald* (December 5, 1972).

The only way the McMahon Government could have been saved was if the National Trust had been asked to declare it an historic ruin.

Fred Daly

TO JIM KILLEN

Fred Daly explained in his book, *From Curtin to Kerr* (1977), that Killen's comments had often to be clarified to determine whether he, Daly, was being praised or insulted. In October 1973, Killen accused Daly of suffering from the 'Munchausen syndrome'. Daly, somewhat perplexed, visited the library and next day replied:

I am now able to inform the House that Baron Munchausen . . . was a gentleman much prone to exaggeration. I also understand that he was given to talking to monkeys.

The imputation that I might, at any time, be guilty of exaggeration is quite without foundation, as every member of this House knows. The second imputation regarding monkeys, however, as I look across this chamber, I can hardly deny. To be fair to the honourable member for Moreton [Jim Killen], it may be that he was referring to another of the Baron's well-known exploits. The good Baron claimed that he had once, with a single shot, brought down sixty-eight ducks. As honourable members know for a fact, without any exaggeration, I regularly come close to emulating this feat. Quite often in this place I am to be seen shooting down fifty-eight galahs with a single well-aimed gag.

Fred Daly

FRED DALY VERSUS JIM KILLEN

See Fred Daly, *From Curtin to Kerr* (1977).

Daly: 'Every time I look at the Honourable Member I know why the jails are full.'
Killen: 'Obviously their numbers are one deficient because that is the proper place for the Minister.'

. . .

Daly (with reference to Killen's legal capabilities): [Killen should] 'get back to his small debts practice in Brisbane.'
Killen: 'Say it again, my practice has trebled since your national advertisement over the ABC.'

. . .

Killen (after 'what I [Daly] considered one of my reasonably good speeches'): 'The speech of the Minister reminds me of the Irishman in the dock. The judge said, "How do you plead?" "I don't know," said the Irishman. "I haven't heard the evidence yet."'

Sir Billy Snedden

ON GOUGH WHITLAM

Mr Snedden, as Leader of the Opposition, was roused to anger by the Prime Minister, Mr Whitlam, when the latter alleged that a former Liberal Minister, Dr Forbes, had had too much to drink after a parliamentary reception.
Mr Snedden's remarks were reported in the Melbourne *Herald* of November 20, 1973.

[Mr Whitlam's statements were] reprehensible and contemptible. They were the outpourings of a man whose mind knows no boundaries. His big head was too big to contain them.

Doug Anthony

DINGO JIBE AT GOUGH WHITLAM

The following remarks by Doug Anthony, Leader of the Country Party, were prompted by the comments, alluded to above, of Gough Whitlam.
Quoted in the Melbourne *Herald* of November 20, 1973.

In plain Australian language the Prime Minister is nothing more than a dingo. No man has been more vile in past years in vilifying Members of this House.

The Prime Minister has reached a state of intoxication with power, and he thinks he can get away unchallenged with attacks on Members of this Parliament.

He will be met with retaliation not only from the Opposition parties but also from the people of Australia.

This is the blackest day I have ever seen in Parliament.

Bruce Dawe

A PLEA ON BEHALF OF A NEWLY ELECTED
POLITICIAN

Bruce Dawe (1930–   ) is a Victorian-born poet much concerned with contemporary
social issues.
From Bruce Dawe, *Sometimes Gladness* (1978).

Ask not too much of this:
   It blinks its eyes,
Will, with the right incentive,
   Sit or rise,
Vote yes or no,
   Ascend somewhere a rostrum
And given half a chance
   Prescribe a nostrum,
Shake a smooth hand or two,
   Enter a room
And with one glance around
   Say who is whom . . .
Ask not too much of this,
   Which still can claim
Its present substance out of
   Nothing came
— A miracle of sorts
   Being this day born
Out of some electorate's
   Bored yawn,
Sustained in office
   For the thing it is
— The offspring of a ho-hum
   And a zizz.

Barry Humphries

TO AL GRASSBY

- Barry Humphries, Melbourne-born actor, entertainer, satirist and wit, hiding behind
his Barry McKenzie creation in 1974, delivered this serve to the then Federal Labor
politician, Mr Al Grassby, who was known for his somewhat flashy dress.
Quoted in Bill Hornadge, *The Australian Slanguage* (1980).

88

If Al Grassby wants to convert me or any other clean-living Australians into getting dressed up like Lord Muck and getting round kitted up like a flamin' pox doctor's clerk, old Grazza's going to have his time cut out.

Sydney Morning Herald

ON AUSTRALIAN POLITICIANS

From the *Sydney Morning Herald* (1975), and quoted by Bill Hornadge in *The Australian Slanguage* (1980).

There's no doubt that Australia fields a very poor political team, that our orating drongoes pose a more serious threat to democracy than the falling dominoes of Asia.

Gough Whitlam

ON MALCOLM FRASER AND SIR JOHN KERR

When the Governor-General, Sir John Kerr, sacked the Labor Government on November 11, 1975, and requested Malcolm Fraser to form an Interim Government, the political arena resounded with the thunder of verbal invectives. Gough Whitlam, the deposed Prime Minister, had the following words to say when addressing a crowd at the steps of Parliament.
Quoted in the Melbourne *Age* of December 30, 1975, under the heading 'Some of the Year's Quotable Quotes'.

Malcolm Fraser will undoubtedly go down in history from Rememberance Day, 1975, as Kerr's cur. We may well say 'God Save the Queen', because nothing will save the Governor-General.

Bob Hawke

ON MALCOLM FRASER

Bob Hawke, during the constitutional crisis in November 1975, was reported by the Melbourne *Age* to have directed this insult at Malcolm Fraser.

Malcolm Fraser could be described as a cutlery man. He was

From A Decade of Pickering (1980)

From *A Decade of Pickering* (1980)

born with a silver spoon in his mouth and he uses knives to stab his colleagues in the back.

Fred Daly

ON MALCOLM FRASER

See Fred Daly, *From Curtin to Kerr* (1977).

Uninspiring and unimaginative, his lengthy parliamentary career has been noticeable for its ultra-conservatism. Politically he seems to be slightly to the left of Rhodesian Prime Minister Ian Smith and to the right of Ivan the Terrible. It seems his policies were written about that period.
. . . To date Fraser is best remembered for the ludicrous slogan: 'Life wasn't meant to be easy'.

The Melbourne *Sunday Observer*

ON POLITICIANS

From an editorial in 1978, quoted by Bill Hornadge in *The Australian Slanguage* (1980).

Many of our so-called leaders proved themselves lazy, two-faced bludgers at the opening of Federal Parliament in Canberra . . . Until now not one newspaper has bothered to point out the outrageous antics of these powder-puff thespians of the Parliamentary stage.

Phillip Adams

NOW, THE FIRST LARRIKING

Phillip Adams, satirical writer for the Melbourne *Age* and other newspapers and journals, and widely known for his instigation of the 'Life Be In It' campaign, has aimed his verbal darts at many politicians. Here he lampoons Joh Bjelke-Petersen as the winner of the terrorist of the year award. Joh Bjelke-Petersen has been Premier of Queensland since 1968.
See Phillip Adams, *More Unspeakable Adams* (1979).

. . . the most successful political desperado of the decade who, having blown holes in the Constitution and hijacked Parliament House, is now showing his tender mercies to those unfortunate enough to be Aborigines or to have cancer.

Ladies and gentlemen, I give you the lethal Lutheran, the Creature from the Black Billabong—the Premier of Queensland.

Not in her wildest political fantasies could Ulrike Meinhoff have conceived of such success. Australia's smallest, noisiest and most irresponsible minority (one man with a handful of neanderthal henchmen) has kidnapped an entire state. While the middle class were told to fear the sound of thongs flopping down the main street, the real danger lay in those few pairs of jackboots clomping down the corridors of power . . .

But just as Godzilla, Japan's irradiated dinosaur, grew in strength as it munched powerlines, Bjelke seems nourished by all forms of opposition and particularly by southern satire. All it does is vindicate him in the dim eyes of those troglodytes who see him as saviour . . .

. . . While other terrorists have relied on hand grenades and machine guns, Bjelke has shown the awesome power of the rough end of the pineapple . . .

Phillip Adams

ON MALCOLM FRASER

See Phillip Adams, *More Unspeakable Adams* (1979).

To avoid death, I make a compact with the Devil. It doesn't involve selling what's left of my soul as the Devil would hardly be interested in such a thing of rags and tatters. But I come to a special arrangement that should guarantee me something approaching infinite life.

I will die the day that Malcolm Fraser throws back his head and laughs.

...AND I'VE A SNEAKY
SUSPICION WE
WOULDN'T NEED
ABORTIONS AT ALL
IF IT WEREN'T FOR
THAT OTHER NASTY
HABIT!!'

From *A Decade of Pickering* (1980)

Bill Hayden

BILL HAYDEN VERSUS JIM KILLEN

From a report on Federal Parliament in the *Age* (March 29, 1981).

It sounded like something from the 'fifties. As the Minister for Defence, Mr Killen, struggled against Opposition pressure to answer a question on the state of preparedness of Australia's defence forces, he turned on the Leader of the Opposition, Mr Hayden, and said: 'Unlike the honorable gentleman, I did wear a uniform.'

The Opposition erupted, and the Government back-benchers looked sheepish. Former policeman Hayden replied that he had in fact worn one and had had to deal with the likes of Mr Killen. The Government front bench seemed to find Mr Hayden's comment more amusing than Mr Killen's.

Late last night Mr Hayden counter-attacked again, saying that in the last six weeks of World War II, Mr Killen had been the 'chief drink waiter in the air-gunners' mess'.

Mr Hayden had drawn the Killen comment by raising a point of order, saying that he had asked the Minister a very serious question and it deserved a direct answer: 'The armed services need more than a bristling moustache and florid rhetoric to defend the country,' he said.

Later the House did get some serious debating . . .

Bill Hayden

BILL HAYDEN VERSUS COMMUNICATIONS MINISTER IAN SINCLAIR

The following extract concerning Federal Parliament appeared in Mungo MacCallum's column, 'The Legislators', in the Melbourne *Age* (June 3, 1981).

. . . it immediately became apparent that question time was to be devoted almost entirely to trying to force Communications Minister Ian Sinclair to admit that he had communicated copies of the proposed amendments to the Broadcasting and Television Act to 'media interests', which apparently meant Rupert Murdoch and his almost equally terrifying colleague, Kerry Packer.

Getting a direct answer out of any Minister on such a touchy subject is like pulling teeth; in the case of Mr Sinclair, it is closer to extracting the horn of an unhappy rhinoceros. However, some forty minutes and five questions later, Mr Sinclair had moved from the general position that he had consultations and discussions with a lot of people to the more definable position that he had shown drafts of the amendments (though not the final draft) to various media people. This seemed to satisfy the Opposition for the time being, or at least exhaust their quest for something a little more specific. Maybe they were simply tired out by the effort of getting that far.

The general tone of the interrogation is well summed up in the following exchange:

Mr Hayden: With a reputation like yours how do you expect us to believe you?

Mr Sinclair: With a reputation like yours, I'd be afraid to hang my head in public.

Mungo MacCallum

ON THE LEGISLATORS

From the Melbourne *Age* (June 6, 1981).

CANBERRA.—It is a sign of the desperate greyness of the present Federal Parliament that Housing Minister Tom McVeigh can be regarded as a character indeed, by some of his more excitable colleagues even as a wit.

Admittedly, parliamentary jesters are somewhat thin on the ground. Many have gone tó that great members' bar in the sky, while others such as a former Labor frontbencher are racing the Taxation Commissioner around the lecture circuit. Of the few that are left, the only one in the great tradition is Defence Minister Jim Killen, and even Mr Killen's jokes are now applauded more from a respect for tradition than because of any intrinsic merit.

Indeed, a churlish observer would probably conclude that while Mr Killen's sense of timing remains impeccable, his previous verbal dexterity has now degenerated to the point where many of his quips are merely solecisms — which are nonetheless greeted with enthusiastic, if not always comprehending, laughter from those sitting behind him.

Still, no replacement resident clown is in sight, and for want of something better, Mr McVeigh appears to be being groomed for the part. Or, perhaps more accurately, he appears to be grooming himself. Certainly his nine years on the back bench had given no hint of the fact that inside his laconic National Party frame there lurked a possible successor to . . . well, perhaps not quite, Bert Newton.

Mr McVeigh's written record is sparse: his 'Who's Who' entry records no more than the fact that he was elected as member for the Queensland seat of Darling Downs in 1972, and can be contacted through a Toowoomba Post Office box number (although it leaves the distinct impression that he would rather not be).

However, the man himself is anything but sparse. His style is modelled less on the Fred Dalys and Jim Killens of this world than on his predecessor in the seat and a former Minister in the conservative governments of the sixties and early seventies, Sir Reginald (Curly) Swartz.

Sir Reginald was an amiable bald person who was called on by successive governments whenever things seemed to be getting out of control. He was almost invariably able to calm them down, largely through an ability to filibuster at stupefying length on any subject within his portfolio and a large number that were not. Or at least we think they were not. After Sir Reginald had been on his feet for a while (say about twelve seconds) people tended to stop listening to what he was saying and simply be lulled.

Mr McVeigh still has a fair way to go. While his style is undoubtedly monotonous, repetitious and usually irrelevant (although regrettably not under the very broad rules applied by Speaker Sir Billy Snedden), it is not yet soporific. It will almost certainly become so when the novelty wears off, but at present he, at least, has curiosity value.

Mr McVeigh's interest is based largely on the fact that he does not use notes in answering questions. He has apparently learned by heart a long string of figures more or less connected to the fields of housing and construction, and he trots them out in belligerent tones whenever he gets the chance.

Needless to say, these figures seldom amount to an answer to the question he has been asked, and in any case, as far as is known, no one has yet bothered to check that they are all correct . . .

In normal circumstances Mr McVeigh would be pushing to last half a minute on 'Young Talent Time'. The sad thing is that the competition in the House of Representatives makes him sound like Peter Ustinov.

The Melbourne *Herald*

STAND UP TO JOH!

From the *Herald* editorial column (July 22, 1981).

How very decent it is of Joh Bjelke-Petersen, the great white papa of the Queensland Aboriginals, to let them have a fifty-year lease of land which has been theirs for thousands of years! In this lucky country (for the whites), none of the legislative authorities has particularly clean hands when it comes to the question of Aboriginal land rights. But Queensland's are the dirtiest of all.

Robert Haupt

A NOSTALGIC LOOK AT PARLIAMENT HOUSE

From the Melbourne *Age* (August 15, 1981).

There were pranks and larrikinism then. Jim Killen, exponent of both, played a complicated trick on Gil Duthie, a Methodist lay preacher from Tasmania, who rose to the rank of Labor Whip and took himself seriously, as lay preachers sometimes do.

Duthie had taken to the vogue of wearing brightly colored shirts, and on a day when he wore a particularly violent shade, Killen rang him and introduced himself as the editor of *Tailor & Cutter* magazine, who happened to be in Orstralia and had heard of Mr Duthie's sartorial reputation.

Might he arrange an interview for his magazine? Too right!

For days and then weeks, negotiations continued as an apologetic Killen and an eager Duthie tried to agree on a time to meet. This was turning into a problem for Killen when, one day, he looked up to the Press Gallery and saw Michael Boddy, gourmet and writer. He looked vast, a real two-chair job, and his shirt, tie and coat were having trouble complying with parliamentary requirement that they be done up.

Down below, Duthie got a note telling him that his *Tailor & Cutter* man had arrived, and where he was sitting. Duthie came out on the floor of the House to look, then knew he had been had.

Killen once took the stockwhip that hangs on the wall of the Government Whip's office and cracked it, in the Government lobby, right behind the Speaker's chair. In that confined space, it sounded like a shotgun, and people rushed to see who had gone down.

Bill Hayden

ON MALCOLM FRASER

Quoted in the Melbourne *Age* (August 29, 1981).

The Prime Minister is cocooned in a comfortable lifestyle sustained by a $100 000 salary and a $1 million farm property that effectively ensures that he has nothing in common with 98 per cent of his 15 million fellow-Australians.

Thomas Warburton

PROSPECTIVE MIGRANT

Letter to the Melbourne *Age* (August 6, 1981)

I've been wondering if Mr Fraser on his twenty-sixth visit to Australia may at some time consider taking up permanent residency.

Paul Keating

ON IAN VINER

Ian Viner, Industrial Relations Minister, came under attack from all sides over his part in the Federal Government's attempt to deregister the Builders Labourers' Federation in 1981. One of his gaffes was his inadvertent disclosure that Costain had been co-operating with the Government. The following exchange between Labor front bencher, Paul Keating, and the Speaker, Sir Billy Snedden, was reported in the *National Times* (September 27–October 3, 1981).

Keating: 'What about those honourable members opposite who are sympathetic to the honourable Member for Kooyong? How do they sit there and let that sort of thing go on, seeing a snivelling, crawling, contemptuous thing like Viner come in here and attack him in this way?'

Snedden: 'Order. The Honourable Member will use the appropriate term, "the Minister".'

None of Viner's colleagues felt compelled to call for Keating to withdraw his adjectives. And so Viner went into Hansard as a liar, an incompetent and a few other choice accolades.

Phillip Adams

ON NEW ZEALAND PRIME MINISTER
MR MULDOON

Prime Minister of New Zealand, Mr Robert Muldoon, seemed intent on catching the attention of the Press while in Melbourne during the CHOGM conference in 1981. Phillip Adams made the following remarks in his column in the Melbourne *Age* (October 17, 1981).

Then there was the way the Australian Press encouraged that Dog Patch demagogue, the Jubilation T. Cornpone from New Zealand. It was absurd to give such emphasis to the antics of Piggy Muldoon, turning the event into a circus for his electoral benefit. Piggy was allowed to hog the headlines and his every oink of ignorance and bigotry was gleefully reported. There's something about these 'populist' politicians—like Bjelke-Petersen—that brings out the worst in Australian journalism, striking an unpleasantly vulgar response that says, in effect, 'you've got to admire a Muldoon'.

From the Melbourne *Herald* (August 8, 1981)

But you don't have to admire him, or any of his thoroughly unpleasant ilk.

Laurie Oakes

SOME PARLIAMENTARIANS

Quoted in the Melbourne *Age* (October 28, 1981).

Their only real contribution is to vote in parliamentary divisions. For much of the rest of the time they loaf, become frustrated and often frequent the members' bar at Parliament House.

Mungo MacCallum

FEDERAL PARLIAMENT'S SPRING SESSION – DULL ENOUGH FOR DAY-TIME TELEVISION

From the Melbourne *Age* (October 29, 1981).

If it had not been for the continual gaffes of the Industrial Relations Minister, Ian Viner, and the continual allegations about the Communications Minister, Ian Sinclair, the whole thing would have been quite suitable for day-time television, which is one of the nastiest things that can be said about any form of public entertainment. Even the rapidly ageing pretender, Andrew Peacock, seems to have lost both his zing and his tan—it is perhaps ominous that at the end of the session Liberal Deputy Sir Phillip Lynch looks a couple of shades browner than he does.

The Politicians

SOME PARLIAMENTARY ONE-LINERS

I recognize that in this country the less you know about anything the better qualified you are to be in Parliament. (King O'Malley, quoted in Dorothy Catts, *King O'Malley*, 1957)

.   .   .

102

From the Melbourne *Age* (October 28, 1981)

A man with the body of an ox and the mind of a troglodyte. (John Curtin on Joe Abbott)

. . .

If the Minister would scrape the filth of East Sydney out of his ears he would be able to hear me. (General Rankin to Eddie Ward)

. . .

This must be the only asylum in the world where the inmates are in charge. (Max Falstein describing Parliament)

. . .

My greatest ambition when I am finally heaved out of office is to travel by sea forever. Opposition colleagues believe I've been at sea all my political life, anyway. (Sir Robert Menzies, quoted in *The Wit of Sir Robert Menzies*, 1966)

. . .

When I am in office I always keep members of Parliament talking. If they stopped they might start thinking. (Sir Robert Menzies in 1952, quoted in *The Wit of Sir Robert Menzies*, 1966)

. . .

A lightweight who couldn't go two rounds with a revolving door. (Vincent Gair on Sir Billy Snedden, then Leader of the Opposition)

. . .

He couldn't make an impression on a pin cushion. (Vincent Gair on Sir Billy Snedden)

. . .

It must be the first time that the burglar has been made the caretaker. (Gough Whitlam on Malcolm Fraser during the constitutional crisis, November, 1975)

. . .

The Victorian Country Party is now furiously trying to pick the maggots off its bum.

.   .   .

He is like the Condamine Bell. He has a great tongue and a head full of nothingness.

.   .   .

The Labor Party's rural policy is as full of kid as a pregnant goat.

.   .   .

Politicians are like bananas: they come in green, turn yellow and there's not a straight one in the bunch.

.   .   .

You can't shut him up; he'd talk under wet cement.

.   .   .

He has a penchant for opening his mouth and letting the wind blow his tongue about.

.   .   .

He is an insensitive totalitarian toff. (On Malcolm Fraser)

.   .   .

That is the greatest heap of bulldust since Marx first enunciated his *Mein Kampf* or whatever it was! (Liberal Senator Sir Magnus Cormack to Labor Senator George Georges, during a debate in the Senate in 1978)

.   .   .

The only pain I've got is in the neck and that is Charles Perkins. (Joh Bjelke-Petersen after being 'sung to death' in 1975)

.   .   .

Australians love a good loser and this man showed he was a good loser. (Jim Killen of Sir Billy Snedden, March 1975)

.   .   .

From the Melbourne *Age* (August 25, 1981)

If you wanted to haunt a house, wouldn't you make Doug Anthony first cab off the rank? (Fred Daly, October, 1975)

. . .

That bible-bashing bastard. (Gough Whitlam on Joh Bjelke-Petersen, 1975)

. . .

Pull out, dig. The dogs are pissing on your swag! (Note from a parliamentarian to a colleague in mid-speech)

. . .

Of course 'Waltzing Matilda' is close to Malcolm Fraser's heart; he's a squatter isn't he? (Xavier Herbert, 1976)

. . .

Old grandpa . . . a poor pathetic little man . . . a dishonest little bastard. (Bob Hawke on Sir William McMahon. From the Melbourne *Herald*, March 25, 1981)

. . .

He will grab at any statistics to support his view. (Bob Hawke on Employment Minister Ian Viner. Reported in the Melbourne *Herald*, March 25, 1981)

. . .

He is grossly disloyal [and possessed of a] manic obssession to get his own way. (Andrew Peacock on Malcolm Fraser, April, 1981)

. . .

Some editorials have described me as the ordinary man's ordinary man—I'm proud to wear that badge with distinction. (Frank Wilkes, reported by the Melbourne *Age*, June 20, 1981)

. . .

Malcolm Fraser has more twists to him than a bottle of worms. (Fred Daly. See the Melbourne *Age*, August 18, 1981)

. . .

107

The Budget included an allocation of $3.7 million for the removal of sewage and garbage from the political centre of Australia, Canberra. (From 'Odd Spot' in the Melbourne *Age*, August 19, 1981)

.   .   .

The only times Malcolm Fraser seems to make it to Canberra — or indeed Australia — these days is when he needs a medical check-up and a bit of convalescence. (Liberal MP, reported in the Melbourne *Age*, August 26, 1981)

.   .   .

Labor frontbencher, Mr Jones, told the House yesterday that the Prime Minister, Mr Fraser, was the greatest assailant on intellectual values of any Government leader since Attila the Hun. (Report in the Melbourne *Age*, September 11, 1981)

4

'THE LAST OF LANDS'

Australia, Australians and Other Coves

Governor Lachlan Macquarie

IN A LETTER TO LORD BATHURST (1822)

There are only two classes of person in New South Wales.
Those who have been convicted and those who ought to have
been.

G. H. Gibson

ON OUTBACK PERILS

The following is an extract from a poem by G. H. Gibson and quoted in Bill
Hornadge, *The Australian Slanguage* (1980).

> Sing a song of saltbush,
> Sandy Blight an' drought.
> Forty thousand weaners
> Slowly pegging out.

Anon

DAMN!

The following is a Western Australian prospectors' 'toast'.

> Damn the teamsters, damn the track,
> Damn Coolgardie, there and back,
> Damn the goldfields, damn the weather,
> Damn the bloody country altogether!

Charles Thatcher

LINES UPON A SQUATTER
AFTER THE STYLE OF *HOGG*, IMPROVED
BY *LAMB*

Thatcher, whose merits as a satirist are displayed elsewhere in this collection, was
most unkindly disposed towards the Victorian squatters—the colonial landed gentry
—of the 1850s and 1860s. He expressed the general view of the gold-diggers of that

110

time that the squatters, while complaining that the gold-rushes were ruining them financially, were nevertheless making tidy profits from the sale of poor-quality meat to the diggers.

Oh, you stupid, grumbling chap,
At you I means to have a rap;
For you always are complaining
Of your bad luck here, and feigning
That by the discovery of gold
You fellows are completely sold;
But had not gold been found out here,
You all might then have, p'raps, looked queer,
And found no customers, I fear,
    For that bad, scabby mutton.
But now you sell your crops like fun;
Hay at an awful price per ton;
And that's the way we coves are done,
    You avaricious glutton.

Signed, BILLY NUTTS.

Jack Bradshaw

FRANK GARDINER: 'A DIRTY TERROR TO POOR TRAVELLERS'

From Jack Bradshaw's *The True History of the Australian Bushrangers* (1930). Bradshaw, who claimed to have known Gardiner, the famous bushranger of the early 1860s, poured contempt on his name and exploits. Ironically, Bradshaw himself was arrested and jailed for taking part in the hold-up of a bank at Quirindi (NSW) in 1880 — the haul being £2000.

As for Frank Gardiner, I have not much to say in his favour. He was a dirty terror to poor travellers and the King Gee villain who led astray all the other good Australian lads, who might have been a credit to their country if Gardiner was never born. These fine youths of Australia were either hanged or shot down like dogs, excepting Jack Vane or Gardiner himself, who escaped the rope by his long-practised adroitness as a consummate vagabond. . . Gardiner never had a conscience, no principle, wrapped up in self, who would rather make a dollar by plundering than a hundred by fair and honourable means.

111

Henry Kendall

ON AN UNWORTHY FOE

From *The Bronze Trumpet* (1866).

Some churls have whispered, (let me say it low)
That thou art, after all, a sorry foe—
That 'heavy vanity and heavy lead
Fill up the crannies' of thy 'ponderous head!'
But *I*—I don't believe it! I have tried
And found—nor lead nor anything beside!

Henry Kendall

A HYDE PARK LARRIKIN

The term 'larrikin' came into general use in the 1870s, in Victoria and New South Wales, to denote a street hooligan, or tough.

What sort of 'gospel' do you preach?
    What 'Bible' is your Bible?
There's worse than wormwood in your speech,
    You livid living libel!

How many lives are growing grey
    Through your depraved behaviour!
I tell you plainly—every day
    You crucify the Saviour!

Henry Kendall

NED THE LARRIKIN

A blossom of blackness indeed—
    of Satan a sinister fruit!
Far better the centipede's seed—
    the spawn of the adder or newt!

Than terror of talon or fang
    this imp of the alleys is worse:
His speech is a poisonous slang—
    his phrases are coloured with curse.

112

Louis Boussenard

A TRAVERS L'AUSTRALIE &c., c. 1875

Quoted in Kathleen Fitzpatrick, *Sir John Franklin in Tasmania* (1949).

I am suffocating here. Your Australian civilization exasperates me. Let me escape from its luxury to the deserts, the free life and the open air . . . Enough of high collars and black coats and official dinners.

E. J. Brady

THE KELLYS

Edwin James Brady (1869–1952), journalist, poet and publicist, made a name for himself with his book of sea ballads, *The Ways of Many Waters* (1899) and a volume of bush verse, *Bells and Hobbles* (1911). His attitude to the Kelly Gang of bushrangers was shared by many of his literary contemporaries. It is embedded in an interesting book he published in 1944: *Two Frontiers*.

The Kellys were rotten, root and branch, not to be classed in criminology with light-hearted led-away riders like the Burkes and Johnny Vane. They were devoid of a humanity which Ben Hall and 'Thunderbolt' Ward retained; were without the intelligence of Mount, and lacked the ferocious courage of black Dan Morgan, who never shunned an open fight. Old New South Wales troopers always conceded that the duel between Morgan and Sergeant McGinnerty had been a fair fight. They would never admit that the Kellys were anything more than cowardly murderers. They killed Sergeant Kennedy, a wounded and disarmed man, who begged to be spared for the sake of his wife and children.

Specious arguments by which Ned Kelly and his criminal relations endeavoured to justify this inhuman deed, carried no conviction. Mistaken writers, dramatists and film producers have invested the Kellys and their deeds with a glamour they do not deserve.

113

Anon

OLD BUSH BALLAD

Quoted in Bill Hornadge, *The Australian Slanguage* (1980).

Fair Australia, Oh what a dump.
All you get to eat is crocodile's rump,
Bandicoot's brains and catfish pie.
Let me go home again before I die!

The Sydney *Bulletin*

AUSTRALIAN 'SASSIETY'

From an issue of the paper in 1887.

Australian 'sassiety' is a hollow heartless bedizened swarm of
sycophantic snobs and snobbesses.

Francis Adams

IF

From *Poetical Works* (1887).

'If I were you and you were me' —
Let us thank God that cannot be!

Francis Adams

TO AN INFAMOUS LORD

From 'Lord Leitrim', in *Songs of the Army of the Night* (1888).

My Lord, at last you have it! Now we know
truth's not a phase, justice an idle show.
Your life ran red with murder, green with lust.
Blood has washed blood clean, and, in the
        final dust,
your carrion will be purified. Yet, see,
though your body perish, for your soul shall be
an immortality of infamy!

114

From an issue of the Sydney *Bulletin* during the 1890s.

John Norton (?)

ON DEEMING THE MURDERER

Frederick Bayley Deeming, multiple murderer, inspired much Press comment during his trial in Melbourne, in 1892, for the murder of one of his wives. The following, from Sydney *Truth*, suggests John Norton's hand.
Quoted in J. S. O'Sullivan's *A Most Unique Ruffian* (1968).

The dastard demoniac, dubbed Deeming, deserves the doom of a degrading dog's death for diabolical deeds, if demonstrated without doubt that he is the doer.

Chief Justice Madden

ON THE COLONIAL TWANG (1892)

Quoted in Bill Hornadge, *The Australian Slanguage* (1980).

The colonial twang was never at the beginning anything better than the twang of Cockney vulgarity. We imported it long before rabbits, sparrows, snails and other British nuisances were grafted upon our budding civilisation.

The Sydney *Bulletin*

ON THE AUSTRALIAN TWANG

From a poem in the Sydney *Bulletin* (1894), and quoted in Bill Hornadge, *The Australian Slanguage* (1980).

Twere better if thou never sang,
Than voiced it in Australian Twang.

'Magnet'

THE FAT MAN AND THE WAR

A poem from *The Bulletin Reciter* (1940), expressing antipathy towards Australian participation in the Boer War.

They sing of the pride of battle,
They sing of the Dogs of War,

116

Of the men that are slain like cattle
    On African soil afar.

They sing of the gallant legions
    A-bearin' the battle's brunt
Out in them torrid regions
    A-fightin' the foe in front.

They sing of Mauser and Maxim,
    And their doin's across the foam,
But I hear none sing of the Fat Man
    Who sits at his ease at home,

Contrivin' another measure
    For scoopin' a lump o' tin,
New coffers to hoard the treasure
    That his brothers' blood sweeps in;

Chock-full o' zeal for speedin'
    The sword of his Queen's behest,
But other men's legs to bear it
    Is the notion that suits him best.

Nothin' he knows of fightin';
    He never was built that way;
But the game of War is excitin'
    When the stake's worth more than the play.

An' a fat little time is comin',
    When the turmoil has settled down,
An' the Dogs of War are silent,
    And the veldt is bare an' brown;

When the sun has licked the blood up
    An' the brown earth hid the bones,
His miners will go out seekin'
    For gold and precious stones.

Like a ghoul from the reekin' shambles
    He grubs out his filthy pelf,
Reapin' a cursed harvest
    Where he dursn't have sown himself.

Now, this is one man's opinion,
    An' I think it is fair an' right:

If he wants the land of the Dutchman
Let him go like a man and fight.

If the African mines have treasure,
And the Fat Man wants a bone,
Let him go by himself an' find it,
Let him trek for the Front alone!

Victor Daley

ON WOMEN

The following remark is attributed to the poet and politician, Victor Daley, in 1906.
Quoted by A. G. Stephens in the Sydney *Bulletin* (January 18, 1906).

I'd sooner talk to a man than a woman any day. Ten minutes
exhausts them.

Henry Lawson

THE SEX PROBLEM AGAIN

From Henry Lawson, *Send Round the Hat* (1907).

Some men want to be considered gods in their own homes;
you'll generally find that sort of men very small potatoes
outside; if they weren't they wouldn't bother so much about
being cocks on their own little dunghills.

Victor Daley

A BACHELOR'S VIEW OF MARRIAGE

This poem by Victor Daley, 'The Australian Bachelor's Soliloquy', is from *Victor
Daley* (Australian Poets series, 1963).

What have I lost? The dear domestic joys!
A howling horde of hungry girls and boys;
A wife made sour by constant motherhood,
A ceaseless struggle to buy clothes and food,
The need to keep a face of haggard cheer

Before the world from dismal year to year; —
The voice that once was musical and low
Grown shrill and acid as the sound a bow
Gone dry makes on an untuned violin;
The grace that pleased—when I was still to win—
And all the charming coquetry of dress
Debased to slippers, wrappers, dowdiness; —
The squalid fear I never felt before
To hear the landlord knocking at the door—
They say 'tis like the knocking in Macbeth,
And dreadful as the call of sudden Death; —
And when I have grown grey with years of strife,
Ungrateful children and a wizened wife . . .
He may who will—but I shall never be
The Haggard Father of a Family.

Dame Nellie Melba (Attributed)

ADVICE TO DAME CLARA BUTT

Madame Melba strongly denied Dame Clara Butt's assertion that she (Melba) had offered the 'sing 'em muck' advice to the contralto, prior to a professional tour of Australia (c. 1907). Folklore perpetuates the story, however.

So you're going to Australia? Well, *I* made twenty thousand pounds on my tour there, but of course *that* will never be done again. Still, it's a wonderful country, and you'll have a good time. What are you going to sing? All I can say is—sing 'em muck! It's all they can understand!

D. H. Lawrence

ON THE AUSTRALIAN PEOPLE

D. H. Lawrence made the following observations in 1922 while visiting Australia.

You NEVER knew anything so nothing, Nichts, Nullus, niente as the life here. Australians are always vaguely on the go. That's what the life in a new country does to you; it makes you so material, so outward, that your real inner life and your inner self dies out, and you clatter around like so many mechanical animals . . .

119

Anon

DEPRESSION SONG

Collected by Mr Merv Lilley from Mr J. Bates, a ship's fireman, and quoted in *Singabout* (Summer, 1958).

I'm spending my days in the doss house,
I'm spending my days on the street,
I'm searching for work but I find none—
I wish I had something to eat.

Chorus:
Soup, soup, soup, soup,
They gave me a big plate of loop-the-loop,
Soup, soup, soup, soup,
They gave me a big plate of soup.

I went and I fought for my country,
I went out to bleed and to die,
I thought that my country would help me,
But this was my country's reply:

Soup, soup, soup, soup,
They gave me a big plate of loop-the-loop,
Soup, soup, soup, soup,
They gave me a big plate of soup.

J. K. McDougall

LICKSPITTLES

From *Beasts of the Blood Trail and Other Verses* (1939).

They crawl to royalty and riches,
In common and in courtly britches;
Throughout a realm as foul as hell is,
They crawl for notice on their bellies.

They crawl in orthodox battalions,
To win a knighthood or medallions;
They crawl in millions on their stomachs,
Their buttocks uppermost like hummocks.

They crawl—the rich and poor together—
To fools that wear a star or feather;
They honour lords with sturdy haunches:
Their pride is less in sense than paunches.

Anon

ADVANCE AUSTRALIA

Quoted in Sidney J. Baker, *Australia Speaks* (1953).

Wowsers, whingers, ratbags, narks,
Silvertails, galahs and sharks,
Knockers, larrikins, and chromos,
Bengal lancers, bludgers, homos,
Botts and polers, spielers, lairs,
Advance Australia—you are theirs!

Sir John Medley

ON MARRIAGE

From Sir John Medley, *An Australian Alphabet* (1953).

Oh! Betting and Beer are the basis
    Of the only respectable life.
Much better to go to the races
    Than moulder at home with the wife.

Anon

SCHOOL-YARD SONG

Quoted in Bill Hornadge, *The Australian Slanguage* (1980).

Boys are strong,
Like King Kong.
Girls are weak,
Chuck 'em in the creek.

Sidney J. Baker

THE AUSTRALIAN FEMALE

From Sidney J. Baker, *The Drum* (1959).

Since Australian females lack practice in conversational exchanges with the opposite sex they, too, are frequently shy. Even at their best their verbal offerings are often shallow and repetitious. They are poor conversational entertainers. They are almost totally lacking in a self-critical sense of humour. Their thinking tends to be of a *non sequitur* variety that would send all but the most complaisant male up the wall. And because of these things, they are usually tense, wary and given to private dreams about knights in shining armour which males rightly scorn. So, because of shyness on both sides, there is little verbal ease between our males and females. And this takes us near to the heart of the problem. Here is a situation that grew out of male diffidence, was sanctified by frontierland courtesy, became static because of female inexperience, and, with nothing to modify it, became fixed into a tradition. If, as a consequence, the Australian male is prepared to wash his hands of the whole affair and confine its correction to manoeuvres on the couch, one can hardly blame him.

George Wallace

TO A FOOD WAITER

Quoted in Bill Hornadge, *The Australian Slanguage* (1980).

'What will you have?' said the waiter,
   reflectively picking his nose.
'I'll have two boiled eggs, you bastard,
   you can't put your finger in those.'

Geoffrey Dutton

THOUGHTS, HOME FROM ABROAD 1966

This poem is evocative of the 'fifties and early 'sixties and is critical of what the poet

122

sees as Australia's somewhat blind allegiance to Britain.
Quoted in Garth Boomer, Morris Hood (Eds.) *The Endless Circle* (1973).

All down the main street the Union Jacks are waving
Windy loyalty to the flag of another country,
And it is headlines the Queen is having another baby.
On the Terrace, erect and frustrated on a pedestal
Surrounded by bare-breasted ladies, is still standing
Edward VII, King and Emperor, it says on the inscription.
George V is somewhere else, but somehow nobody
Has got around yet to perpetuating George VI.
Two Melbourne bachelors are building a yacht in Scotland
Which, if it wins the America's Cup, will win for Britain,
(But we, of course, are British to our arse-holes.)
A knighted ENT physician with a wife whose ear-lobes
Peep from blue hair, has just come Orient Line
From several months at home and on the Continent.
In the flat model town of Elizabeth the only high spots,
Two blocks of flats, are called Oxford and Cambridge;
The streets are Somerset and Kent, the airfield Edinburgh.
(Is there a single street in all Australia
Called after an artist, a poet or a scientist?)   .
My country, my country, what can you call your own?

The Holden. 99%. According to the taxi-driver
'Everybody knows the Holden's the best bloody unit,
But look at that bloke in a Jap job. There's always got to be
Some dumb bastard who wants to be different.'
There is a proposal to run a cable car for tired tourists
To the top of Ayers Rock; the album for the snapshots
Is decorated on the cover with Abos throwing boomerangs.
(The stones we throw at Alabama come from Namatjira's
        grave.)
In Kapunda, a country town, the old bluestone bank is
        demolished,
The earth ready for concrete and glass expanses,
And on every important corner there is now a service
        station.
Broadcast Canberra still clogs the official airwaves,
Covering a nation listening to horses and disc-jockeys,
Though the member for Parkes knows what theatre is good
        for the people,

123

For the decent, down-to-earth people who are not wanting
Plays about incest or tramps or foetuses in ash-cans.
Around our indefensible coastline, under the rockets,
Still runs our brave mud wall of morality
Where our white guardians of printed literature
Defend the decent and the dirty-minded minority
From Lawrence, Nabokov and the Negro Baldwin.

What other country could give one such a welcome?
And what other country lifts one with such sunlight,
Curves its flat miles with magpies singing,
Throws petals of fire and evening from the white tree-trunks,
Galah, rosella, grass-parrot, cockatoo, budgerigar,
Draws plumes of red dust from winter-scarred bush-tracks,
Has people neither obsequious nor patronizing,
People no authoritarian has yet made cheerless,
People whose give-it-a-go is also a fair go,
People of 'youth and beauty and the sun' — ah yes,
People who obey old men in courts and cabinets and offices,
Old men in unions, factory committees and caucuses,
People who stand up for another country's anthem,
A people of grown-up babies dangling from their hairy
      bellies
The shrivelled, sacred umbilical cord.

Robin Boyd

AUSTRALIAN SUBURBIA

Robin Boyd, Melbourne architect and author of *The Australian Ugliness*, a book which
caused considerable controversy when published in 1960, is well-known for his
criticism of some of the less attractive features of Australian life.
Quoted in Garth Boomer, Morris Hood (Eds.) *The Endless Circle* (1973) which states
George Johnston, *The Australians*, as its source.

The Australian town-dweller spent a century in the acquisition of his toy: an emasculated garden, a five-roomed cottage
of his very own, different from its neighbours by a minor
contortion of window or porch — its difference significant to
no one but himself. He skimped and saved for it, and fought
two World Wars with it figuring prominently in the back of

124

his mind. Whenever an Australian boy spoke to an Australian girl of marriage, he meant, and she understood him to mean, a life in a five-roomed house.

Robin Boyd

DRESSED IN BORROWED ROBES

From Robin Boyd's *The Australian Ugliness* (1960).

In expressing ourselves in the arts of our daily way of life, we avoid committing ourselves. We are frightened of bold and original ideas. While denying opportunities to the true artists, we dress the borrowed background of our lives with meaningless features — vivid colours, textures, ornaments. Australia has become a land of 'featurists'.

A. D. Hope

AUSTRALIA

From A. D. Hope's *Collected Poems 1930–1970* (1972).

A Nation of trees, drab green and desolate grey
In the field uniform of modern wars,
Darkens her hills, those endless, outstretched paws
Of Sphinx demolished or stone lion worn away.

They call her a young country, but they lie:
She is the last of lands, the emptiest,
A woman beyond her change of life, a breast
Still tender but within the womb is dry.

Without songs, architecture, history:
The emotions and superstitions of younger lands,
Her rivers of water drown among inland sands,
The river of her immense stupidity

Floods her monotonous tribes from Cairns to Perth.
In them at last the ultimate men arrive
Whose boast is not: 'we live' but 'we survive',
A type who will inhabit the dying earth.

125

And her five cities, like five teeming sores,
Each drains her: a vast parasite robber-state
Where second-hand Europeans pullulate
Timidly on the edge of alien shores.

Yet there are some like me turn gladly home
From the lush jungle of modern thought, to find
The Arabian desert of the human mind,
Hoping, if still from the deserts the prophets come,

Such savage and scarlet as no green hills dare
Springs in that waste, some spirit which escapes
The learned doubt, the chatter of cultured apes
Which is called civilization over there.

Alan Renouf

DIPLOMATIC WIVES

Alan Renouf reportedly made this statement in 1968, when he was permanent head
of the Department of Foreign Affairs.
Quoted in Bill Hornadge, *The Australian Slanguage* (1980).

If you find yourself stuck with the wife of an Australian
diplomat overseas, she'll talk to you about holidays, about
children, but she'll never say anything that will interest you.

B. A. Breen

O'FLAHERTY TO HIS MISTRESS

From B. A. Breen, *Behind My Eyes* (1968).

Now thickened
ankles. God! girl
how you danced, your
belly circling out
to raze my eyes; arms high-held
bunching and tightening breasts
that droop now
and the long
line of you from breast to hip

126

From the Melbourne *Herald* (November 12, 1981)

127

is a tide now, and the thighs
once taut and tight and telling my
every nerve now
squelch under my hand
and chuckle like jelly.

Chris Wallace-Crabbe

THE WIFE'S STORY

Melbourne-born poet and critic, Chris Wallace-Crabbe (1934–   ), is Reader in English
at the University of Melbourne.
Quoted in David Campbell (Ed.) *Modern Australian Poetry* (1970).

What with his taking bets upon the footy,
While keeping out a sharp eye for the Bulls,
And what with laying off among other bookies
Who masqueraded as both knaves and fools;

What with his ringing up those drunken mates —
The one who sang 'Jack Doolan' in the bar,
The fat one and the one with smelly feet —
And talking to the bloke who tuned his car;

What with his ringing up the spirit merchant
And with those calls he made too low to hear
But which, she long suspected, were his urgent
Demands on girls with easy yellow hair;

And what with the invitations he'd refuse,
The telephone was never hers to use.

Kath Walker

NO MORE BOOMERANG

An indictment of modern Australian society by Aboriginal poet, Kath Walker. See
Kath Walker *My People* (1970).

No more boomerang
No more spear;
Now all civilized —
Colour bar and beer.

No more corroboree,
Gay dance and din.
Now we got movies,
And pay to go in.

No more sharing
What the hunter brings.
Now we work for money,
Then pay it back for things.

Now we track bosses
To catch a few bob,
Now we go walkabout
On bus to the job.

One time naked,
Who never knew shame;
Now we put clothes on
To hide whatsaname.

No more gunya,
Now bungalow,
Paid by hire purchase
In twenty year or so.

Lay down the stone axe,
Take up the steel,
And work like a nigger
For a white man meal.

No more firesticks
That made the whites scoff.
Now all electric,
And no better off.

Bunyip he finish,
Now got instead
White fella Bunyip,
Call him Red.

Abstract picture now —
What they coming at?
Cripes, in our caves we
Did better than that.

Black hunted wallaby,
White hunt dollar;
White fella witch-doctor
Wear dog-collar.

No more message-stick;
Lubras and lads
Got television now,
Mostly ads.

Lay down the woomera,
Lay down the waddy.
Now we got atom-bomb,
End *every*body.

Ronald McCuaig

THE COMMERCIAL TRAVELLER'S WIFE

This poem by Ronald McCuaig (1909–) is from Chris Wallace-Crabbe (Ed.) *The
Golden Apples of the Sun* (1980).

I'm living with a commercial traveller.
He's away, most of the time.
Most I see of him's his wife; as for her:
I'm just home from a show,
And there I am undressing, in my shirt.
I hear midnight chime,
And up flares the curtain at the window.
The door's opened. It's Gert—
That's the wife. Her hair's hanging down.
She's only got her nightgown
Blowing up against her in the wind.
She's fat, and getting fatter.
I said, 'What's the matter?'
'Jack,' she said, 'now's your chance.'
'What chance?' I said. 'You out of your mind?'
She goes over to the bed.
I grab my pants.
'That's enough of that,' I said. 'Now go on; you get out.'
'But Jack,' she said, 'don't you love me?'

130

'I don't know what you're talking about,'
I said. 'Besides, Jim—
    What about him?'
'Yes; Jim,' she said; 'there's always Jim, but he's
Always away. And you don't know
What it's like. I can't stand it. And anyhow,
Jack, don't you want me?'
    'Oh, don't be an ass',
I said. 'Look at yourself in the glass.'
She faced the mirror where she stood
And sort of stiffened there.
Her eyes went still as knots in a bit of wood,
And it all seemed to sigh out of her:
'All right,' she said. 'All right, all right, good night',
As though she didn't know if I heard,
And shuffled out without another word.
Well, I was tired. I went to bed and slept.
In the morning
I thought I'd dreamt the whole thing,
But, at breakfast, I could have wept:
Poor Gert, clattering the dishes
With a dead sort of face
Like a fish's.
I'll have to get a new place.
I'm going out today to have a look.
Trouble is, she's a marvellous cook.

A. G. Chambers

ON THE AUSTRALIAN ACCENT

A statement made by Chambers in 1974 and quoted in Bill Hornadge, *The Australian Slanguage* (1980).

It is safe to say that however it came about no greater millstone was ever tied around the neck of any nation. The Australian accent at its worst brands every one of us, whether we speak it or not, as uncouth, ignorant and a race of second-class people.

The *Australian*

THE FEMALE OCKER

From the *Australian* (September 1, 1975) and quoted in Bill Hornadge, *The Australian Slanguage* (1980).

. . . Fat, lazy and going to seed . . . That's yer spoilt Ocker sheila.

Sir Reginald Ansett

ON AIRLINE HOSTESSES

Sir Reginald Ansett, then head of Ansett Airlines, made this virulent attack on the airline hostesses who were on strike in March 1975.
Quoted in Bill Hornadge, *The Australian Slanguage* (1980).

I'm not joking. I'm not going to have a bar of them. They are a batch of old boilers sitting on their executive. Frankly I've had them. We can run our airline without people to serve drinks.

Nation Review

ON THE CONVERSATION OF WOMEN

The following extract is from a report in *Nation Review* in 1976 concerning dinners at the Australian country home of Rupert Murdoch.
Quoted in Bill Hornadge, *The Australian Slanguage* (1980).

. . . conversation during dinner tends, out of necessity, to involve the women to a greater extent. The fact that they are seated alternately with the men makes it very difficult to ignore them. Perhaps it is due to their greater involvement in the conversation that it becomes noticeably more banal.

Barry Humphries

ON MAX HARRIS

Humphries reportedly made this remark in 1977.
Quoted in Bill Hornadge, *The Australian Slanguage* (1980).

An ocker is a mythical Australian creature like a unicorn or a bunyip. The only person who has ever seen one is Mr Max Harris every time he shaves.

Buzz Kennedy

THE AUSTRALIAN ACCENT

From an article in the *Australian* in 1978 and quoted by Bill Hornadge in *The Australian Slanguage* (1980).

The broad Australian accent is not a lovesome thing, I grant you. At its worst, it is reminiscent of a dehydrated crow uttering its last statement on life from the bough of a dead tree in the middle of a claypan at the peak of a seven-year drought . . .

Phillip Adams

ON A SUBURBAN RITUAL

See Phillip Adams, *More Unspeakable Adams* (1979).

And now, another great mystery from the Ocker occult. It is Monday night and, in dozens of suburbs, people are engaged in a ritual that beggars the imagination and boggles the mind. Here our hidden cameras show you them dragging dustbins down their drives. Galvanised dustbins, dustbins in bright plastic colours. In actuality interviews we've conducted, they explain that the bins are being left out 'for the garbos'. Well, who and what are garbos? Are they wizards or warlocks who insist on bi-weekly supplication? See how one's offerings have to be just right. For if you offer the garbos your garbage in an unsuitable bin, or plonk it in a cardboard box, they'll refuse to accept it. And look at the way they scatter unworthy refuse up and down the street. More evidence, irrefutable evidence, of the existence of demonology in our everyday lives. And spare a thought for the discipline under which these suburbanites live, forever buying and consuming at desperate pace so they'll have enough rubbish to fill their bins, lest the garbos be angered.

133

A. D. Hope

FULL AS A BOOT

This poem is one of three collectively titled 'Three Songs for Monaro Pubs'. The three poems present Australian male chauvinism at its worst.
From A. D. Hope's *The Drifting Continent* (1979).

Full as a boot, lad, full as a boot:
Well, Christ, why shouldn't I be?
That barmaid there, she's a piece of fruit . . .
(Make it rum and cloves for me!)

Full as a boot; but when I was young
They christened me Nevertire Jack.
Rum and cloves and you'ld never go wrong
To lay that piece on her back.

Down with her bottom; up with her heels;
Tackle her tit-for-tat.
Never you mind if she bucks or squeals:
All the better for that!

Never you mind, that's my advice;
Give her one on the floor;
Rum and cloves to her sugar and spice:
She'll tear you apart for more.

I've shore at The Rock, I've roused at Condobolin,
I've rabbited up around Parkes,
And wherever I camped them girls come nosin'
Nosin' around like sharks.

It was: No, Jack, no; I promised me mother!
Or: Geez, you're a bastard, Jack!
But have it your own way, have it the other,
She'ld end up flat on her back.

One girl, I left her in Gerringong,
One up by Capertee;
But that little honey at Cuppacumbalong,
She up and *she* left me.

Oh, she up and she left me there horn mad;
She up and she left me flat.

The best bloody woman that ever I had,
To do a thing like that!

Mr Bruce Gyngell
A REAL AUSTRALIAN?

Quoted in the Melbourne *Age* (June 20, 1981).

I think we have got to recognise the range of cultures to which all Australians are heirs, and that this mixture of people coming together will one day form a unique individual called an Australian.

Barry Humphries
ON AUSTRALIA

From an article called 'The Beastly Beatitudes of Barry H.' in *Mode Australia* (August–September, 1981).

Australia is like a jacuzzi of Bailey's Irish Mist, sort of syrupy and rather too warm.

.   .   .

It's interesting that a country which prides itself on its liberty has so many restrictions on it. But then we have a lot of people here in Australia who are natural public servants. I did a little research and I found that most public servants can trace their ancestry to convicts. They were in the service and prefer to remain so.

Patrick White
THE AUSTRALIAN DESERT

The author of *Voss* and *The Tree of Man* was quoted thus in *Mode Australia* (August–September, 1981):

I've never been very far into the Australian desert. And what's more, I'm determined never to go.

Barry Humphries

A TRUE AUSTRALIAN

Quoted in Bill Hornadge, *The Australian Slanguage* (1980).

To be a true Australian you have to dislike everybody from anywhere else.

Charles O'Neill

SO MUCH AT STEAK

The following verse from a reader was included in Lawrence Money's column in the Melbourne *Herald* (September 1, 1981) during the meat scandal.

Horses for courses make a nice little snack
A bonus for punters away from the track,
And kanga or wally or call it plain 'roo
Beats beef whether corned or boiled or in stew.
Add possum at will if your diet needs changing,
It comes big or small in a series wide-ranging
And platypus bill is rare of the rarest
As Brownlow well knew, the best and the fairest.
Choice cuddly bear and the dash of a wombat
Should steel Mr Reagan for satellite combat.
And last on the list, don't miss our fine emu
It's worth a top billing on your very best menu.

The London *Observer*

THE CURSE OF AUSTRALIA

This comment by Edward Mace, travel writer for the London *Observer*, was quoted in the Melbourne *Age* (October 3, 1981).

Flies are the curse of Australia and probably the reason why Australians tend to be irascible.

Patrick White

ON AUSTRALIA

From Patrick White's most recent book, *Flaws in the Glass* (1981) and quoted in the Melbourne *Herald* (October 13, 1981).

This supposedly sophisticated country is still, alas, a colonial sheep-run.

Brian Sweeney

BACKWOODS AUSTRALIA?

This comment by a Melbourne Cup visitor from Queensland, Brian Sweeney, was quoted in the Melbourne *Age* (November 7, 1981).

In Australia, if you don't live in Sydney, you're camping out.

SOME AUSTRALIAN ONE-LINERS

Many of the following are to be found in Bill Wannan's books and articles.

You're as clumsy as a duck in a ploughed paddock.

.   .   .

She is three bricks short of a load.

.   .   .

May all your chooks turn into emus and kick your dunny over.

.   .   .

He was meaner than a goldfield Chinaman, and sharper than a sewer rat.

.   .   .

He's got more corrugations on his belly than a thousand gallon tank.

.   .   .

137

She was as skinny as a sapling with the wood scraped off.

.   .   .

She was a whopper . . . fully three axe-handles across the hips.

.   .   .

All behind like Barney's Bull.

.   .   .

He's so mean that when a fly lands in the sugar he shakes its feet before he kills it.

.   .   .

She'd talk ten feet under water with a snorkel in her mouth.

.   .   .

Flash as a rat with a gold tooth.

.   .   .

He couldn't knock the skin off a rice pudding.

.   .   .

He wouldn't shout in a shark attack.

.   .   .

If those two blokes were alone in a bar together they'd die of thirst.

.   .   .

Brains! If your brains was gunpowder they wouldn't blow off your hat!

.   .   .

That man was too mean to hang himself.

5

GROWLS FROM GRUB STREET

Writers, Artists, Critics

The Launceston *Advertiser*

CONCERNING THE EDITOR OF THE CORNWALL *CHRONICLE*, WILLIAM LUSHINGTON GOODWIN

The editor of the Tasmanian journal, the Launceston *Advertiser*, mixed vitriol with his printer's ink when he attacked the editor of another Tasmanian paper, the Cornwall *Chronicle*, in his issue of June 23, 1842. See Kathleen Fitzpatrick, *Sir John Franklin in Tasmania* (1949).

. . . the public throw down this journal, disgusted at the foulness of his language, and unanimously agree that if any man be deserving of personal retaliation, that man is WILLIAM LUSHINGTON GOODWIN! They ask themselves whether private character, or the peace of families, has always been respected by *him*? Whether *he* has always held sacred the ties between husband and wife, parents and children? Whether *he* is the man who never disturbed the happiness of a domestic fireside?

Anon

LINES TO BARRON FIELD

Barron Field (1786–1846), a Supreme Court judge in early New South Wales, was the author of a small book of insipid verse, *First Fruits of Australian Poetry*, published in 1819. Even Charles Lamb, a friend of Field, had to strain every critical nerve to say anything good about the book. See Brian Elliott, *Singing to the Cattle* (1947).

Thy poems, Barron Field, I've read,
And thus adjudge their meed—
So poor a crop proclaims thy head
A *barren field* indeed!

Charles Harpur

'THE BALL-ROOM ERCILDOUNE OF BOTANY BAY'

These lines from *The Temple of Infamy* make fun of John Rae, a Sydney company director and amateur poet. He was a Master of Arts of Edinburgh. (Ercildoune, better known as 'Thomas the Rhymer', was a 13th century Scots poet.)

140

A Poetic Fancy.

POET - (out of a billet) "Great opening for poets here — I mean The Harbour"

Of Scottish Scribbleshire a native he,
A province betwixt Prose and Poetry . . .
Fled from his lovely classic mists, to be
(As shame decreed at his nativity)
The ball-room Ercildoune of Botany Bay
And Corporation Laureat.

Charles Harpur

ON A SYDNEY POET

From Harpur's *The Temple of Infamy*. The poet referred to was E. K. Silvester, who
was a Sydney *Herald* staff writer.

Not even the jangle of St Mary's chimes
Is more incongruous than his rag-tag rhymes.

Charles Harpur

ON A SYDNEY EDITOR

From *The Temple of Infamy*. The victim of this satire was Richard Thompson.

He might have been perhaps a man of worth,
If Bacchus had not 'stolen him at birth'.
Even yet, the things of Mind he holds as dear,
Or nearly, as the smaller things of Beer.

The *Sydney Punch*

HENRY KENDALL 'THE RHYMER'

The poet Henry Kendall (1839–1882) stirred the Sydney critics with the publication,
in 1886, of a satirical poem, *The Bronze Trumpet*. It provoked many counter-blasts,
including the one below.

'I sing,' murmured Henry the rhymer,
    'I sing now as often before,
And my song hath the sound of a trumpet,
    Well blown, on one key, evermore.'

The Maryborough and Dunolly *Advertiser*

ON A RIVAL, THE DUNOLLY *EXPRESS*

The Maryborough and Dunolly *Advertiser* (Vic.) thus commented on its newly-founded rival and 'reptile contemporary', the Dunolly *Express* during the year 1862. Quoted in James Flett's *Dunolly* (1956).

We have received what purports to be a newspaper. Except that the back page is printed over one of those inside, and that some of the advertising is upsidedown, that some of the type-matter is missing altogether and at other places runs over the edge of the paper, it would be readable were it not for the ridiculous reading matter. It won't last long.

A. G. Stephens

ON BRUNTON STEPHENS'S POEM, 'CONVICT ONCE'

'Convict Once', a long poem by the Queensland writer, James Brunton Stephens, was first published in 1871, when it was greeted with much critical acclaim.

. . . it is so far from being 'the most highly finished piece of work that has been accomplished in Australia' that one could more correctly say, 'in a hundred pages there is scarcely a line that could not be improved'.

The Sydney *Bulletin*

THE MYSTERY

From the Sydney *Bulletin* of 1883.

> He was a low comedian,
>   Whose forehead bore the brunt
> Of many a votive brick, flung by
>   Admirers, in the front.
>
> And yet though he was dull, almost
>   As a vice-regal speech,
> Those who were with him on the boards
>   When he would smile would screech.

What was the cause? He had no wit,
    No humour and no chaff;
His drink was rum—this was the cause
    Of his 'infectious laugh.'

The Sydney *Bulletin*

OF OSCAR WILDE

From the Sydney *Bulletin* of 1883.

Notwithstanding what the satirists have said about him, we
had some faith in Oscar Wilde, but now we begin to believe
he is a humbug after all. Not a humbug without some genius,
remember, for it takes genius to humbug successfully, and
whatever else he may be, he is a very graceful writer. But
when we read this sort of thing we got ill. He is replying to
an American reporter who asks him about his knee-breeches
and his hair. Thus: 'I have given up knee-breeches for a
time, and I did put myself in the hands of a hairdresser.
Everything has changed. Art has not one form only. It is
only necessary to follow the essence of art, and one may
dress beautifully without wearing knee-breeches. That style
of dress was worn when long, flowing wigs were in vogue.
Removing the knee-breeches necessitated a curtailment of
the hair. Many forms of dress are beautiful if the laws of art
and colour are observed. For the present I shall not wear my
hair long—*not, at least, till I have thoroughly thought the matter
over.*' The emphasis is ours. Just imagine any sane creature
thoroughly thinking over the matter as to whether he should
wear his hair long or short!

        Bah, Oscar! do you think the world
        Cares if your locks are straight or curled
        Or thick, or shed off?
        Or do you think a cuss we'd care
        If, when your barber cut your hair,
        He'd cut your head off?

The Sydney *Truth*

ON THE DEMISE OF THE *DEMOCRAT*

This attack by John Norton's *Truth* illustrates the amount of energy and newsprint
expended by journals on denouncing one another, during the last decade of the 19th
century. The *Democrat* had been an independent Labor paper.
Quoted in Cyril Pearl, *Wild Men of Sydney* (1958).

. . . a puling little rag . . . that circulated widely round the
Bondi sewer and was much execrated by the rats therein.

The Sydney *Truth*

ON THE *BIRD OF FREEDOM*

The *Bird of Freedom* was banned for the second time in 1891.
Quoted in Cyril Pearl, *Wild Men of Sydney* (1958).

Gorged with garbage, filled with foulness, leprous-tainted,
   vicious-vile,
Catering for the harlot's custom, bidding for the wanton's
   smile,
Thinly veiling bawdyism, brutal passion, bestial lust.
Revelling in vile excesses, joying in their fetid must.

Henry Lawson

AUSTRALIAN BARDS AND BUSH REVIEWERS

Henry Lawson (1867–1922) conducted a 'verse debate' with 'Banjo' Paterson (1864–
1941) in the pages of the Sydney *Bulletin* during the year 1892. The idea, which was
mutually agreeable, was that they should 'write against each other about the bush'.
Lawson claimed that Paterson's portrayal of bush life in his verse and fiction was an
idealised one; the outback was no paradise but a harsh and barren place. Paterson
claimed that there was as much of beauty as of harshness in the back country, and that
there was more of cheerfulness and hope there than of the bitter despair so often
encountered in Lawson's writings. Paterson summed up:
   'For the bush will never suit you, and you'll never suit the bush.'
Lawson, in 'Australian Bards and Bush Reviewers' and 'My Literary Friend' indicated
some of the hazards that beset the poet's path in this country.

While you use your best endeavour to immortalize in verse
The gambling and the drink which are your country's
   greatest curse,

While you glorify the bully and you take the spieler's part—
You're a clever southern writer, scarce inferior to Bret Harte.

If you sing of waving grasses when the plains are dry as
    bricks,
And discover shining rivers where there's only mud and
    sticks;
If you picture mighty forests where the mulga spoils the
    view—
You're superior to Kendall, and ahead of Gordon too.

If you swear there's not a country like the land that gave you
    birth,
And its sons are just the noblest and most glorious chaps on
    earth;
If in every girl a Venus your poetic eye discerns—
You are gracefully referred to as the 'Young Australian
    Burns'.

But should you find that Bushmen—spite of all the poets
    say—
Are just common brother-sinners, and you're quite as good
    as they—
You're a drunkard, and a liar, and a cynic, and a sneak,
Your grammar's simply awful, and your intellect is weak.

Henry Lawson

MY LITERARY FRIEND

Once I wrote a little poem that I thought was very fine,
And I showed the printer's copy to a critic friend of mine;
First he praised the thing a little, then he found a little fault;
'The ideas are good,' he muttered, 'but the rhythm seems to
    halt.'

So I straightened up the rhythm where he marked it with his
    pen,
And I copied it and showed it to my clever friend again,
'You've improved the metre greatly, but the rhymes are
    bad,' he said
As he read it slowly, scratching surplus wisdom from his
    head.

147

So I worked as he suggested (I believe in taking time),
And I burnt the midnight taper while I straightened up the
 rhyme.
'It is better now,' he muttered, 'you go on and you'll succeed,
It has got a ring about it—the ideas are what you need.'

So I worked for hours upon it (I go on when I commence)
And I kept in view the rhythm and the jingle and the sense,
And I copied it and took it to my solemn friend once more—
It reminded him of something he had somehwere read
 before!

. . .

Now the people say I'd never put such horrors into print
If I wasn't too conceited to accept a friendly hint,
And my dearest friends are certain that I'd profit in the end
If I'd always show my copy to a literary friend.

Sir Charles Dilke

PARKES'S POETRY

Sir Henry Parkes, the noted politician, published six volumes of unpretentious verse
between 1842 and 1895.

His debts, his poetry, are powerless to sink him.

John Haynes

TO SIR HENRY PARKES

John Haynes was co-founder with J. F. Archibald of the Sydney *Bulletin*.
Quoted in P. S. Cleary, *Australia's Debt to the Irish Nation Builders* (1933).

Sir Henry (on meeting Haynes in the parliamentary library):
 'Ah, Mr Haynes, have I caught you writing poetry?'
John Haynes: 'No, Sir Henry. Like yourself, I never wrote a
 line of poetry in my life.'

W. E. Fitz Henry

OF JOHN FELTHAM ARCHIBALD

From W. E. Fitz Henry, 'J. F. Archibald, Editor', in the Sydney *Bulletin* (January 11,
1956).

It is doubtful whether Archibald wrote a dozen leading-articles in all his years. He wrote ten thousand pungent lines, however, and he made phrases, said a colleague, 'as other men make good resolutions and put them to much more effective use'.

The Sydney *Worker*
'THE TYPICAL DAILY NEWSPAPER'

From the Sydney *Worker* (July 29, 1893).

[The typical daily newspaper] wants boiling down to the size of a sheet of notepaper and then frying with disinfecting fluid and cayenne pepper to make it wholesome and refreshing.

Henry Lawson
AN UNCULTURED RHYMER TO HIS CRITICS

From Henry Lawson, *An Uncultured Rhymer to his Critics* (1897).

You were quick to pick on a faulty line
That I strove to put my soul in:
Your eyes were keen for a dash of mine
In the place of a semi-colon —
And blind to the rest. And is it for such
As you I must brook restriction?
'I was taught too little?' I learnt too much
To care for a pedant's diction!

The *Innocents of Sydney*
ON A 'REPTILE CONTEMPORARY', SYDNEY *TRUTH*

During the late 1890s the *Innocents of Sydney*, a scandal-sheet, castigated its contemporary, Sydney *Truth*, founded in 1879. Quoted in Cyril Pearl's *Wild Men of Sydney* (1958).

The lackbrain, yelping, shady-pated, chowder-skulled, and

obscenely ridiculous promulgators of piddling, babbling, frothy, doting nonsense, under the prostituted word of *Truth*, are at their old lunes, and have made one more abortive, plaintive, miscarriage sort of effort to 'catchpenny' a few threepences.

Nicholas Eugene Coxon

JOHN NORTON: 'CRAFTY, CONCUPISCENT COCKATRICE'

Norton, who as a proprietor and frequent contributor to Sydney *Truth* used its columns for vicious, verbal assaults on innumerable public people who somehow incurred his ire, was in his turn assailed in print from many journalistic quarters.

The community of the Commonwealth is at present being menaced by a miserable mite of human malformation, known in this country as John Norton, a crafty, concupiscent cockatrice whose gluttony, drunkenness and lusts, which he admits he allowed to run riot in his youth, seem to have been raging more violently than ever during the past twelve months.

· · ·

Coxon also wrote a poem on Norton, which appeared in the *Jury*.
Quoted in Cyril Pearl, *Wild Men of Sydney* (1958).

> Who lives upon poor women's tears
> Of men who shrink from venomed ink
> John Norton
> Who walks the streets in fear and dread
> Of vengeance on his hairless head
> And smites with pen defenceless men
> John Norton
> Who boasts with valour to the skies
> And blackens women's weeping eyes
> Half brute, half man, the Charlatan
> John Norton
> Whose croak re-echoes to the toads
> And through his neck the filth explodes

The land's foul blot and drunken sot
John Norton

Joseph Furphy
ON *GEOFFRY HAMLYN*

Joseph Furphy, author of *Such is Life* (published by the Sydney *Bulletin* in 1903), made the following comment on the male characters in *Geoffry Hamlyn*, a novel by Henry Kingsley.
Quoted in Vance Palmer, *The Legend of the Nineties* (1954).

[The male characters are] slender-witted, virgin-souled over-grown schoolboys who fill Henry Kingsley's exceedingly trashy and misleading novel with their insufferable twaddle.

A. G. Stephens
ON HENRY KINGSLEY'S *GEOFFRY HAMLYN*

Alfred George Stephens (1865–1933) was literary editor of the Sydney *Bulletin* for many years, and that journal's most penetrating and sensitive literary critic, during a vital period in the development of Australian writing.

Geoffry Hamlyn is a pleasant, rambling story of the old school, patchy in interest, and very patchy in merit. It is never quite dull enough to bore, and rarely bright enough to excite. You put it down without difficulty, and take it up without anticipation.

A. G. Stephens
ON DOUGLAS SLADEN

Douglas Sladen (1856–1947), English-born author, was a prolific writer of fiction and verse, some of the latter being concerned with Australia.

Mr Sladen's work in relation to this country has been characterized by energy and incompetence.

151

Victor Daley

THE MODEL JOURNALIST

Victor Daley, using the pen-name 'Creeve Roe', wrote this poem in Sydney in 1903. See *Creeve Roe, Poetry by Victor Daley*, edited by Muir Holburn and Marjorie Pizer (1947).

[*Referring to the proposal of Pulitzer, the American newspaper proprietor, for the establishment of a School of Journalism, the* Sydney Morning Herald *says: 'If a School of Journalism can further the honourable traditions and principles of journalism as it is known to Britons and fostered by the atmosphere and traditions of the British press, it is surely welcome to try the experiment.'*]

> Young men who would succeed
>   As pressmen, unimperilled
> By foolish notions, read
>   The Gospel of the *Herald*—
>
> Be safe, be slow, be sure,
>   Take nothing upon rumour,
> And ever more be pure
>   And wholesome in your humour.
>
> Be sparing in your jests—
>   'Tis safer to be solemn;
> For Vested Interests
>   There is no Funny Column.
>
> Take views as calm and high
>   As Newton did, or Herschel;
> But always keep your eye
>   Upon the Things Commercial.
>
> Cast Creeds of Change afar,
>   No quarter to them giving;
> That things are as they are
>   Is our excuse for living.
>
> Go dead against Reform—
>   We stand or fall together—
> While we are snug and warm,
>   Who cares about cold weather?

Remember Property,
   Like the great goddess Isis,
'Is, has been, and shall be' —
   The crux of every crisis.

But let the Public see,
   When you have abstract reasons,
How liberal you can be
   In proper times and seasons.

Proclaim undying war,
   In leaders fierce and murky,
'Gainst Russian Horrors, or
   The Tyranny of Turkey.

Write boldly, cut and thrust,
   'Gainst wrong in some unseen land;
Denounce the Blubber Trust
   That paralyses Greenland:

.   .   .

Be hard on Ancient Rome —
   Things dead, or at a distance,
Are safe — but take at home
   The line of least resistance.

Pose as the People's Friend,
   Its candid, calm adviser —
But never dare offend
   The Lord God Advertiser.

Then you will happy be
   And will fulfil your mission,
And well uphold the free
   Old British Press Tradition.

A. G. Stephens

OF 'G. B. LANCASTER' (EDITH JOAN LYTTLETON)

From A. G. Stephens, 'Review' of 'G. B. Lancaster's' *Sons o' Men*, in the Sydney *Bulletin* (September 6, 1906).

Lancaster's poverty of ideas is as noticeable as [her] wealth of perceptions. Nor does excess of manner compensate for deficiency of matter: for the motive, when there is one, is usually lost in uncouth verbiage. Style is strained till it shrieks. It is said of Macauley that one never needed to read his sentences twice to discover their meaning; but often one reads Lancaster's thrice to discover them barren.

Victor Daley

AN URGENT CASE FOR WOMEN'S LIB.

I have provided my own title for this verse, which appeared as 'Two of a Trade' in the *Lone Hand* (July 1, 1907).

I

Green grew the grey Port Jackson sky —
Another day was drawing nigh.

Above the waters wan and weird
The Angel of the Dawn appeared.

The sleeping city turned and woke:
The houses shook their plumes of smoke.

A sound upon the stillness stole —
The Poet's wife was breaking coal.

She said, 'My love lies fast asleep.
His slumber it is calm and deep.

'He tarries in the Land of Dreams,
And walks by visionary streams.

'With long, white, languid nymphs and dames
Who bear outlandish Pagan names,

'And wear no clothes — because says he,
The weather's warm in Arcady.

'Would I could to his height aspire,
And touch like him the living lyre!

154

'But vain are my imaginings!
My spirit mounts on penguin's wings.

'It cannot soar in those strange skies
Wherein his eagle spirit flies.

'I have not his poetic soul,'
She sighed—and went on breaking coal.

II

The Poet at this moment woke
Into the world of common folk,

And rose, with patronising yawn,
To note the colour-scheme of dawn.

Then gazing down into the yard
He saw his small wife slogging hard.

'My tender Love! My sweet white rose!
My angel-wife! she little knows

'That what she's doing now,' said he,
'Is quintessential poetry—

'No finer any Muse need ask.
The humble, homely, daily task,

'Performed in cheerful style and free,
Is Earth's divinest melody—

'And Heav'n can boast no grander strain,'
He said, and went to bed again.

III

All day she roamed from room to room
With listless, unconvincing broom.

She saw not where, in corners, lay
The dust:—Her thoughts were far away.

155

She did not even once—alas!—
Gaze fondly in the looking-glass.

She hardly saw her way about,
But wandered in, and wandered out,

And fell, in her abstraction pure,
All over her scant furniture

And barked her fair shins many times—
For she was ruminating rhymes.

She dipped a pen in ink blood-red;
'I'll write a poem now!' she said.

In tones between a laugh and cry—
'I'll write a poem, if I die.'

Her brow was knit in thoughtful frown;
Her hair, unbrushed, hung loosely down.

Her tongue dropped gently from the South-
West corner of her pretty mouth.

With smiles, and tears, and blots she wrote—
I wish I could her poem quote!

She ended it, with flourish grand—
The proudest woman in the land.

'This poem is about,' she said,
'My sweet Love, and his dear, bald head.

'And when I've made a copy clean,
I'll send it to a magazine;

'And he, with joy beyond control,
Will say his 'Liza has a soul.'

IV

That tender poem, young and green—
It never reached that magazine.

Beneath the hearth-rug, neatly slipped,
The Poet found the manuscript,

156

While searching, with a spirit sore,
For sixpence hid the night before.

He read it slowly; read it through—
His face became a livid blue.

'Good God! what have I done,' cried he,
'That this should happen unto me!'

He called his wife; that gentle dame,
With sweet, expectant blushes, came.

Alas! his face looked stern and hard
As white, repulsive, frozen lard.

He gazed on her with beetling brow—
'I've loved you long,' he said, 'but now

'I tear your image from my heart—
The time has come for us to part.'

She fell upon her knees, and cried—
'O, dearest, turn not thus aside!

'Forgive your 'Liza, love,' cried she—
'My lord! my prince of poetry!

'How did I dare to reach the plane
Where you above all rivals reign?'

The Poet softened visibly—
'Come to my heart once more,' said he.

'I pardon you—but learn, my dear,
To keep within your proper sphere.'

                .   .   .

By marriage, genius oft is marred—
Not so with the foregoing Bard,

He still in verse outpours his soul;
His wife continues breaking coal.

John Norton

FROM 'AN OPEN LETTER TO MADAME MELBA CONCERNING HER CHAMPAGNE CAPERS, BREACHES OF PUBLIC FAITH, OUTRAGES AGAINST GOOD MANNERS, AND INSULTS TO AUSTRALIAN CITIZENS!'

This typical piece of Nortonian scurrility is quoted in John Hetherington's admirable biography, *Melba* (1967).

Madame—Marvellous Melba, Mellifluous Melba, Supreme Singer, Crowned Cantatrice, and Monarch of Matchless Music though you be, your public and private conduct during your short six months sojourn in Australia makes it compulsory that you should be told the truth. Genius is mostly eccentric; the eccentricities of genius are generally pardoned—up to a certain point. You have great genius, which is only excelled by your eccentricity. The public have heard too little of the first, and a great deal too much of the last. The turpitude of a talented termagant can be forgiven ten times ten, but there is a limit of licence which cannot be condoned. You have so often transgressed that limit that the public has at last become tired of your truculent tricks and vicious vagaries. Public patience is exhausted; public opinion exasperated; and in that style of language to which you have shown that you are not a stranger, you have to be told, on behalf of an abused and outraged community, that 'it's time you took a pull,' or were 'pulled up with a round turn'. Your scandalous breaches of public faith, and private propriety are no longer to be borne without protest. That protest I now make; and if you resent it, I invite you to vindicate yourself by civil or criminal process in a Court of Law. I tell you frankly that I court such a contest . . .

I am not going to dig up the squalid scandal of your married life, nor to resuscitate the sordid story of your alleged intrigue with the French royal rotter, the Duke of Orleans, nor to revive the details of the celebrated motion for *crim con* brought against you and him . . . I want to confine myself to your conduct here in Australia . . .

Surely you have made enough money out of your offended and outraged countrymen and countrywomen, and given so little of your easily gotten superfluity to the deserving charities of your native land, to enable you to deal not only fairly but liberally with the few second-rate artistes who accompany, and with two such responsible and deserving attendants as your private secretary and your personal companion. It is altogether too bad to add to the truculence of the termagant, the vagaries of the virago, and the proclivities of the poculent pocharde those of a miserable miser, who, while revelling in wealth and swigging champagne, balances and buncoes dependants who have kept better faith with her than she has kept with the public who have paid her so liberally, and generously forgiven her so much.

Madame, I've done with you for the meantime. Perhaps now that I've done with you you'll think it about time to begin with me. Be it so, but be sure you count the cost before commencing . . . Maintenant il faut que je vous fasse mes adieux, en chantant to the classic air of *Dolly Gray*.

'Good-bye, Nellie, I must leave you!
Give up swigging dry champagne;
Else your friends will surely leave you
In disgust and poignant pain.'

C. J. Dennis

POETS

From *Random Verse* (1952).

Of all the poetry I've read
I've never yet seen one (he said)
That couldn't be, far as it goes,
Much better written out in prose.
It's what they eat, I often think;
Or, yet more likely, what they drink.
Aw, poets! All the tribe, by heck,
Give me a swift pain in the neck.

Norman Lindsay (?)

THE MADHOUSE

The extract given here is from an article in *Vision* (No. 2, August, 1923). Although not signed, the article was probably written by Norman Lindsay, well-known for his scathing attacks on modern art, or possibly his son Jack Lindsay, one of the editors of *Vision*.

It is a well-known condition of madness, part of its general condition of disassociation, that a patient will see a face staring at him in a crack on the wall, or that he will evolve images that appear to him perfectly real, either of terror or fascination, from the hint of a wall-paper pattern. The reason is, of course, that all conscious control of mental processes has lapsed, and the disintegrated subconscious is let loose to play as it likes with the medley of unrelated and incoherent imagery that passes through it.

But we need not go to the padded cell to cull examples of this disarticulation. Modernistic studies and editorial rooms reveal the same condition. It is true they are not legally certified as asylums for the insane, but Matisse, for instance, in his drawings shows the same disintegration of mind as the lunatic who sees defined forms in what is really only an amorphous stain in the ceiling. The only difference is that Matisse transcribes his vague visions to paper or canvas, while the other remains in ecstatic contemplation. It is as absurd to question the sincerity of Matisse as to question the sincerity of our second exhibit, the grinning lunatic. Matisse himself clinches the matter by stating that he works without any help from his intellect, i.e., he lets his disordered subconscious parade its vague incoherencies without any effort of mind.

But the citic is not to be outdone in this competition for mental vacuity. He is the simple lunatic finding articulation. Instead of looking out of his window and seeing devils making faces at him in the pattern of the leaves against the glass, he stands in front of a modern primitive picture and discourses on the wonderful suggestion of infinity in a splotch of white, or of the grandeur of life in a bubonic sunflower by Van Gogh, or the marvellous solidity of objects in Cézanne.

J. A. V. Stevens

OF JAMES JOYCE'S *FINNEGAN'S WAKE*

From J. A. V. Stevens, 'Joyce's Choice', in *Bohemia* (May, 1939).

I wonder whether Jimmie Joyce
Produces tomes like that from choice,
Or whether he's impelled thereto
By something which, to me and you,
Is quite incomprehensible,
Some force from which he takes his cue,
And judges indispensable
In writing those queer, tangled tales
At which the hapless critic quails.

.   .   .

Let him who likes to have his brain
Befuddled by such puzzles gain
What e'er he can from that which lurks
Within the maze of Joyce's works;
As lief my plain mentality
I'd test on books inscribed by Turks,
Or some such nationality.
Yes, Jimmie's art may be the sort
That's known as long — but life's too short.

Lennie Lower

LENNIE LOWER VERSUS NOEL COWARD

Lennie Lower, dragooned into attending a big reception for Noel Coward when the latter visited Sydney in 1940, clashed with the celebrity, after having imbibed not wisely but too well.
Quoted in Bill Hornadge, *The Australian Slanguage* (1980).

When Noel Coward was introduced to Lower he rather condescendingly exclaimed, 'Ah, the King of the Australian humorists, one presumes!' to which Lower retorted: 'Ah, the great Quean of the English stage, one presumes!'

161

Lennie Lower

ON JOURNALISTS

The following two extracts are from *The Best of Lennie Lower Presented by Cyril Pearl and Wep* (1963).

Journalists are born. Why, nobody knows.

.   .   .

Journalists' hotels are easy to pick out by the noise. Invariably one can get credit there. Otherwise, it wouldn't be a journalists' hangout. The conversation in these places is mostly lewd and profane, and you will hear any amount of marvellous news stories that were canned by a moron sub-editor because he had no more brains than a wart-hog and words to that effect.

Sir Lionel Lindsay

ON MODERN ART

Sir Lionel Lindsay was an advocate of Royal Academy art. He heaped abuse on modern art, refusing to appreciate Picasso and Matisse.
The following extracts are from Lionel Lindsay, *Addled Art* (1942).

Modernism in art is a freak, not a natural, evolutional growth.

.   .   .

Except in Australia, the most intellectually backward country of European origin in the world, modern art is already moribund. The Jew dealers are dispersed and the novelty makers have no new dishes to tickle the palates of *fin de siècle* decadents. The dope demands a larger dose, the stinger must be laced with hard alcohol, sensation calls for fresh sensation, and when it cannot be provided inevitable boredom, the demon that pursues all chasers of distraction, invades the lives of the devotees of time-killing.

If modern art accurately reflects the spirit of the age, then our case is desperate and the sooner the arts crash the better for mankind; for here there is no road to a decent future or a renaissance of the spirit.

.   .   .

162

If the public rests content with modern art—which I am convinced it will not—it deserves to be exploited by the cheapjacks. As for the artist, bemused by inane theories and fallacious premises, who has bartered his birthright for a mess of Montmartre pottage, let him swelter in his revolutionary maze or win free of his folly. It is nobody's business but his own.

Sir Lionel Lindsay

ON THE ADVOCATES OF MODERN ART

André Breton (1896–1966), referred to in this extract, was the high priest of surrealism, its chief theorist and exponent.
From Lionel Lindsay, *Addled Art* (1942).

For the champions of modernism are plain sophists. Assertive, often truculent, and given to the use of categorical imperative, they neither dispute nor reason, having learned well the first rule of propaganda, which is that anything wrapped in a little mystery and proclaimed in tones of authority will find believers. At times I find their cant almost worse than the pictures they prate about. Far too shrewd to write straight French or English or German, they employ a metaphysical and pseudo-scientific Esperanto to dazzle their disciples and stupefy snobs . . . André Breton, bear-leader to the surrealists, rows in another galley, in which the Mad Hatter and the March Hare ply an oar.

Sir Lionel Lindsay

ON FREUD AND SURREALISM

From Lionel Lindsay, *Addled Art* (1942).

[Freud was] a pseudo-scientist, an unconscious charlatan whose monstrous theories have been discredited, like those of his master, Charcot (who invented hysteria, which he confused with nymphomania) upon which the pupil erected his crazy dream castle.

It follows naturally that surrealism, which emanates from the study of Freud, must share in the original imposture; and that its pretensions are equally suspect and fraudulent.

A. D. Hope

CONFESSIONS OF A ZOMBIE

A. D. Hope, reviewing the novel, *The Vegetative Eye*, must have virtually annihilated its author, the young Max Harris.
From *Meanjin Papers* (Autumn, 1944).

The Vegetative Eye reminds me of a one-man band. It is about Mr Max Harris, the well-known manager of the Educated Womb, written by Mr Max Harris, published by Mr Max Harris, and advertised with fearless praise by Mr Max Harris in Mr Max Harris's journal *Angry Penguins*. Nearly all the characters in the book turn out to be Mr Max Harris, too. Apart from that the book owes very little to Mr Max Harris. It reads like a guide to all the more fashionable literary enthusiasms of the last thirty years . . .

Dostoevsky wrote novels on two levels of consciousness. Mr Harris writes on so many levels at once that he whizzes from one to another with the mechanical agility of a lift-driver. Various writers have used the stream of consciousness technique for telling a story. Mr Harris's stream of consciousness has as many tributaries as the Amazon. Baudelaire gave us an example of the artist as the analyst of his own moral sickness. Mr Harris is morally sick and discusses his symptoms with the gusto of an old woman showing the vicar her ulcerated leg . . .

One is charmed by such examples of acute observation as: '*The burning alcohol was soft now, like a baby in her guts.*' Pregnancy is obviously one of the few experiences that Mr Harris has never enjoyed . . .

He is pathetically anxious to reveal his sources and to quote his authorities . . . These naive endorsements of the writer's *bona fides* are like the hotel labels which some travellers carefully preserve on their luggage to impress others with the fact that they have been around. Mr Harris's luggage is completely covered with labels . . . The plain fact is that Mr Harris cannot write . . .

At other times the narrative slushes along through the illiterate mannerisms of the pulp magazines . . .

It is all in the dream world. Had the writer's ability matched his conception we should have had the picture of a living man. As it is, we have a Zombie, a composite corpse, assembled from the undigested fragments of authors Mr Harris has swallowed without chewing and animated by psychological voodoo.

If, therefore, Mr Harris should be inclined to be wounded by this article, I can safely assure him that no reference in it is intended to any living person.

Robert Peel

ON THE EDIFICATION OF ERN MALLEY BY MAX HARRIS

The *Meanjin Papers* (Vol. 3, No. 2, 1944) contained an article by Robert Peel concerning the 1944 Autumn Number of the magazine *Angry Penguins*, edited by Max Harris and John Reed, which had devoted 'thirty-three pages to *The Darkening Ecliptic*, a batch of verse by Ern Malley, an alleged Sydney garage mechanic and insurance salesman, who died at the age of twenty-five from Grave's disease, and was cremated at Rockwood cemetery in July, 1943. His sister, Ethel, sent the manuscript to *Angry Penguins'* editors, who published a Malley commemorative issue, claiming the new poet to be "one of the two giants of contemporary Australian poetry". It was subsequently revealed that the "poems" were written during one afternoon by two Sydney graduates [James McAuley and Harold Stewart] by weaving misquotations and haphazardly chosen phrases and clichés with deliberately fashioned nonsense.' The 'debunking' of the modern literary movement was claimed to be the object of the deception.

[Peel claimed *Angry Penguins* to be a] . . . load of undigested rhetoric, cliché, didacticism, and indiscriminate optimism . . .

The appalling error, the real give-away, comes in the value placed by Harris on this poetry, his own and his friends' as well as Ern's. To see the latter as 'working through a disciplined and restrained kind of statement into the deepest wells of human experience' and its author as one of the 'giants' of modern Australian poetry is to abandon all serious standards of judgement in favour of an intellectual frivolity

165

disguised as superior sensibility . . . Is it to be wondered at that unregenerate Philistines rock with joy at the exposure of what they rightly judge to be dilettantism, faddism, and wilful obscurantism?

Harris writes of being diverted in his 'green age' from 'the gaunt Babel of the apes to the personal edifice'. What a pity that such brilliant energy should have immured itself from the one place where it could come to terms with humanity, to terms of understanding and love. Yeats in his aristocratic lonely tower, turning with aversion from the 'horrible green parrots' of a crass society, never lost his realistic sense of the human cost of such an isolation, and in that awareness partly transcended it. Not so Mr Harris in his private and paltry Babel.

A. D. Hope

ON ARTHUR MURPHY

A. D. Hope's review of Arthur Murphy's *First Harvest* included the following criticism. See C. B. Christesen (Ed.) *Meanjin Papers* (Vol. 3, No. 2, Winter, 1944).

First Harvest, by Arthur Murphy, is a collection of short lyrics which show that the writer can write singing verse. He has not yet acquired a language or an idiom of his own, and though the verse sings, it is someone else's music.

Australian Artists

IN 'ARCHIBALD PRIZE FIGHT'

A number of artists challenged the award of the 1943 Archibald prize for portrait painting to William Dobell for his painting of Joshua Smith, his friend and fellow artist. The artists claimed that the picture was not a portrait at all. The challenge was taken to court, and bitter, fiery scenes ensued. The court had to decide whether the painting was a portrait or a caricature or merely a fantasy. Mr Dwyer, K.C., declared that the suit (which subsequently was dismissed) to set aside the award of the prize to William Dobell was 'conceived in jealousy and born in spite'. Dobell was devastated and hurt by the case and to a large extent withdrew from the public eye.

The *Argus* reported the case under the headline 'Archibald Prize Fight' (October 24, 1944).

[J. S. MacDonald, former Director of the National Gallery of Victoria (1937–1939) was in the witness box.] Dobell's painting he regarded as a pictorial defamation of character. It was a fantasy, a satirical caricature. If somebody said to him, 'This [i.e. the subject of the painting] is a portrait painter,' he would reply, 'No, that man could not paint a portrait. He is a poor maimed creature.' . . .

Mr MacDonald said also that the figure in the painting did not look like a normal person. It looked like an ailing person, sick in body and brain.

[25 October 1944] The crier's busy time began when Dr Vivian Benjafield, well-known Macquarie St doctor, who was called for the plaintiffs as an expert on human anatomy, diagnosed the painting of Mr Smith as a portrait of a man who had been dead some months. (Laughter)

Mr Kitto, K.C., for the National Gallery Trustees, objected to the admission of Dr Benjafield's evidence.

'If he says the figure is like a corpse I shall have to call other witnesses from Macquarie St to say it is alive,' said Mr Kitto.

Mr Barwick, K.C., (for plaintiffs) said he could call an undertaker to speak as an expert on corpses . . .

Then, to witness (Dr Benjafield), Mr Barwick said: 'What is the state of Mr Smith's physical existence as represented in the picture?'

Witness (looking critically at the picture): 'I should say it represents the body of a man who had died in that position and remained in that position for some months and dried up.' (Laughter)

Dr Benjafield also made some gruesome comparisons between certain features of the picture, and those of a corpse. He said, too, that the normal neck had several vertebrae, but there would need to be at least ten to produce a neck like the one in the picture.

Mr John Henry Young, art valuer, and until recently acting director of Sydney National Gallery, said he had known Joshua Smith for some years and was dumbfounded and shocked when he saw Mr Dobell's painting of him. He did not regard it as a portrait. It was a thoroughly fantastic conception. It might be called a fantasy of Joshua Smith. He

167

could not think of any portrait which was considered great, or even good, where distortion was obvious.

'I find it hard to discuss this picture in terms of reality,' witness added. 'It is a biological absurdity.' . . .

.   .   .

Mr Barwick produced a small plaster bust modelling of Mr Weaver, Opposition leader in the NSW Parliament. It had a very prominent nose, extremely prominent.

'What would you say of that?' Mr Barwick asked the witness (Mr Richard Horton James, lecturer and broadcaster on art, a Fellow of the Royal Society of Arts, London, and a member of the Contemporary Art Society, who had defended Dobell's portrait).

'I think it was done in a spirit of fun. It is not a work of art at all. It is a joke.'

A well-known Sydney artist rose in the body of the court and called in a loud voice, 'That was done in all seriousness.' (Laughter)

[26 October 1944] [Mr Barwick, on cross-examining Paul Haefliger, artist and art critic for the *Sydney Morning Herald*] asked what he thought about a statement by a previous witness that Picasso had painted a pile of packing cases and called it 'Portrait of My Father'.

Witness said he had not seen such portrait, but an artist could paint in any form to express his spiritual reaction.

Mr Barwick: 'So if an artist wanted to paint his mother-in-law according to his spiritual reaction, he could paint a coil of barbed wire and that would be a portrait?' (Loud laughter) . . .

Dobell later said under cross-examination by Mr Barwick [that] he painted Mr Smith as he appeared to him.

'I admit the neck is elongated,' said witness, 'but that is only part of the whole, and I might just as well criticise the conduct of your case by the angle of your wig.' (Laughter)

[27 October 1944] 'If this is a portrait,' said Mr Barwick, 'There is no limit to portrait painting. There is no principle, no logical point to stop at. Your Honour is asked by defendants to open the door. No one can gainsay that.'

Randolph Bedford

ON BENNETT'S *EVENING NEWS*

From Randolph Bedford, *Naught to Thirty-three* (1944).

And first in Pitt Street [Sydney] and then in Market Street was the most slipshod journal between Sydney Harbour and Spitzbergen — Bennett's *Evening News*. Its music critic once wrote of Madame Melba:

'Mrs Armstrong took well and gave pleasure to all.'

James Stuart MacDonald

PERVERSION OF ART

J. S. MacDonald, Director of the National Gallery of Victoria from 1937 to 1939 and a 'foremost Australian art critic', wrote a trenchant criticism of modern art which he considered to be 'alien from Australian life and tone'. The extracts given here constitute only a small part of the rather lengthy article, all of which is expressed in like terms!

From the Sydney *Daily Mirror* (February 5, 1945).

The condign approbrium visited by public opinion on that majority of the trustees of the National Art Gallery who awarded the Archibald Prize wrongly in 1943, and then, without due apology, attempted to retrieve their position by a volte face, cannot be monopolised by them alone. The exponents, teachers, partisans and writers concerned in this debauching of the public mind (through urging this leprous cult, miscalled Art) must share the obloquy.

... The members of this mouldy, cinglutination of paranoics, whichever they might be, trumpeted it to the world that they were a band of heroes besieging the sun; but they really were only a larrikin pack of degenerates, out on a street lamp-breaking foray.

... due to the efforts of the advocates of 'the latest thing', germs of this pestilence, this black plague, have been brought in and cultivated with all the diabolical industry of destructive fanatics.

Why should they be hell-bent on inoculating us with this loathsome, corrupting, foreign pus is beyond conception to all but themselves.

169

... For reprehensible reasons of their own, certain persons in high places are urging this evil on the people ... They get out of it either profit, or a sadistic gratification. It amuses them.

Sir Robert Menzies

ON JOURNALISM

From Ray Robinson, *The Wit of Sir Robert Menzies* (1966).

Years ago, a South Australian Premier, Sir Thomas Playford, told me: 'You never get into trouble for what you don't say.' There's a great deal of truth in that, though in my experience what you don't say is frequently reported.

Mike McColl Jones

EARLY DAYS OF TELEVISION

Mike McColl Jones, script and gag writer for such television personalities as Graham Kennedy and Bert Newton, records some of the jokes and amusing experiences of the early days of Australian television in his book, *My Funny Friends* (1979).

On the Channel 9 Canteen

We used to call the place 'The Bureau of Missing Portions', and would suggest that before flies landed on the food there they would have tetanus injections. One night we showed [on *In Melbourne Tonight*] a skeleton sitting at a table and explained that it was just somebody waiting to be served ... The canteen manager was not amused!

Graham Kennedy on Philip Brady

Graham Kennedy introducing Philip Brady on *In Melbourne Tonight*: 'Some people have it, some people don't. Philip Brady doesn't even know what *it* is!'

On Ita Buttrose

Don Lane introducing Bobby Limb: 'Bobby Limb is to music, what Ita Buttrose is to elocution.'

170

On Eric Pearce

I wouldn't say that Eric Pearce is old, but his driving licence number is 2.

.　　　.　　　.

Eric is on the show tonight because when he woke up this morning he checked the death announcements in the newspaper and found he wasn't in them. So he came to work!

Bert Newton's Big Chance

On the morning that President Kennedy was assassinated, someone in the business was taking a cab and mentioned it to his driver. 'Isn't it terrible news about Kennedy being killed?' he said. The driver instantly reacted with 'Horrible. I didn't know about it. Yes, it's real bad . . . but, I guess, maybe now Bert Newton will get his chance?'

J. S. Manifold

A HAT IN THE RING

This poem takes the form of a dialogue between two persons, one of whom is severely critical of the value of poetry. The lines quoted are from the first few stanzas only. From Chris Wallace-Crabbe (Ed.) *The Golden Apples of the Sun* (1980).

N.　Verse? Writing verse? Dear man, are you insane?
　　To think I used to think you had a brain!
　　This is not Arcady; the days are gone
　　When Phyllis babbled verse to Corydon.
　　Wake up! Queen Anne is dead, and Pope as well.
　　So's Burns, so's Keats, so's Byron . . .

M.　Go to hell.
　　Talk to your friends or rollick in a stew,
　　Go anywhere, but go. I've got work to do.

N.　You call it work? I call it waste of time
　　To brood and curse and mumble scraps of rhyme.
　　For what's to show? No publisher prevails
　　On press and populace to swell your sales.

171

Novels, I grant, and travel books are sound,
But verse will never bring you fifty pound:
Books may be published, bought and read, it's true,
But not in verse, and not by such as you.
What sort of thing's a poet when all's said?
A gutless creature with an empty head
Given to sandals, corduroys, and beard
And curious vices too from all I've heard.

Sir Robert Menzies
ON PRESS REPORTING

From an address given at the twenty-fifth anniversary dinner of the Journalists' Club in Sydney, in 1964. From Ray Robinson's *The Wit of Sir Robert Menzies* (1966).

I have always been an admirer of the great art of reporting...
now so sadly neglected.

John Pinkney
ON BOB HOPE

From the Melbourne *Age* (April 6, 1973).

[Bob] Hope hoes into humour like a cornered heavyweight fighting for his laugh—and thereby uses more dead weight than discrimination.

Helen Frizell
ON *BARRY McKENZIE HOLDS HIS OWN*

Bill Hornadge in *The Australian Slanguage* (1980) quotes the view of former *Sydney Morning Herald* literary editor, Helen Frizell, expressed in 1974, regarding the Australian film.

Personally, I've had a gutful of watching Bazza (McKenzie) and his mates boozing away, showering one another with the amber fluid, and doing their Ugly Australian act abroad. And, although some may consider it transcendentally witty for Bazza to vomit into the camera lens, once you've seen this you've seen it, and an almost Technicolour yawn was my reaction. The Ockerish audience seemed to love this, but then the film was made about Ockers for Ockers.

Phillip Adams

ON *CLOSE ENCOUNTERS OF THE THIRD KIND*

In *More Unspeakable Adams* (1979) the author, in a discourse on the American film, *Close Encounters of the Third Kind*, ridicules what he sees as the foolish gullibility of those who believe in the supernatural:

Once upon a time and camels, three wise men followed a star to a manger, where they beheld the birth of a new religion. Long fascinated by matters theological, I undertook a similar trek. Along with myriad true believers, I followed a strange glow to a mangy cinema in San Francisco where buttered popcorn and Hershey bars substitute for frankincense and myrrh. In this unprepossessing locale, America is witnessing a remarkable resurgence of faith.

I speak of *Close Encounters of the Third Kind*, the messianic movie that's New Testament to the Old Testament of *Star Wars* . . . In the UFO phenomenon, we are witnessing an attempt by technological society to create a god in its own image. Make no mistake, ufology is a faith, as transcendental as the most pentecostal Christian cult. Like hillbillies draping themselves in rattlesnakes, an entire generation is jibbering in the Monty Pythonic coils of this moronic film . . .

[In regard to some cuts made to the film after the first preview] I only wish he'd kept cutting . . . and let us get on with the job of coping, thinking, surviving.

Dennis Pryor

ON BOOKS FOR BURNING

Dennis Pryor, in an article entitled 'Burnt any books lately?' in the Melbourne *Age* (March 23, 1981), made a satirical comment on the news from Hay-on-Wye (Wales) concerning its 'most notorious resident, the bibliophile eccentric Mr Richard Booth'.

173

In a piece of pure economic Thatcherism, he has decided to go into the solid fuel business. The Thatcherites keep closing down coal mines, so, he argues, why not use the mine of combustible material which stays unsold on his shelves?

He is offering assorted books at $3 a carload, which is a snip when you consider the price of solid fuel in Britain. He claims they burn well with a bit of wood to help them.

Here we have the first commercially creative act of book burning. Were I Mr Booth (and sometimes I wonder if I am, when hit on the head by a domestic bookslide) the problem would be how to select the most appropriate candidates for the fire.

For me the romantic novelists would be the ladies for burning. Barbara Cartland would be the first hackneyed cab off the rank and I should probably have the support of the Free Wales guerillas, since Ms Cartland is about to become a remote connection of the Prince of Wales after his marriage.

Next the sociologists, who write too much and too badly. The self-help manuals would also go into the boot of the first customer, all those books teaching you how to meditate on a macrobiotic diet while going into transactional analysis with a primal-screaming birth-counsellor.

Mr Booth has his own views. His incendiary priorities are for Latin, theology and legal textbooks. And books on educational techniques, of which he says: 'If you saw some of the textbooks produced for modern universities you would think I was doing the trade a favor.'

That's the kind of vice-chancellor our universities need.

Barry Humphries

A WORD FROM SIR LES PATTERSON

In 1981 Barry Humphries, in the guise of Sir Les Patterson, cultural attaché and 'Australia's number one Socialist elder statesman overseas', made what he termed 'some *totally* unsubsidised hard-hitting political comment' in regard to the cutbacks in art subsidies from Canberra.

I got the big knock-back from Canberra myself a couple of months ago when I put the hard word on The Yartz boys

174

there to swing me a five-figure Project Development Grant with respect to my life story.

Incredible isn't it, if you remember the golden days of Gough, when the cheque always came back by return of post?

Incredible and sickening.

. . . *My goodself*, Les Patterson K.B.E., has been largely the only left-wing voice in terms of Australian theatre since a *coup* and two rigged elections cut our home-grown writers off from the huge sums they ought to bloody well be getting in order to shove a bit of political comment into their shows.

Are you with me?

Phillip Adams

YOU DON'T SAY, MARCEL

Phillip Adams, in an 'interview' with the great French mime artiste, Marcel Marceau, found himself doing all the talking! A few extracts only are given here. From the Melbourne *Age* (August 15, 1981).

PA: . . . Well, moving right along, what are your first . . .
MM:
PA: Pardon e moi, *second* impressions of Melbourne?
MM:
PA: Could you elaborate on that . . .?
MM:
PA: Well, isn't that bloody typical. Some frog lands at Tulla and within cinq minutes he's a bloody expert. If there's one thing that gives me a pain in the derrière it's you celebrities coming ici and mal-mouthing us Melburnians. I bet you haven't even seen the Paris end of Collins Rue? Or been to some of our bon frog cafés. Well, let me tell you un thing or deux. I reckon that Paris'd be très bon if it wasn't for the Frenchmen. Talk about arrogant! Looking down their nez at we tourists. Cripes, I lost count of the temps I wanted to give your taxi drivers a knuckle sandwich.
MM:
PA: Don't you mime at me like that!
MM:

PA: Don't you raise your gestures at me! I didn't come ici to be insulte par vous!

MM:

PA: What didn't you say to me? How dare you not say a thing like that! If you think I'm going to sit here and not listen to your insults you've got another think coming!

MM:

PA: So I am a bit gros. At least I don't go mincing around in long underpants and ballet shoes. With my visage all covered in paint blanc. With un fleur sticking out of mon chapeau! I told 'em I didn't bloody well want to interview vous anyway. A ratbag who wanders around the stage all nuit en silence! At the prix you're charging for les billets you'd expect a bloody soundtrack! Who do you think you are anyway? Harpo Marx?

MM:

PA: Just you gesture that encore! Just you step à l'extérieur and mime that!

MM:

PA: How dare you say that about our Prime Minister! Anyway, Mitterand's a poofter!

MM: !!

PA: And Gough Whitlam could beat Napoleon any time! Anyway, the spire on our Arts Centre's going to make the Eiffel Tower look like a bill spike! And what about your rotten bombe atomique tests dans le Pacific.

MM: (thump)

PA: Ouch! You've given me a bloody nez! You better watch it Marceau. My big frère est un gendarme!

At this point, the interview est fini.

Barry Humphries

AT THE 104th OLD MELBURNIAN DINNER

Barry Humphries, as speaker at the 1981 Old Melburnian dinner, pulled in a record crowd of 920, to be compared with past attendances for Malcolm Fraser (400) and Sir Zelman Cowan (450). Humphries took his wife, Diane — the first woman to attend the boys-only night! This report appeared in the Melbourne *Herald* (August 21, 1981).

Everyone there wore a dinner suit and black tie, except, of

course, Diane and a lonely-looking three in lounge suits.

After his speech I was talking to Barry, who was in my year at school, when a young man holding a beer and wearing a grey suit with red-spotted tie slightly askew, trotted up and said, 'Barry, I thought you would do Les Patterson.'

Barry replied: 'I thought you would wear a dinner suit.'

Then as our young man in grey did not look like leaving he added: 'Furthermore, I only do Les Patterson for money, so may I assume, sir, that you only wear a dinner suit for money and you are, I assume, one of the waiters.'

Brian Courtis

A BOTTOMLESS WELL OF HUMOR

From the Melbourne *Age*'s television 'In View' column (August 28, 1981).

If our national sense of humor was to be judged on the state of our television comedies, Australia would be considered a dull, dour, and underprivileged country indeed.

New York Advertisement

FOR *GALLIPOLI*

An American advertisement for the Australian film *Gallipoli* was quoted in the Melbourne *Age* (August 29, 1981).

From a country you've never heard of—a story you'll never forget.

Doug Anthony

ON POLITICAL COMMENTATORS

When the Prime Minister, Mr Fraser, was convalescing due to a viral infection in September 1981, the acting Prime Minister, Mr Anthony, criticised the 'silly' rumours about Mr Fraser's health.
From the Melbourne *Age* (September 2, 1981).

The main trouble I see with his taking sick leave is that it sparks off a frenzy of activity in our political commentators. Every cough is analysed for its political significance and every medical bulletin read with the care of a fortune teller reading tea leaves.

Public Reaction

TO THE YELLOW PERIL

The saga of the Melbourne City Square sculpture, *The Vault*, by Ronald Robertson-Swann, has been a long, emotional, mud-slinging affair. Journalist Noel Hawken described what he saw as the regrettable reaction by the public to what became popularly known as the 'Yellow Peril'.
From the Melbourne *Herald* (July 22, 1981).

What was this? It didn't look like Burke and Wills, or the fairy tree in the Fitzroy Gardens, or Winston Churchill, or Disneyland! It didn't even look like a hamburger or a plaster bust of Innocence Weeping!

It was just a creation of shape and surface, weight and light, planes and shadow-varied color . . . just standing there, like.

So what the bloody hell was the use! Give Little Willy a few tin trays, and he could do something as good in the backyard!

Mr Robertson-Swann called it, *The Vault*. What could that mean for heaven's sake? Vault? That's for banks to put money in, eh? And people do it with a big pole over a bar . . .

On to the sculpture we heaped our self-distrust and inferiority; our guilt about not knowing about 'art'; our fear of the new; our crudity of popular taste; our ignorance of levels of achievement . . .

Dr John Carroll

YELLOW SCAPEGOAT

The views held by Dr John Carroll, lecturer in the sociology of Australian culture at La Trobe University, were reported in the Melbourne *Age* (September 2, 1981).

Morally, in terms of what we Melburnians needed to go in

178

From the Melbourne *Herald* (March 25, 1981)

179

that space, the sculpture couldn't be worse. It's a totally impersonal object, not allowing any possibility for human identification.

Its shape is totally abstract and geometric, symbolising the inhumanity of the modern city, which is exactly what it shouldn't be doing. It needed in some way to be a strong sacred object, to fulfil the role of a totem pole, something before which the people of the city need to have some respect and awe, and take some pride in. The need to write graffiti on it shows that it's seen as a defilement. It needed to be warm and powerful to give it some sacred aspect.

Hence the legitimate revolt against it, and it deserved to be dumped in the mud. This was psychologically satisfying for most Melburnians. You couldn't imagine an object less likely to gain the sympathy of a significant number of people. In fact, it got the sympathy of a few people who used it as a cause against conservative, philistine councillors.

Garrie Hutchinson

ON *THE DUNSTAN DOCUMENTARIES*

The following extract is from a review entitled 'Dunstan's Nightmare', by Garrie Hutchinson, dealing with the 1981 series, 'grandiloquently entitled' *The Dunstan Documentaries*, written and hosted by South Australia's ex-Premier, Mr Don Dunstan. From the 'Green Guide' of the Melbourne *Age* (September 3, 1981).

I don't mean to be nasty, but rarely in the field of documentaries has a series been more monumentally mediocre than this one.

Barry Humphries

ON AUSTRALIAN AUDIENCES

From an interview reported in the local Melbourne newspaper *Green Place* (September, 1981).

Humphries laconically observed that Australians were the 'most transcendentally vulgar people in the world', that one of the great distinguishing things about the Australian

180

audiences is that they eat, that they seem to associate Theatre with oral mastication . . . 'a primaeval urge to devour . . . perhaps to sweeten some (bitter truth that might project across the footlights)'. However, Mr. Humphries hastened to add that on his return to Australia—'I am happy to see that they are still eating, and still there.'

Mode Australia

ON PETER ALLEN

An article in the Australian magazine *Mode Australia* (August–September, 1981) described singer and entertainer, Peter Allen, thus:

[He] looks a cross between a weasel and a mother's endearing, toothy little boy.

Robert Hughes

OF ART CRITICISM

Australian-born Robert Hughes, art critic for *Time* magazine and author of *The Shock of the New*, was quoted recently in *Mode Australia* (August–September, 1981):

Most art criticism . . . is a desert of bad writing and over-elaborated small thought.

Barry Humphries

CULTURE DISSEMINATION BY THE ABC

Quoted in an article in *Mode Australia* (August–September, 1981).

The ABC has this habit of taking an Australian book of some merit and attempting to turn it into a classic. What happens is that they grind it small on the wheel of culture.

The Press

OF RUPERT MURDOCH

The following observations are quoted in *Mode Australia* (August–September, 1981).

The **Dirty** Digger. (Britain's *Private Eye*)

. . .

Send this wallaby back, Jack. (Pre-takeover graffiti on the office walls of the *New York Magazine*)

. . .

[Murdoch practises] mean, ugly, violent journalism. (Executive editor, Abe Rosenthal, of the *New York Times*)

Chris Wallace-Crabbe

MEDIOCRE POET WRITES UNMEMORABLE LETTERS

From a review of Stephen Spender, *Letters to Christopher*, by Chris Wallace-Crabbe, in the Melbourne *Age* (September 5, 1981).

From my earliest acquaintance with his writings and with any writing about him, Stephen Spender presented me with an absolutely consistent image. Despite random felicities like *Landscape near an Aerodrome* it was plain all the way that he was a 'wet', in the good old schoolboy sense of that category rather than in the coarsened usage which Mrs Thatcher has gone so energetically far to popularise . . .

It is a hard thing to say of a book, but I found not one sentence anywhere in Spender's letters or journals which seemed worth noting or remembering . . .

If readers should still be looking for a portrait of this mediocre poet and ardent sitter upon committees, I suggest that they take the fictive version: his presentation as Mark Members in Anthony Powell's *The Music of Time*. Comic is always better than pathetic.

Hal Porter

AUTOBIOGRAPHER'S FREAK SHOW

The Melbourne *Age* of October 24, 1981, carried a review by noted Australian

'Sorry Sir! In order to compensate for the iniquitous Govt. sales tax, the publishers were forced to delete the last 2½% of pages!'

From the *Bulletin* (October 20, 1981)

author, Hal Porter, of the self-portrait *Flaws in the Glass* (1981) by Patrick White. A small extract only is given here.

[The novels and plays of Mr White] bamboozle and irritate me. My fault? His? After examining this self-portrait I'm now as near as I'll ever be to knowing why Mr White writes as he does, and from which limited sources he gets the inspiration for his self-indulgent works with their *longueurs*, obsessively frequent use of certain dirty words, kinky and dotty characters, and over-all tone of high-camp mysticism and low-camp waspishness.

'FOR WHERE WE ARE IS HELL'

Places Unpleasant

Anon

HAIL SOUTH AUSTRALIA!

First published in 1843, this anonymous denigration of South Australia is quoted in Freedom on the Wallaby, *edited by Marjorie Pizer (n.d.).*

Hail South Australia! blessed clime,
　　Thou lovely land of my adoption;
(I never meant to see the spot
　　If I had had the slightest option.)

Hail charming plains of bounteous growth!
　　Where tufted vegetation smiles.
(Those dull, atrocious endless flats,
　　And no plain less than thirteen miles.)

Hail tuneful choristers of air!
　　Who open wide your tiny throats.
(There's not a bird on any tree
　　Can twitter half a dozen notes.)

Hail glorious gums of matchless height!
　　Whose heads the very skies pervade;
Whose tops and trunks yield vast supplies
　　(But not a particle of shade.)

Hail far-famed Torrens, graceful stream!
　　On whose sweet banks I often linger,
Soothed by the murmur of thy waves;
　　(And plumb the bottom with my finger.)

Hail *June*, our grateful *winter* month!
　　Which never bring'st us wintry rigours;
And when *sweet February* comes
　　(It finds us steaming like the niggers.)

Hail balmy rains! in showers come down,
　　To do both town and country good;
(To give to each on reaching home
　　The blessings of a ton of mud.)

Hail land! where all the wants of life
　　Flow in cheap streams of milk and honey;

186

Where all are sure of daily bread
(If they can fork out ready money.)

Hail *South Australia*! once more hail!
That man indeed is surely rash
Who cannot live content in thee,
Or wants for anything (but cash).

Anon

'LAND OF PROMISE'

From A. B. Paterson's collection, *Old Bush Songs* (1905). Paterson noted: 'Mr Jordan was sent to England by the Queensland Government in 1858, 1859, and 1860 to lecture on the advantages of immigration, and told the most extraordinary tales about the place.'

Air: Four and Twenty Blackbirds

Now Jordan's land of promise is the burden of my song.
Perhaps you've heard him lecture, and blow about it strong.
To hear him talk you'd think it was a heaven upon earth,
But listen and I'll tell you now the plain unvarnished truth.

Here mutton, beef, and damper are all you'll get to eat
From Monday morn till Sunday night, all through the
     blessed week.
And if the flour-bag should run short, then mutton, beef,
     and tea
Will be your lot, and whether or not, 'twill have to do, you'll
     see.

Here snakes and all vile reptiles crawl around you as you
     walk,
But these you never hear about in Mr Jordan's talk;
Mosquitoes, too, and sandflies, they will tease you all the
     night,
And until you get colonized you'll be a pretty sight.

Here are boundless plains where it seldom rains, and you'll
     maybe die of thirst;
But should you so dispose your bones, you'll scarcely be the
     first,

187

For there's many a strong and stalwart man come out to
    make his pile
Who never leaves the fatal shore of this thrice accursed isle.

To sum it up in few short words, the place is only fit
For those who were sent out here, for from it they cannot flit.
But any other men who come a living here to try
Will vegetate a little while, and then lie down and die.

John Boyle O'Reilly

'NATION OF SUN AND SIN'

Born in Ireland in 1844, John Boyle O'Reilly was transported to Western Australia in
1867–68 for his part in Fenian activities. A year after his arrival he escaped aboard a
whaling vessel to the United States. He wrote works of fiction and a number of poems
with an Australian background. He died in 1890.

Nation of sun and sin,
Thy flowers and crimes are red,
And thy heart is sore within
While the glory crowns thy head.
Land of the songless birds,
What was thine ancient crime,
Burning through lapse of time
Like a prophet's cursing words?

Sir John Robertson

SOUTH OF THE MURRAY

Sir John Robertson (1816–1891), a landholder in the Liverpool Plains district of New
South Wales, subsequently became Premier of that colony on five occasions. His
speech had the rough flavour of the bush.

Victoria! What the hell do I care for Victoria? A bloody
country to the south of the Murray, inhabited by bloody
savages!

         .   .   .

We cannot stand that progressive colony; they are rather too
insolent.

188

Anon

THE BUSHMAN'S FAREWELL TO QUEENSLAND

There are several versions of this bit of old folklore still in circulation. The present one has been slightly abbreviated, not for reasons of censorship but because it seemed to me boringly over-long.

Queensland, thou art a land of pests;
For flies and fleas one never rests.
E'en now mosquitoes round me revel—
In fact they are the very devil.
Sandflies and hornets, just as bad,
They nearly drive a fellow mad;
With scorpion and centipede
And stinging ants of every breed;
Fever and ague, with the shakes,
Tarantulas and poisonous snakes;
Iguanas, lizards, cockatoos,
Bushrangers and jackaroos,
Bandicoots and swarms of rats,
Bulldog ants and native cats;
Stunted timber, thirsty plains,
Parched-up deserts, scanty rains;
There's rivers here you can't sail ships on,
There's native women without shifts on;
There's humpies, huts, and wooden houses,
And native men who don't wear trousers;
There's Barcoo rot and sandy-blight,
There's dingoes howling all the night;
There's curlew's wail, and croaking frogs,
There's savage blacks and native dogs. . .
To stay in thee, O land of mutton,
I wouldn't give a single button,
But bid thee now a long farewell,
Thou scorching, sunburnt land of hell!

Matt Ferris

THE ITALIAN COCKY'S LAMENT

From Bill Wannan, *Fair Go, Spinner* (1964).

Me bloody full of da Queensland,
Your country verra dry;
Me never maka no fortune
No matter how me try.

Banana getta da bunchy top,
Tomato getta da blight;
Cabbage getta da aphis:
He looka da rotten sight.

Grub he eata da peanut,
I losa da crop of corn:
Cockatoo he eata da crop
At night and early morn.

One week verra cold,
Da next week verra hot;
Den you getta da thunderstorm
An' drowna da bloody lot.

Someone doctor my red bull,
Maka him verra sick;
Cow she kicka da bucket—
Too much da cattle tick.

Just den I getta da cart horse,
I calla him Stars-d'-Stripes:
Only driva him two times twice,
Den da cussa getta da gripes.

I getta dam disgusted,
I gonna maka da tracks,
When da Labor Party writa me
Abouta da income tax.

Dey writa da nasty letter
To givva da man da fright,
So I writa back to tell 'im
Da money bloody tight.

Shire Council he writa also,
He sticka up da rate;
So I writa back to tell 'im
To putta 'im on da slate.

190

Now watta in hell to grin about?
'Tainta no time to laugh —
Your country bloody rotten
No doubt in more dan half.

I go up to da auctioneer
An' tella 'im dis yarn:
I hopa da cripes you bloody quick
To sella da rotten farm.

I mortgage ever' bloody thing
To da Agricult'ral Bank —
Twenty year in Queensland
An' I drawa da bloody blank.

Anon

WESTERN AUSTRALIA

The land of sin, sweat, sorrow, and Sir John Forrest.

The Sydney *Bulletin*

THE MELBOURNE DRAINS
(An Ode to Their Odours)

From a *Bulletin* issue of 1883.

The smells are gently rising,
    Gently rising to my nose;
And this fact there's no disguising —
    That the 'perfume of the rose'
Is, at best, but a misnomer
    As compared with Melbourne drains,
When the strength of their aroma
    Is enhanced by recent rains.

Filled with freshest fairy fragrance
    All the summer breezes seem,
As I watch the little vagrants
    Floating corks adown the stream.

191

People prate about sweet-briar,
    And the scented clover plains—
But, what more can they desire
    Than the perfumed Melbourne drains?

In my memory will I treasure
    All those sweetly subtle smells,
Then when wandering at my leisure
    'Mid a field of asphodels;
Or among the blooming heather,
    Aye, as long as life remains,
I can ne'er forget the zephyr
    Wafting perfume from the drains.

The Sydney *Bulletin*

ODE TO THE YARRA

A poem published in an 1889 issue of the *Bulletin*.

Gigantic gutter! sewer-receiving stream,
Across whose breast the ferry-boat doth steam,
Thou who dost cherish many a mystic stink,
And fostereth many more upon thy brink,
At whose delicious scent e'en angels wink,
    I think.

Where can we find a blacker, inkier flood?
Where sit the tranquil rats upon the mud,
And whisper to the decomposing cat—
No more thou wilt scare away the gentle rat,
Or sit and yowl upon the doorstep mat.
    I wot.

The sad-eyed puppy and the gloomy goat
Together on thy peaceful bosom float—
Deeming their tasks on earth are all complete,
Not dreaming they'll be used for sausage-meat
To heaven they point in resignation sweet,
    Their feet.

The anxious butcher with a hook in hand
Upon thy brink with eager eye doth stand,

In order to augment his weekly wages,
The reason why his time he thus engages
It grieves us to record upon these pages.
      Sau-sages!

Sweet innocents oft sport upon thy bank,
All heedless of their mother's threatened spank;
Too oft, alas! they tumble in, are drowned,
Thou buriest them—alas! not underground,
But when the diver comes a-scraping round,
      They're found!

Crawl on! thou dark and dismal Yarra, crawl,
While we with bated breath thy praises scrawl,
By fertile meadows and by gum-trees tall,
By Merri Creek, by Kew Asylum's wall,
Thy sweetest stream on this terrestrial ball,
      We bawl.

Francis Adams

MELBOURNE

From Francis Adams, *The Australians* (1893).

In Melbourne there is plenty of vigour and eagerness, but
there is nothing worth being eager or vigorous about.

Anon

FAR COOKTOWN

Things are quiet in far Cooktown,
  The days are dull and cold,
The festive goat has ceased to skip
  Upon the mountain bold.

The Chinamen who run the show
  Are tired, and broke, and weak;
The pub has got its shutters up—
  The barmaid's in the creek.

No more the sweet, rich scent of rum
  Will roll across the plain;

For cash is gone, and tick is done:
The red blind glares in vain.

A busy city by the sea
Has sunk and settled down—
A goat, two Chinkies and a dog
Now own the bloody town.

Anon

THINGS ARE CROOK

Things are crook
In Tallarook.
There's no work
In bloody Bourke.
There's s.f.a.
At Batemans Bay.
There's no tobaccer
At Euraka.
The girls are bandy
At Urandangie.
It's up the shit
At Murrabit.
You'll rue the day
You go to Hay.
But the worst of all
Is Booligal.

A. B. ('Banjo') Paterson

ON DARWIN (NORTHERN TERRITORY)

Quoted in William Linklater and Lynda Tapp, *Gather No Moss* (1968).

The city of booze, blow, and blasphemy.

Anon

McQUADE'S CURSE
Upon Being Refused a Drink at a Pub in Tallarook

These lines have the ring of the Celtic curse about them. They were collected in
Seymour (Vic.) in 1962, and a version has been circulated by the Folklore Society of
Victoria. Several allusions suggest a late 19th century origin. See W. Fearn-Wannan,
Australian Folklore (1970).

May Satan, with a rusty crook,
Catch every goat in Tallarook;
May Mrs Melton's latest spook
Haunt all old maids in Tallarook;
May China's oldest pig-tailed cook
Spoil chops and steaks in Tallarook;
May all the frogs in Doogalook
Sing every night in Tallarook;
May Reedy Creek create a brook
To swamp the flats in Tallarook;
May rabbits ever find a nook
To breed apace in Tallarook;
May Sin Ye Sun and Sam Ah Fook
Steal all the fowls in Tallarook;
May Ikey Moses make a book
To stiffen sport in Tallarook;
May sirens fair as Lalla Rookh
Tempt all old men in Tallarook;
May every paddock yield a stook
Of smutty wheat in Tallarook;
May good Saint Peter overlook
The good deeds done in Tallarook;
May each Don Juan who forsook
His sweetheart live in Tallarook;
May all who Matthew's pledges took
Get rolling drunk in Tallarook;
May every pigeon breed a rook
To spoil the crops in Tallarook;
May I get ague, gout and fluke
If I drink rum in Tallarook!

Lyndall Haddow

ON THE BARCOO

Quoted in *Bill Wannan's Folk Medicine* (1970).

On the far Barcoo
  Where they eat Nardoo,
Jumbuck giblets and pigweed stew.·
  Fever and ague
And scurvy plague you
  And the Barcoo rot;
But the worst of the lot
  Is the Bel-y-ando spew.

C. W. Chandler

DARKEST ADELAIDE

From C. W. Chandler, *Darkest Adelaide* (1911) and quoted in Bill Hornadge, *The Australian Slanguage* (1980).

. . . that bludging has been reduced to a fine art in Adelaide
cannot be gainsaid. Here the bludger is an institution . . .
There is no need to send missionaries to China or India's
coral strand — we have so many Heathens nearer home.

Ernestine Hill

DARWIN

Quoted in William Linklater and Lynda Tapp, *Gather No Moss* (1968).

Ernestine Hill has said that over many decades the citizens
of Darwin fell into two categories — those who were paid to
stay there, and those who had no money to leave.

Sir Tyrone Guthrie

PERTH

Quoted in the Sydney *Bulletin* (July 24, 1967).

A boring, materialistic quicksand of sun-drenched steak-fed
vacuity.

197

Ava Gardner

ON MELBOURNE

When in Melbourne for the filming of Stanley Kramer's *On the Beach*, actress Ava Gardner thus described Melbourne:

On the Beach is a film about the end of the world and I couldn't think of a better place to film it.

Sir Robert Menzies

SYDNEY

Quoted in Ray Robinson, *The Wit of Sir Robert Menzies* (1966).

It was put to me that Sydney was the obvious place to begin an All Nations Club, since Sydney is always in need of civilizing influences.

B. A. Breen

O'FLAHERTY PASSING THROUGH

The insulting nature of these lines is inherent in the poet's use of understatement.
From B. A. Breen, *Behind My Eyes* (1968).

> I had
> a beer in their bars and used
> their piss-houses and met
> a talkative drunk in a hotel
> yard, I slept
> in a room where the cobwebs
> talked   moved
> on next day   they say
> it's a bloody nice little
> town that.

From the Melbourne *Herald* (November 7, 1981)

Chris Wallace-Crabbe

MELBOURNE

From David Campbell (Ed.) *Modern Australian Poetry* (1970).

Not on the ocean, on a muted bay
Where the broad rays drift slowly over mud
And flathead loll on sand, a city bloats
Between the plains of water and of loam.
If surf beats, it is faint and far away;
If slogans blow around, we stay at home.

And, like the bay, our blood flows easily,
Not warm, not cold (in all things moderate),
Following our familiar tides. Elsewhere
Victims are bleeding, sun is beating down
On patriot, guerilla, refugee.
We see the newsreels when we dine in town.

Ideas are grown in other gardens while
This chocolate soil throws up its harvest of
Imported and deciduous platitudes,
None of them flowering boldly or for long;
And we, the gardeners, securely smile
Humming a bar or two of rusty song.

Old tunes are good enough if sing we must;
Old images, re-vamped *ad nauseam*,
Will sate the burgher's eye and keep him quiet
As the great wheels run on. And should he seek
Variety, there's wind, there's heat, there's frost
To feed his conversation all the week.

Highway by highway, the remorseless cars
Strangle the city, put it out of pain,
Its limbs still kicking feebly on the hills.
Nobody cares. The artists sail at dawn
For brisker ports, or rot in public bars.
Though much has died here, nothing has been born.

Hal Porter

BEHIND THAT SUN-SPLASHED
TOURIST POSTER

From Hal Porter, *In an Australian Country Graveyard and Other Poems* (1974).

TO SHELLEY BEACH the painted fingers point.
No point in this: the season's over.
Dunes are bald and loutless; summer's spayed;
   the furled and salt-starched ice-cream awnings fade;
and now no bed-and-bawd-bent tripper ever
   hunts pick-ups on the drizzling Esplanade—
all's
   out of
      joint.

No one to litter, loiter, swindle, spend.
No juke-box keens. No carnies gabble.
One yacht, turned turtle, silly in the sand . . .
One gap-toothed neon for night's no-man's-land:
   one ISH & IPS on Nick the Greek's tin gable . . .
One guest, a leftist vicar, at the Grand—
   he's
     round
      the bend.

Each kiosk's rusted shut. The tide-line's fringed
   with kelp, wrack, trawler muck. It's later
than he thinks, the one-eyed odd-job-man
   who, wine-hot in the rain-wet caravan,
awaits his abo, skin-and-bone Lolita.
   The tide's today run wryer than they ran—
the
   time's
     unhinged.

So's the beach-combing spinster at her sport:
the Furies are her dotty sisters.
   She squeaks with glee to find the drowned girl there
with crab-torn thighs, and sea-lice-beaded hair

(unmissed though missing, NIL in known disasters),
and reads an answer in the socket's stare—

x

    equals
      nought.

Waterside Worker

ON WYNDHAM

Athol Thomas, in an article in the *Bulletin* in 1978, related how he had once wandered into the Port Hotel in Wyndham, in Western Australia, where he encountered a waterside worker wearing grubby shorts, boots without socks and a black singlet.
From Bill Hornadge, *The Australian Slanguage* (1980).

'So you are up here to write about us,' the wharfie said after getting acquainted, adding, 'Put this in, mate, Cambridge Gulf is the arsehole of the world and Wyndham is sixty-five miles up it.'

Phillip Adams

ON TASMANIA

While satirically considering that war would help boost the Australian economy, Adams eliminates Tasmania as a possible worthy enemy 'for all its geographic convenience'.
See Phillip Adams, *More Unspeakable Adams* (1979).

In any case, it just wouldn't be cricket. Their army is so disadvantaged. Even if the officers managed to say 'quick march' despite their cleft palates, the troops couldn't oblige because of club feet.

Phillip Adams

MELBOURNE

From Phillip Adams, *More Unspeakable Adams* (1979).

. . . our citizens have a suburban instinct which pursues them to the grave. Visit any of our cemeteries and you find a microcosm of the sprawl, complete with slums, ghettos and middle-class pretensions. There are snooty, two-storey graves, triple-fronted tombs and any number of desirable, wrought iron graves that echo the aesthetic of the Victorian

202

terraces. So much so it's a wonder that the trendies haven't exhumed the decayed occupants and moved in.

Dennis Pryor

BRECON IN SOUTH WALES

From an article by journalist Dennis Pryor in the Melbourne *Age* (March 23, 1981).

[Brecon is] the birthplace that I managed to escape from. Now Brecon was (and still is) so sleepy a place that it makes Nar Nar Goon look like Times Square. It sulks below the Brecon Beacons, a range of hills trodden by muscular hikers and tough, ill-tempered sheep.

Barry Oakley

MY MELBOURNE

Journalist James Murray recorded a piece of Melbourne nostalgia from Barry Oakley, author of *A Salute to the Great McCarthy* and *A Walk Through Tigerland*. Barry Oakley is currently living in Sydney.
From the Melbourne *Herald* (August 20, 1981).

When I get into a tram, I feel I am getting into the essence of Melbourne. Men in the outer part, women in the saloon part.

David Williamson

ON SYDNEY

Melbourne-born playwright, David Williamson (1942–), expressed his feelings about Sydney (where he now lives) in an article in the Melbourne *Herald* (August 20, 1981).

[At a Sydney dinner party] all you get between mouthfuls is gossip about who is doing what. It is almost seen as a mark of adolescence to have thoughts or emotions about what is happening in the Third World . . .
[Compared to the majesty of the Victorian bush] In New South Wales, the bush merely straggles . . .
In Sydney, people don't have friendships which go back twenty years. Contacts are half business, half social.
This is Deal City . . .
Playboy, derivative, culturally nondescript, is Sydney . . .

203

James Murray

KING'S CROSS

From an article by journalist James Murray in the Melbourne *Herald* (August 20, 1981).

. . . the sleaze of King's Cross. There the last straight businesses hold out against barbaric porn behind ramparts of chocolate cakes.

Graeme Blundell

SYDNEY

Melbourne actor Graeme Blundell, living in Sydney, misses Melbourne's quality of intensity. See the Melbourne *Herald* (August 20, 1981).

The reason I go to the gym every day in Sydney is to make up physically for the intellectual work-outs I no longer get.

H. R. Freedman

BACK IN THE OL' HOME TOWN

A Melbourne *Herald* journalist gives her impressions of returning to Melbourne after an absence of five and a half years.
From the Melbourne *Herald* (August 22, 1981).

. . . being home is rather like turning on a favorite soap opera again. New York spoils you; coming back to Melbourne you realise fast that most of the drama has been edited out. If you've missed a few episodes (five and a half year's worth in my case) you can come right back into it and pick up where you left off.

Ray Barrett

OF SURFERS' PARADISE

This comment by film actor, Ray Barrett, was quoted in the Melbourne *Age* (August 29, 1981).

Tinsel is what the film industry is all about and tinsel is what we have here in Surfers' Paradise.

Errol Simper

BRUSSELS

Journalist Errol Simper reported on the countries of the European Common Market in the *Australian* (August 29, 1981). Here is an extract.

Brussels isn't quite like it should be. You have a pre-conceived notion that the unofficial capital of the European Economic Community is a glass and plastic monstrosity, gradually fuelled skywards by the relative affluence of the EEC bureaucracy.

Bob Ellis

THE ATTRACTION OF SURFERS' PARADISE!

Quoted in the *Australian* (August 29, 1981).

[The southern elderly migrate north] like beetles to lie down in the sun and die.

John Hargreaves

ON SURFERS' PARADISE

The *Australian* (August 29, 1981) quoted the actor, John Hargreaves, who three years before, while filming *The Odd Angry Shot* in the Gold Coast hinterland, described Surfers as:

God's waiting room.

Adrian McGregor

ON SURFERS' PARADISE

From an article by journalist Adrian McGregor in the *Australian* (August 29, 1981).

Surfers' has no national culture, except boobs, bums and brass.

Barry Humphries

OF SYDNEY AND MELBOURNE

Quoted in *Mode Australia* (August–September, 1981).

People say that Sydney will soon be like Paris in the 1890s—
there is not a chance of a possibility it will be.

.   .   .

[The most bizarre thing Humphries has ever done] was to be
born in an English provincial town in South East Asia
[Melbourne!].

7

CONTEMPT OF COURTS

Judges, Advocates and the Law

Judge A. Montagu

AN ATTACK ON AN ATTORNEY-GENERAL

The victim of this personal attack by Mr Justice Montagu was Alfred Stephen, Attorney-General in Van Diemen's Land during the administrations of Sir George Arthur and his successor, Sir John Franklin. Stephen later became the very able Chief Justice of New South Wales. Quoted in John West, *The History of Tasmania* (1852).

No, sir; in your official capacity I shall always treat you with the courtesy and respect due to you. Were you elsewhere, I should treat you, after your conduct, with less courtesy than a dog.

Henry Kendall

ON JUDGE FRANCIS AS A LECTURER

His Honour, Mr Justice H. R. Francis, had given the poet Henry Kendall cause for offence in one of his public lectures, delivered in Sydney early in 1865. In his satirical work, *The Bronze Trumpet* (1866), Kendall took his revenge on the judge:

Then sound the trumpet! Let our Francis grace
His petty audience with his nightly face;
Yea, let him twist his mouth, and snarl and sneer,
On bench and platform, yelping year by year!
What though the Herald dubs his lectures 'treats',
Those changeless dishes of familiar meats:
Are they the newer? Will they tickle more
Because we've heard them fifty times before?

The Melbourne *Herald*

ON MR JUSTICE WILLIAMS

Mr Justice Williams, a Judge of the Supreme Court, was the President of the Melbourne Bicycle Club. In 1883 he toured various towns in Victoria on his 'safety machine', presiding over cases in each town. At Ballarat he received a guard of honour from the Ballarat Bicycle Club. The *Herald* was shocked at such unseemly behaviour!
Quoted in Keith Dunstan, *Sports* (1973).

Three Chinese gardeners were recently fined for working on Sunday in Sydney. Here is a portrait of the judge who declines to eat vegetables grown on Sunday, or meat that has been fattened on Sunday.

From the early Sydney *Bulletin* and reproduced in Patricia Rolfe (Ed.)
Clotted Rot for Clots and Rotters (1980)

209

That the whole legal profession is scandalized at the burlesquing of the dignity of the judicial bench by Mr Justice Williams going circuit on a bicycle. What a contrast, they say, to the pomp and ceremony attending the entry of the judges in English assize towns, where they ride in splendid equipage and are received by a High Sheriff and other officials, and the Judges attend church in State on the Sunday.

Fancy a Judge of the Supreme Court of Victoria entering a large city like Ballarat on a velocipede and being met, not by the sheriff and other functionaries, but by half a dozen boobies on bicycles.

A Sydney Shark

SOME LEGAL THOUGHTS AND MAXIMS

From the Sydney *Bulletin* of 1892, and reprinted in Patricia Rolfe (Ed.) *Clotted Rot for Clots and Rotters* (1980).

'In the multitude of counsellors there is wisdom.'
— *Salomons*, Q.C.

.   .   .

When briefed to appear in five cases on one day in five different Courts, you will best and most conscientiously earn your fees by going on a fishing excursion twenty miles away.

.   .   .

There are a good many lawrikins in the Courts.

John Norton

FROM AN 'OPEN LETTER TO JUDGE DOCKER'

'Norton,' wrote Cyril Pearl in *Wild Men of Sydney*, 'was fairly catholic in his choice of targets but Judge Docker, whom he often referred to as "Dingo" Docker, seems to have aroused his greatest ballistic fervour. Docker was not only an irresponsible, savage, and class-biassed judge; he was also one of that wretched tribe of judicial jesters, who enjoy the servile titter that greets the feeblest witticism from the Bench.' Judge Docker was prominent in New South Wales in the late 1890s.

From an early edition of the Sydney *Bulletin* and reproduced in Patricia Rolfe (Ed.)
Clotted Rot for Clots and Rotters (1980)

I propose that you are utterly unfit for your position . . . and to expose and denounce you on the best evidence as a disgrace to the Bench . . .

If I state what is not true, or what being true is not justifiable on the highest public grounds, you know enough of law—although the quantity and quality of your law is like your temper, very limited and damned bad—to know that you can indict me for scandalous libel.

Your consistent conduct on the subordinate bench has been alternately that of an idiot and a brutal bewigged bully. Some of your judicial *obiter dicta*—the obstreperous observations of an ignorant, irascible, jury-ranter—would seem to indicate that a padded room at Callan Park would be a fit and proper abiding place for you . . .

You are one of the opprobrious spawn of the old Convict system and would, had not Providence delayed your advent to this world in order to curse our Courts, have made an admirable member of the military rum-selling mob of martinets who mercilessly murdered, by the mockery of judicial process, men and women at the triangles and on the gallows.

You are the hereditary lay descendant of that old parsonical pirate, the 'Reverend' Samuel Marsden . . .

Your vagaries on the bench recall the pothouse vapourings of a drunken man. A special session of Parliament ought to be called to put an end to your official existence. I remain,

Your present Accuser,

And Prospective Impeacher,

John Norton.

Paris Nesbitt

AN INSULT FOR A JUDGE

This turn-of-the-century anecdote, and the one concerning Walter Coldham, which follows, are quoted in P. A. Jacobs's excellent book of legal reminiscence, *A Lawyer Tells* (1949).

Mr Paris Nesbitt, K.C., who was in the habit of living and talking dangerously, caused a flutter in the High Court on the hearing of an appeal in which he acted as counsel. In the course of his argument, he made some statement relating to the law of trusts.

'That sounds rather startling,' said Sir Samuel Griffith; 'what is your authority for that proposition?'

'I should have thought,' Nesbitt replied, 'that it was unnecessary to require authority for anything so obvious.' Turning to the solicitor instructing him, he said, 'Get me a text-book on the Law of Trusts from the Supreme Court Library.' As the solicitor was approaching the door leading out of the Court, Nesbitt called out, in the hearing of everyone, 'Any *elementary* book will do!'

Walter Coldham

'NOT WISER, PERHAPS'

Walter Coldham, a Victorian barrister of an earlier time, once reprimanded a judge who, after listening for a considerable time to Coldham's arguments on a particular point of law, said sombrely, 'Well, Mr Coldham, after hearing you at great length, I don't know whether I am any wiser than I was before you began.'

'Not wiser, perhaps,' replied Coldham, smiling, 'but better informed, I hope.'

Richard Birnie

ON LAW COURTS

Quoted by A. G. Stephens in the Sydney *Bulletin* (June 30, 1904).

What a fusty stench pervades the full court! What snug homes, cradles, and receptacles for unmentionable entomologies.

NONE IN THE MARKET

JUST-APPOINTED JAYPEE (who will have his little joke): '*That's a good moke, Father, too good for a priest. Our Saviour used to ride an ass.*'

FATHER McGINTY: '*That's so, my friend. But they've been making magistrates of all the asses round here and I can't get one for love or money.*'

From the Sydney *Bulletin* (1890s) and reproduced in Patricia Rolfe (Ed.) *Clotted Rot for Clots and Rotters* (1980)

A. G. Stephens

THE HANGING JUDGE

Alfred George Stephens (1865–1933), although now chiefly remembered for the
excellence of his literary criticism in the old Sydney *Bulletin*, and for his fostering of
young writers' talents, wrote some fiction and a large amount of unremarkable verse.
The extract from 'The Hanging Judge', given below, suggests the vein of irony that
ran through much of Stephens's writing.

I am the Judge. I like to dine
Before I charge: then, flushed with wine,
I bully the jury into submission
And rise to the height of judicial ambition.
O how I thrill deliciously
At the wretch in anguish under me!
I gather my brows in a terrible frown,
The slow beads drop from his forehead down;
I lower my voice, and my eyes I roll:
'The Lord have mercy upon your soul!'
He lifts his hands; but — 'Sheriff!' I shout,
And his knees give way as they drag him out.
Into eternity he shall trudge.
    I am the Judge.

I am the Judge. A Judge should be
A pattern of humble piety.
A week well spent brings Sabbath content:
To church my steps are piously bent.
When the holy man reads the holy book
I grieve for the god, by gods forsook,
So clumsily crucified: pity rises,
He was not a remanet to My assizes!
But when at the door they stand aside
To watch me pass, how I swell with pride
To hear them say, 'That's Him all right!
He hanged another one yesterday night!
The jury cried mercy, he wouldn't budge,
    He is the Judge!'

Kath Walker

DARK UNMARRIED MOTHERS

Kath Walker, in the following poem, expresses her feelings about the hypocrisy of
the law in Australia.
From Kath Walker, *My People* (1970).

All about the country,
From earliest teens,
Dark unmarried mothers,
Fair game for lechers—
Bosses and station hands,
And in town and city
Low-grade animals
Prowl for safe prey.
Nothing done about it,
No one to protect them—
But hush, you mustn't say so,
Bad taste or something
To challenge the accepted,
Disturbing the established.
Turn the blind eye,
Wash the hands like Pilate.

Consent? Even with consent
It is still seduction.
Is it a white girl?
Then court case and headline
Stern talk of maintenance.
Is it a dark girl?
Then safe immunity;
He takes what he wants
And walks off like a dog.
Was ever even one,
One of all the thousands
Ever made responsible?
For dark unmarried mothers
The law does not run.
No blame for the guilty
But blame uttered only
For anyone made angry

'There now. See what a good lawyer c i do. Drawing and
quartering to run concurrently!'

From the *Bulletin* (October 20, 1981)

217

Who dares even mention it,
Challenging old usage,
Established, accepted
And therefore condoned.
Shrug away the problem,
The shame, the injustice;
Turn the blind eye,
Wash the hands like Pilate.

Jack Galbally

ON HIS BROTHER FRANK

In 1975 Frank Galbally, renowned Criminal lawyer, who had previously supported the Labor Party, changed his vote in favour of the Federal Liberal Party. This comment by his brother Jack, then Labor Leader in the Legislative Council, was quoted in the *National Times* (August 23–29, 1981).

Frank is a superb advocate, but a howler of a judge . . .

8

ANTI-CLERICAL CHOLERS

The Clergy

Convict Women

'HOLY WILLIE' BEDFORD INSULTED

The Rev. William Bedford became Church of England Chaplain at Hobart Town, Tasmania, in 1822. He incurred the enmity of many folk in that colony by his irritating piety and his stern attempts to combat the 'moral laxity' he found everywhere. He was particularly disliked by the female convicts, whose hair he ordered to be cut off for even the most insignificant offences. From John Butler Cooper's *The History of Tasmania* (1915) the following extract is taken.

How the convict women loved 'Holy Willie Bedford' may be judged by an experience he had at the Female Barracks a few days after he had cast a stone and bore witness against Phillis Jones. He went to the barracks to exhort them to lead virtuous lives and to shun fornication and adultery as they should the devil and all his wiles. The women were not taking any of that sort of tinned Christianity from Bedford, and with one accord, led by the most desperate characters, they set upon him, and had him down on the floor of the prison before he could defend himself. The women made a determined attempt to permanently maim or injure him. Bedford howled as loud as a stuck pig squeals, and had it not been for the prompt assistance of Chief Constable Pitt and his assistants the women would have succeeded in ruining Bedford if they had stopped at murdering him. It was with great difficulty he was rescued out of their hands, and he afterwards presented a very sick and sorry appearance, natural to a man who had come through such a very trying ordeal.

.   .   .

In *The Convict, a Tale Founded on Fact*, an unpublished manuscript novel, written by Robert Crooke, a former convict chaplain, in 1886, and quoted by Kathleen Fitzpatrick in her *Sir John Franklin in Tasmania* (1949), there is a vivid description of the incident described above, concluding with the following lines.
See W. Fearn-Wannan, *Australian Folklore*: A Dictionary of Lore, Legends and Popular Allusions (1970).

These women had had quite enough of Mr Bedford; they were compelled to listen to his long stupid sermons, and knew his character, and that he loved roast turkey and ham with a bottle or two of port wine much better than he loved his Bible, and when he commenced to preach they with one accord endeavoured to cough him down, and upon the warders proclaiming silence they all with one impulse turned round, raised their clothes and smacked their posteriors with a loud report.

Governor Macquarie

THE REVEREND SAMUEL MARSDEN ADMONISHED

Samuel Marsden (1764–1838) began his religious duties in the colony of New South Wales as Assistant Chaplain. He acquired large land holdings and was a successful pioneer breeder of fine-wooled sheep. As a magistrate he dealt harshly with convict offenders; and his conservative political views and narrow self-interest caused him to be a thorn in the flesh of Governors Macquarie and Brisbane. See Bill Wannan, *Early Colonial Scandals* (1972).

I have long known, Mr Marsden, that you are a secret enemy of mine, and as long as you continued a secret one I despised too much your malicious attempts to injure my character to take any notice of your treacherous conduct; but now that you have thrown off the mask and have openly and publicly manifested your hostile and factious opposition to me, I can no longer, consistently with what I owe to my own high station, and the tranquillity of the country I have the honour to govern, pass over unnoticed a recent and most daring act of insolence and insubordination of which you have been guilty . . .

Viewing you now, sir, as the head of a seditious, low cabal, and consequently unworthy of mixing in private society or intercourse with me, I beg to inform you that I never wish to see you, excepting on public duty, and I cannot help deeply lamenting that any man of your sacred profession should be so much lost to every good feeling of justice, generosity and gratitude as to manifest such deep-rooted malice and vindictive spite against one who has never injured you, but on the contrary has conferred several acts of kindness on yourself and family.

Kenneth Slessor

OF THE REVEREND SAMUEL MARSDEN

In early New South Wales the Reverend Samuel Marsden was known as the 'Flogging Parson'.
From Kenneth Slessor's poem 'Vesper Song of the Reverend Samuel Marsden'.

> And make me, God, Your Overseer,
> But if the veins of Saints be dead,
> Grant me a whip in Hell instead,
> Where blood is not so hard to fetch.

Sir William Denison

DR JOHN DUNMORE LANG: 'A NOISY LIAR'

The Rev. Dr John Dunmore Lang (1799–1878) was the founder of the Presbyterian Church in Australia, as well as being an ardent promoter of Scottish migration to this country, and a staunch republican. The choice example of character assassination which follows is from a private letter from Sir William Denison, Governor of Tasmania, to Deas Thomson, the Colonial Secretary in Sydney, written during May, 1850.

There is a degree of ignorance as to the state and condition of the colonies which it is difficult to understand. It originated, I imagine, in the universal tendency to lie which takes possession of people like Dr Lang, who thrust themselves and their falsehoods upon the Colonial Office while modest truth hides itself behind the green doors of the entrance and is not seen or heard. A noisy liar like Lang, who has neither honesty nor conscience, does an infinity of harm. People at home do not know his character and he gets the credit of being interested in the welfare of the colony when in point of fact he is only looking to his own selfish interests. I judge of the man from his career, his language, his propositions. He may, it is true, belong to that class of impostors who have managed to deceive themselves as well as the world. They are, however, equally as bad as those who deceive the world purposely and deliberately and should be opposed as energetically.

The Sydney *Bulletin*

LUNATIC DRIVEL

From the Sydney *Bulletin* of 1882 and reprinted in Patricia Rolfe (Ed.) *Clotted Rot for Clots and Rotters* (1980).

Christian reader:— wipe the froth off your mouth and listen. Did you ever notice that when some unfortunate wretch of a gospel slinger is cornered and hauled up to have the usual 'address and testimonial' inflicted upon him, the agony is always heightened by the lunatic drivel of a few of the 'most influential citizens'. Only the other day, a Roman Catholic clergyman was presented with a pawn-office set of plate, and half a mile of epistle, by the leading inhabitants of Dead Dog Gully, and after making a speech as long as a late breakfast, the presenting orator wound up by saying, he 'felt it an' honor, an a—an a—an a JOOTY to hand over this illegint testymonyil to the Rivirind Father Doolin—the frind av' the poor, un' th' father av' half de counthry. Will ye playze keep soilince down the rume there'.

The Sydney *Bulletin*

WANTED—DEAD BISHOPS

From the Sydney *Bulletin* of 1886 and reproduced in Patricia Rolfe (Ed.) *Clotted Rot for Clots and Rotters* (1980).

Speaking of Dr Pearson's translation, 'Atlas' in the *World* says: 'That Bishop Moorhouse's patronage is well bestowed no one can for an instant doubt; but one cannot but call to mind the saying of a wise man, that the most effective aid to the Colonial Church would be the graves of a few of its bishops in their dioceses.' Excellent! This is a matter that must be attended to—

WANTED—DEAD BISHOPS

Our bishops are birds of passage
        Who never for long remain—
They bring us the Master's message,

Then fly away 'home' again;
  Oh, we notice, with secret sorrow,
    That the bishop who's here to-day
  Is most certainly gone to-morrow—
    Right tiddleiumtitay.

For as soon as an English billet
    Is offered (with larger screw)
They're off like a shot to fill it,
    And bid us a fond adieu;
They leave us their hearts best wishes,
    Most beautiful things they say,
As they go for the loaves and fishes—
    Right tiddleiumtitay.

This state of affairs is awful;
    The Colonial Church can't thrive;
It ought to be made unlawful
    For the b's to go back alive;
'Tis their bodies are badly wanted,
    But they carry them safe away—
All our bishops at home are 'planted'
    Right tiddleiumtitay.

Though the notion a trifle odd is
    (A necessity we deplore)
We must-write home, at once, for bodies
    Of bishops who've 'gone before';
Then, possessed of such saintly treasure,
    Our Church will rejoice away—
Oh! we'll bury the lot with pleasure,
    Right tiddleiumtitay.

The Sydney *Bulletin*

SHADE OF ST PETER

An anecdote from the Sydney *Bulletin* of 1887 and reprinted in Patricia Rolfe (Ed.) *Clotted Rot for Clots and Rotters* (1980).

Kyardinal Moran is disgusted with the dilatoriness of Manly Beach Council. He has expended £60000 of Bridget the cook and Patsy the coachman's hard-earned savings on his palace and seminary, and yet 'the Council have not thought it to be their duty to make a decent approach to the building'. His Eminence's own words are: 'I may say that it would be next to an impossibility for me to have my carriage driven from my residence to the wharf.' My carriage! Shade of St Peter, the fisherman! The Devil!

The Sydney *Bulletin*

MATTERS OF FAITH

The following anecdotes appeared in the early Sydney *Bulletin* during the 1880s and 1890s.
See Patricia Rolfe (Ed.) *Clotted Rot for Clots and Rotters* (1980).

There is a 'Rambling Club' in connection with the Melbourne Young Men's Christian Association. We suppose the Rambling Club is designed for the cultivation and elaboration of pulpit discourses. (1889)

. . .

Queer Sydney advt:
TENDERS required up to October 15, for the PURCHASE of the FREE CHURCH of ENGLAND, Kogarah, with land, fittings, &c., complete; organ also, if desired. Brilliantly lighted with gas. The church is closed, amidst feelings of deepest regret, after four years of most remarkable success, ONLY because the object of the establishment has been consummated. Terms can be arranged.
'Consummated' is most excellent. Have all the Sunday-school marms got married, or has the parson made his pile? (1889)

. . .

A man died in a Sandhurst (Vic.) church during the progress of the sermon on the Sunday before last. Some men will go to any extremes to avoid the collection. (1889)

. . .

'Yes, father was connected with Mr Nolan's church,' said the daughter of the poor, hard-up, bailiff-tortured ex-soldier,

225

who made a sensation at North Sydney (North Sydney again!) last week by cutting his own and his wife's throat. 'We had prayers each morning. Father was very good to the church, and taught a Bible-class at the lecture-hall, where the Wesleyan classes meet.' My son, paste this in your hat: The road to mania lies through the gate of sincere religion. The imitation pietists—the sugar-sanding grocer, the plate-passing elder who absconds with the savings of the widow and orphan, *these* are mentally as tough as leather. But the fervent believer with the narrow head, and the protruding eye, and the scanty hair, and the galvanic lurch—*he* is safe only within the four walls of an asylum. (1893)

. . .

A woman from the country recently went into St. Francis Xavier's Cathedral, Adelaide, and, leaving a bundle near the entrance, advanced to the Lady Altar to pay her devotions. When she returned, her property was gone. She complained to the verger, who said: 'My good woman, you should never leave anything about in this cathedral, because Protestants and all sorts come in here.' (1897)

Francis Adams

NEW GUINEA 'CONVERTS'

From *Songs of the Army of the Night* (1888).

> I saw them as they were born,
> erect and fearless and free,
> facing the sun and the wind
> of the hills and the sea.
>
> I saw them naked, superb,
> like the Greeks long ago,
> with shield and spear and arrow
> ready to strike and throw.
>
> I saw them as they were made
> by the Christianising crows,
> blinking, stupid, clumsy,
> in their greasy ill-cut clothes.

I heard their gibbering cant,
and they sang those hymns that smell
of poor souls besotted, degraded
with the fear of 'God' and 'Hell' ...

O Jesus, O man of the People,
who died to abolish all this—
the Pharisee rank and respectable,
the Scribe and the scabrous Priest—

O Jesus, O sacred Socialist,
you would die again of shame,
if you were alive and could see
what things are done in your Name.

Adolphus George Taylor

THE CLERGY

A. G. Taylor was the original editor of the Sydney *Truth*, from 1890 to 1896. In the early 1920s he entered the Legislative Assembly as senior member for Mudgee and remained in parliament for nearly ten years. The following extract is from a satire called *The Marble Man* and is quoted in Cyril Pearl, *Wild Men of Sydney* (1958).

Here we see, in its naked deformity, this sphere of sweat and struggle ... The bitterest enemy of mankind is Man, and the religion of humanity is rivetted to the rock of selfishness ...

You have noted the two men in the background with repulsive faces and without canonicals. They are, as yet, only honorary members of the corps clerical—no nearer in affinity than accredited acolytes. Yes, they are—the flogger and the hangman ...

Why do we erect scaffolds? Why do we retain whipping-posts? .... To please the Clergy and High Churchmen. The Anglican and Dissenting Sections are the worst offenders therein.

Edward Kinglake

ON VESTRYMEN

From Edward Kinglake, *The Australian at Home* (1891).

THE ONLY INFERENCE

PARSON: *'When I was a boy, my father never knew me to go fishing on Sundays.'*
BOY: *'My word! I wish I could have humbugged my father as well as that.'*

Vestrymen are proverbially quarrelsome. The elders, deacons, and churchwardens in Australia are the most pragmatical and cantankerous set of people it is possible to imagine. Only an angel from heaven could please them, and he, even if he suited one section, would *ipso facto*, displease another.

John Norton

A CARNIVAL OF CANT

This typical piece of Nortonian invective from 1896, directed at the Anglican bishops, is quoted by Cyril Pearl in *Wild Men of Sydney* (1958).

During nearly the whole week the public of this continent have been treated to a carnival of cant, organised and conducted by a religious rabble comprising Anglican Bishops in lawn sleeves and with well-filled paunches, and Wesleyan Methodist tub-thumpers of impoverished abdominal anatomy, and dight in dirty dickies which conceal still dirtier under-linen, or the entire absence of any linen at all—dirty or clean . . . The game began on Sunday morning at St Andrews with a grand grunting grab performance by that Gargantuan, full-fleshed, wine-flushed lover of the Lord, Bishop Saumarez-Smith who made the text from the 10th chapter of Nehemiah 'We will not forsake the home of the Lord' a pretext for plunging his leg-of-mutton fist into the partially empty pockets of his impoverished congregation . . . This is the same benign Bishop who was nicknamed 'Some-More-O-Yez' Smith by the Darlinghurst cabmen for declining to pay them more than a paltry shilling for conveying his corpulent carcass to the city, whereas slenderer men, with more heart and less belly, always paid at least one shilling and sixpence for the same journey. Some Christians deserve to be driven to town in Chinese dung-carts.

John Norton

ON DR HENRY LOWTHER CLARKE

Clarke was the Anglican Archbishop of Melbourne from 1905 to 1926.
From Cyril Pearl, *Wild Men of Sydney* (1958).

... devious, disgusting, dastard ... the Anglican Archnight-
man of Smelbourne ... You have turned the church into a
bestial clerical cloacina ... Whenever we smell a stink we
suspect 'the nightman' is on the job.

As a churchman you're a cronk, as a Christian you're
crook, and as a man, a moral mongrel.

F. J. Mills

ON CHRISTIAN HYPOCRISY

From 'The Twinkler' (F. J. Mills), *Dinkum Oil* (1917).

Some of us go to church to reveal that we are Christians.
Others to hide the fact that they are not.

Anon

'I DRAW THE LINE AT CLERICS'

In his *Great Australian Folk Songs* (1965) John Lahey gave the following version of an
old Western Australian ditty titled 'I am a Tolerant Man', which originally appeared
in the Kalgoorlie *Sun*.

I don't mind blokes who digs or stokes,
Who fettle or work on derricks;
I can even stand a German band,
But I draw the line at clerics.

Chorus:
Why, strike me pink, I'd sooner drink
With a cove sent up for arson
Than a rain-beseeching, preaching, teaching,
Blanky, cranky parson.

I snort and jibe at the whole of the tribe,
Whatever their sect or class is—
From lawn-sleeved ranters to kerbstone canters,
From bishops to Army lasses.

Give *me* the blaspheming, scheming, screaming,
Barracking football garcons—

In preference to the reverent gents,
The blithering, blathering parsons!

Padre Herbert Hayes

A BISHOP'S PUNISHMENT

An Anglican clergyman, Padre Herbert Hayes of Mernda (Vic.), published a volume
of verse, *Centenary Songs and a Parson's Nonsense*, in Melbourne in 1934. This book, as
Frederick T. Macartney noted in his edition of the Morris Miller bibliography,
Australian Literature (1956), as well as other publications, involved Hayes 'in an
ecclesiastical action before the Church courts'. 'A Bishop's Punishment' is given here
in an abbreviated form. See George Blaikie, *Remember Smith's Weekly?* (1966).

Squeeze his mitre
Tighter and tighter.
Burst all his veins
Squeeze out his brains.
How his eyes stare,
Through bloody hair.
Imps burn his nose
Red as a rose.
Pound his fat belly
Into a jelly.
With a rusty pin
Score all his skin.
Strip him quite bare,
Singe all his hair.
Roast his entrails,
Tear out his nails.
Pluck out his tongue,
Let it be hung
To be used as a bell
In the service of hell;
And if nothing is worse
Let him read this grim verse.

Sir Lionel Lindsay

OF BILLY GRAHAM

Quoted in Daryl Lindsay, *The Leafy Tree* (1956).

This go-getting commercial traveller for J.C. Inc.

Thomas W. Shapcott

THREE KINGS CAME

From David Campbell (Ed.) *Modern Australian Poetry* (1970).

Three Kings came
with hard gifts of gold
to pay their way
to another world.

Three Kings came
with bribes of myrrh
to please the gods
and to gain favour.

Three Kings came
with frankincense

and the people saw
their few flung pence
and full of awe
they grovelled deep.

The child himself stayed fast asleep.

Bruce Dawe

THE DECAY OF PREACHING

From Bruce Dawe, *Condolences of the Season* (1971).

Dear reverend fathers (one or two)
I dedicate this poem to you,
A nothing, a mere widow's mite
— From your rich store select a trite
Metaphor to suit the case . . .
I'm here to celebrate the race
You run from one week to the next
Around the treadmill of your text,
The sleep-inducing sermon whose
Machinery creaks from over-use.

If lively preaching is the key
To every Protestant heresy,

Then, laity and clergy both,
Sleep on! for this our current sloth
Is but the instrument of the Lord
—Salvation lies in being bored!
As bored we are for being given
A steep and tedious road to heaven
(All doomed, it seems, to purge desires
In such keen purgatorial fires
Damnation for eternity
Becomes a matter of degree).

Give us for God's sake (and our own)
A living Lord of flesh and bone;
All our humanity refutes
Effeminate bloodless substitutes:
We'd rather, every time, the shabby
Tiger than the presbytery tabby!

Spare us the eloquence that feeds
On self, not sacerdotal needs.
What good were Bossuet's gifts apart
From a warm, understanding heart?
And to Our Lady, reverend sirs,
Extend the dignity that's hers
By birth and which she shares in common
With every other blessed woman,
Down to the saddest drab that ever
Sought a cheap exit in a river . . .

Take a day off from ranting still
At some new contraception pill,
Or gloating over the increased rate
Of Catholic births, as though the State
Were nothing but a fish-pond where
Research is carried out with care,
And, with the right conclusions drawn,
Only the tagged fish free to spawn.

While for those kindred ills as yet
Unspecified, may they beget
Their remedies upon themselves,
Or failing this, may your wide shelves

Of books lie inches deep in dust
Until such time as you have thrust
Your theological noses out-
Of-doors and raised a heathen shout
Of joy to see the egg-blue sky
And fellow-men like trees walk by . . .

Phillip Adams

AMERICA'S ELECTRONIC EVANGELISTS

From the Melbourne *Age* (June 20, 1981).

There's a marvellous scene in *The Life of Brian* where the camera dwells on a group who've got bad possies for the Sermon on the Mount. Lacking a public address system, Christ can barely make himself heard, and the message gets garbled. 'What does he mean—the Greek will inherit the Earth?' Chapman asks Cleese.

What we had there was a failure to communicate. Little wonder that Christ's latterday salesmen have opted for the neck mike, the zoom lens, the quadraphonic choir and the satellite. Little wonder that the odious Oral Roberts and the monstrous Reverend Jerry Falwell and that fellow Rex Humbard (or is it Humbug?) are now as rich as Croesus. It is to be hoped that these bad Samaritans find it as difficult to enter the Kingdom of Heaven as a dromedary attempting to squeeze through a needle's eye.

Be that as it may, it's possible they will find it a little harder to squeeze money from Australia's gullible as (praise the Lord!) the Nine Network are driving the tithe collectors from the temples of television. For decades, America's electronic evangelists have been passing the cathode plate around their videotic congregation, making millions from 'free' Bible courses and the sale of indulgences. They have preyed on (while pretending to pray for) the lonely, the ill-educated and the sick. Hundreds of Australian families have been influenced by one false prophet alone—Herbert W. Armstrong of *The World Tomorrow* and *Plain Truth* magazine notoriety. (Not content with tithing, Herbert prefers *double*

235

tithing, and I've a bulging file of tragic letters from people whose lives he's affected.) . . .

Principal among Raygun's religious ratbags was, and remains, the aforementioned Falwell. From his network pulpit he's órchestrated one of the nastiest coalitions in political history, linking every reactionary in a holy crusade against communism, unionism, liberalism, humanism, atheism and most of all, social justice. As Falwell boasts 'the pornographers are angry, the amoral secular humanists are livid, the abortionists are furious' . . .

The Reverend Jerry Falwell is a highly intelligent, nuclear-powered version of the Reverend Fred Nile, while his Moral Majority Inc. is a battleship that would drown such dogmatic dinghies as the Right to Life and Festival of Light in its wake. . . .

Ian Dickson

LINES FOR THE REVEREND FRED

From an article by Phillip Adams in the Melbourne *Age* (June 20, 1981).

And now, a ballad from a reader in Balmain, one Ian Dickson. Called 'Lines for the Reverend Fred' it was inspired by an answer Nile gave to the question 'If everyone has a price, what's yours?' Fred immediately responded with 'I suppose my price would be to hear the words "Well done thou good and faithful servant".'

> Australia's Old Testament prophet
> You scourge of the sod and the sot
> (Though I hope for the sake of your missus
> You're no reincarnation of Lot.)
>
> Defender of everything righteous
> The family, the state and the bourse
> If you're pure, patriotic and loaded
> You are saved as a matter of course.

But to deal with the lost and abandoned,
Whose habits aren't blessed by the Lord,
You take a tip from Procrustes
And don't alter the bed but the bawd.

Your purpose on earth is to warn us
To beware lest the flood gates cave in
For we'll all be awash with corruption
And weighed down by the wages of sin.

Hitherto sweet little grannies
Maniacally shrilling with glee
Will recklessly plunder their savings
And purchase a dildo or three.

Bank managers, lewd in leather
Will clank down the streets in their chains
And mild-mannered chartered accountants
Grab their offspring and bash out their brains.

On George Street, we'll frighten the horses,
At Bondi we'll ride in the sand
And we'll be too intent on our pleasure
To notice the enemy land.

For the present destruction of morals
Has been planned, as you know, by the reds
Who will sweep down and conquer the nation
While we're all hard at work in our beds.

So fight for God, country and commerce,
Destroy any canker that blights—
The whore and the sexual inadequate
Are deprived by their nature of rights.

But when the last trumpet is sounding
And you front up to claim your reward
I hope for your sake they don't tell you
It's compassion that counts with the Lord.

A linocut entitled *Parson 1932* by Noel Counihan (1913–   ), and reproduced from
Roger Butler, *Melbourne Woodcuts and Linocuts of the 1920s and 1930s* (1981)

Waitress

TO A BISHOP

This anecdote appeared in the Melbourne *Age* (August 31, 1981).

When a layman had taken his bishop out for dinner, the
waitress had taken the layman's order and then asked what
'robin red breast' would like.

9

WORK WHINGES

Jobs, Bosses, Unionism

Anon

THE SQUATTER'S MAN

From A. B. Paterson's *Old Bush Songs* (1905). The reference in the final stanza to Ben Hall and Gardiner, two notorious outlaws of New South Wales, suggests that the song was written in 1863 or 1864.

Come all ye lads an' list to me,
That's left your homes an' crossed the sea,
To try your fortune, bound or free,
   All in this golden land.
For twelve long months I had to pace,
Humping my swag with a cadging face,
Sleeping in the bush, like the sable race,
   As in my song you'll understand.

Unto this country I did come,
A regular out-and-out new chum;
I then abhorred the sight of rum—
   Teetotal was my plan.
But soon I learned to wet one eye—
Misfortune oft-times made me sigh,
To raise fresh funds I was forced to fly
   And be a squatter's man.

Soon at a station I appeared.
I saw the squatter with his beard,
And up to him I boldly steered
   With my swag and billy-can.
I said, 'Kind sir, I want a job!'
Said he, 'Do you know how to snob,
Or can you break in a bucking cob?'
   Whilst my figure he well did scan.

"Tis now I want a useful cove
To stop at home and not to rove.
The scamps go about—a regular drove—
   I s'pose you're one of the clan?
But I'll give you ten, ten, sugar an' tea;
Ten bob a week, if you'll suit me,
And very soon I hope you'll be
   A handy squatter's man.

UNEMPLOYED

'No chance, Bill! even the blooming moon is full.'

'At daylight you must milk the cows,
Make butter, cheese, an' feed the sows,
Put on the kettle, the cook arouse,
    And clean the family shoes.
The stable and sheep-yard clean out,
And always answer when we shout,
With "Yes, ma'am", and "No, sir"; mind your mouth,
    And my youngsters don't abuse.

'You must fetch wood an' water, bake an' boil,
Act as butcher when we kill;
The corn an' taters you must hill,
    Keep the garden spick and span.
You must not scruple in the rain
To take to market all the grain,
An' be sure you come sober back again
    To be a squatter's man.'

He sent me to an old bark hut,
Inhabited by a greyhound slut
Who put her fangs through my poor fut,
    And, snarling, off she ran.
So once more I'm looking for a job,
Without a copper in my fob.
With Ben Hall or Gardiner I'd rather rob
    Than be a squatter's man.

John Haynes

A MONSTER DEMONSTRATION

Quoted in E. H. Collis, *Lost Years* (1948).

A 'monster Protectionist demonstration' had been advertised
[in Sydney] at the beginning of the 'eighties. The *Evening
News* was a free trade paper, and John Haynes was its sub-
editor. He covered the demonstration and next day the
following paragraph appeared in the *Evening News*: 'Last
night a monster Protectionist demonstration was held at the
Cow and Bull Hotel, Paddington. There were exactly thirteen
monsters present.'

W. Kidston

THE BALLOT IS THE THING

(To be sung to the tune of 'The Wearing of the Green')

During the 1891 shearers' strike in Queensland, a number of songs were written in support of the men's stand, including 'The Ballot is the Thing' by William Kidston of Rockhampton, ironmoulder, trade union activist, and (in 1892) politician. The idea behind 'The Ballot is the Thing' was that workers should strengthen their position in their clashes with employers by gaining parliamentary power through the ballot box. See D. J. Murphy, R. B. Joyce, Colin A. Hughes (Eds.) *Prelude to Power*: The Rise of the Labour Party in Queensland, 1885–1915, published in 1970.

Oh comrades dear! and did you hear the news that's going
    round:
The shearer is by law forbid to camp on camping ground.
Unto the chain-gang's clank again Australian woods shall
    ring,
For they have found a law was made when George the
    Fourth was king.
  It makes the squatters sing, Oh, it makes the squatters
    sing!
  This vile old law that once was made when George the
    Fourth was king.

We used to have the notion that in Queensland men were
    free,
That before the law the squatter was the same as you or me;
But the sturdy bushman now, they say, 'down to his knees
    we'll bring
With this old law that once was made when George the
    Fourth was king'.
  It makes the squatter sing, Oh, it makes the squatter
    sing!
  This vile old law that once was made when George the
    Fourth was king.
And if you are a railway man, I'd have you for to know
You've got to ask your gaffer where your sympathies should
    go.
Your heart, your purse, your conscience to their keeping
    you must bring;
Why, it's even getting hotter than when George the Fourth
    was king.

When George the Fourth was king. When George the
    Fourth was king;
Why, it's even getting hotter than when George the
    Fourth was king.

But keep your heads and tempers, boys. Your time will
    come again.
Remember that your breath has made, and can *un*make
    these men.
When they've to face the ballot-box, it's mighty small they'll
    sing,
These men who'd drag us backward to the time when
    George was king.
    It's mighty small they'll sing, my boys; it's mighty small
        they'll sing,
    These men who'd drag us backward to the time when
        George was king.

Anon

FIVE BOB TO FOUR

This old song of a threshing gang was collected by Mr John Meredith from the
singing of Mr Alf Fuller of Concord (NSW), and included with tune in *Singabout* (Vol.
2, No. 4, May, 1958). John Meredith commented: 'Mr Fuller got this song from his
father who learned it from threshers at Lewis Ponds, New South Wales. Now [almost]
an extinct race, travelling gangs of threshers, harvesters and chaff-cutters were
responsible for spreading many of our folk songs.'

It was over at MacRose's where the threshing first began:
He is a little podgy, a jolly little man;
And every time the whistle blew at the closing of the day,
He was no ways backward in coming with the pay.
Four bob a day
Is all that he could pay—
I hope his cows the measles take, his hens refuse to lay,
For cutting down the wages to four bob a day.
I hope his pumpkins all take rot, his haystacks and his straw,
For cutting down the wages from five bob to four.

246

THE UNEMPLOYED AGAIN

'The man you can git to work for nothing, and board himself, will jest about earn his wages.'
—JOSH BILLINGS

From the Sydney *Bulletin* and reproduced in Patricia Rolfe (Ed.)
Clotted Rot for Clots and Rotters (1980)

Anon

THE CANE CUTTER'S LAMENT

I have no knowledge of the origin of this rhyme, which was sent to me by a reader of
my 'Come in Spinner' column in *Australasian Post*. It refers, of course, to the cutting of
cane by the banks of the Isis River near Bundaberg (Q). The earth in that region is,
I'm told, of a reddish hue.

How we suffered grief and pain
Out on the Isis, cutting cane!
We worked in the mud as red as blood—
And the ganger he drove the spurs right in.

Six months on end we were forced to spend,
And the food was a choice of evils:
There was cat's-meat stew that the flies had blew,
And the damper was crawling with weevils.

The Chinese cook with his cross-eyed look
Tormented our guts with his hashes,
And blocked up our holes with his half-baked rolls
That'd poison the snakes with their ashes.

The cane was bad, the cutters were mad,
And the cook he had shit on the liver;
And never again will I cut cane
On the banks of the Isis River.

I'm cleaning out of this lousy place—
I'll cut no more for this bugger.
He can stand in the mud as red as blood
And cut his own bloody sugar.

J. K. McDougall

THE STRIKE-BREAKER

From J. K. McDougall's *The Golden Road and Other Verses* (1936).

See the scab—the hated scab—
Traitor to his kind and class,
Got between a snake and drab,
Where no lower breed could pass.

See his face—the vilest face,
  Ever trunk of mortal bore;
See him slink with comrades base—
  Bludger, thief and draggled whore.

See him crawl, a reptile loose,
  On his belly doomed to go,
Serving every bastard use,
  Cursed as ev'rything that's low.

See him fawn—no baser cur
  Ever licked a master's boot;
Baser thief or perjurer
  Never risked a rope for loot.

See him wriggle—see him squirm,
  Crooked, covetous and slim;
When he crawls the meanest worm
  Cannot take the dust with him.

Labour's host at Greed's behest
  Basely does he rate and scold,
As a viper bites the breast
  That has warmed its slimy fold.

See him snarl and spit his hate,
  In the pride that heralds doom,
Recreant to man and State—
  Rubbish ready for the broom.

Sir Henry Bolte

ON STRIKING WORKERS IN THE LATROBE VALLEY

Sir Henry Bolte, during a power strike in Gippsland's Latrobe Valley in February
1972, showed little sympathy for the unionists' cause.
Quoted in B. Muir, *Bolte From Bamganie* (1973).

I don't care if they're out seven days or 70.

Hawke was busy getting the unions on-side ...

An' all Australia — all at once ...
beaudy ... beaudy ...

From *A Decade of Pickering* (1980)

Jack Nicholls

ON THE DEATH OF PAT SHANNON

Jack 'Puttynose' Nicholls (1920–1981), Secretary of the Melbourne Painters and Dockers' Union (1974–1981), was elected to his position after the preceding secretary, Pat Shannon, was shot in October 1973. (Nicholls was found dead in his car near Wangaratta, Victoria, with an alleged suicide note beside him, in June, 1981.) Nicholls, on the death of Shannon, broke the union's tradition of silence during such events, to make the following statement.
Quoted in the Melbourne *Herald* (October 18, 1973).

It's a real bastard of an act. Whoever did this is nothing but a mongrel cur.

The Melbourne *Age*

THE DARK WORLD OF THE PAINTERS AND DOCKERS

An article in the Melbourne *Age* (March 29, 1974) decried the violence on the waterfront and the fact that the Melbourne public initiated no word of protest.

Perhaps sedate Melbournites found a touch of Hollywood color in the occasional blaze of gangsterism on the waterfront.

Here was a picturesque piece of violent sub-culture where, just across town, colorful characters with humorous nicknames could cut each other down occasionally, make good headlines and present absolutely no hazard to the normal decent properties.

The Melbourne *Age*

THE WORKERS—OUR BEST LINE OF DEFENCE

A satirical sketch from 'Pinkney Place' in the Melbourne *Age* (November 1, 1975).

Across Australia the shirk ethic is fast replacing the work ethic. Never before have sickie statistics been so steep, or dole-diddlings so widespread . . .

Drones have infiltrated society so deeply that some unions now regard go-slow strikes as medically dangerous.

'Our fear', admitted one shop steward, 'is that if we order the men to labour even more languidly, their respiration and heartbeat might stop.'

Is the New Listlessness turning us into another burnt-out Britain? . . . Paradoxically, Australia's economic decline is in her best strategic interests.

. . . As one RAN commander put it: 'Continued industriousness would have turned us into the hemisphere's richest prize—an irresistible temptation to invasion.

'But now, thank God, with 3000 firms bankrupt since January, and two-thirds of other business under threat, we're too sour a plum for any conqueror to pluck.'

Idlers, it's plain, are our latterday AIF. Every loo in which a leadswinger steals a smoke is a little Kokoda trail—whereupon the nation is made a mite more safe from envious eyes.

Anti-Unionist

OF THE BUILDING BLACK BAN THREAT
ON THE REGENT THEATRE, MELBOURNE

When the Builders Labourers' Federation threatened a black ban on building projects after the City councillors talked of demolishing Melbourne's Regent Theatre, Councillor Moffat claimed to have received 120 telephone calls from the public—110 supporting the theatre's demolition. The typical comments made were quoted in the Melbourne *Sun* (June 6, 1977).

Pull the bloody thing down . . . [It is] just a plaster of Paris replica of a European octopus.

Phillip Adams

NOT RIP BUT RIT

Phillip Adams, while extolling the virtues of tea drinking, made this comment, in *The Unspeakable Adams* (1977):

This nation was built on a cup of tea, a Bex, and a good liedown.

The *Australian*

INDUSTRIAL ABSURDITY

From the *Australian* (August 30, 1977).

From *A Decade of Pickering* (1980)

253

On Saturday we said that Australia seemed to be living in some sort of industrial cloud cuckoo land. The reference was to a recommendation by an arbitration commissioner that workers on a central Melbourne building project be paid for five of the seven weeks for which they had been on strike. Today's continuing story on the matter seems to move us into something like the Mad Hatter's tea party, with all the unreality of thrashing around in the Dormouse's treacle well, trying to make sense out of nonsense.

It would surely seem to be nonsense that it is 'normal' procedure for strikers to be paid for all or part of their time on strike as a condition for returning to work. Yet the secretary of the Builders Laborers' Federation, Mr Gallagher, said yesterday that this had been the practice for fifteen years—and it seems apparent that the practice has not been confined to the building industry but is widespread. That this is so provides one illuminating explanation of why we find ourselves in our present state of industrial disorientation.

The perniciousness of the practice was demonstrated yesterday when the building company refused to float with the tide and pay the $¼ million involved, because it could see little point in paying the money for nothing—work bans in support of a demand for a $30 wage rise would continue, anyway. The unions refused to return to work, apparently on the basis that if they were not to be paid for not working then they would not work for pay.

Quite obviously, employers and their organisations who have countenanced the practice of pay for strike time in the past have made a rod for their own backs and one which may raise many more weals before it is broken. Yet broken it must be, because it is an industrial absurdity. It is no more realistic than employers demanding that unions compensate them for production and revenue lost during strike time—a demand we can expect if everybody is to jump into the treacle well.

254

Norm Gallagher

IN CONFRONTATION WITH THE MASTER BUILDERS' ASSOCIATION

From an article in the Melbourne *Herald* (September 2, 1977).

Action is the key to these disputes. You get respect only when you're strong. When you're weak, the other side will trample all over you.

As someone who used to do a bit of boxing, I was always taught that when you were hurt you never let on because the other bloke will hit you even harder. It's obvious to me—by the way the employers are whingeing now—that they were never taught that lesson.

Jack Mundey

ON NORM GALLAGHER

Jack Mundey, one-time New South Wales State Secretary of the Builders Labourers' Federation, was dismissed, with several others, from the NSW branch in 1974, after the union lost its Federal registration over industrial lawlessness (it regained its registration some months later). It was claimed that the dismissals were organised by Norm Gallagher, Federal Secretary of the BLF.
From the Melbourne *Herald* (June 12, 1978).

I'd take action against him if I didn't think he had delusions of grandeur and would like to be sent to Pentridge.

Jack Mundey

ON GOVERNMENT

Reported in the Melbourne *Herald* (June 12, 1978).

Capitalist or socialist, all governments now are too big, too suffocating, irresponsibly making life-or-death decisions for millions of people in the land they live in.

From *A Decade of Pickering* (1980)

257

Norm Gallagher

THOUGHTS OF CHAIRMAN NORM OF THE BUILDERS LABOURERS' FEDERATION

From the Melbourne *Age* (May 17, 1978; February 3, 1981; February 7, 1981; July 14, 1981; August 4, 1981), the *Financial Review* (May 2, 1979) and the Melbourne *Herald* (August 31, 1981).

After the Mainline building empire crash.

It could not have happened to a greater pack of prize bastards. (1974)

.   .   .

If we have used blackmail tactics, we have had some pretty good teachers.

.   .   .

Disputes do not always end where they begin.

.   .   .

What with guidelines and freezes, I would not even take my mother-in-law to the arbitration court, let alone my union. (1977)

.   .   .

We'll be fighting a coward's war. It will be hit and run tactics all the way. (May, 1978)

.   .   .

You have to soften up the employers first. The best steak is the one you tenderise. (May, 1979)

.   .   .

During the dispute surrounding the resumption of work on the Omega navigation station in South Gippsland.

What you can't win on the battle field you will not win at the conference table. (February, 1981)

.   .   .

258

To Mr Thorley, the Melbourne City Council Chief Commissioner,
on hearing about the threatened removal of the City Square
sculpture.

He will pay dearly. We don't take kindly to people breaking
union bans. (July, 1981)

For every action of the council there will be a reaction from
this union. (July, 1981)

For every act of vandalism from Mr Thorley . . . we will
place a green ban to protect the people's heritage. (July 1981)

I'll just go and put a few more bans on his developer mates
and hit them in the hip pocket if that's the way he wants to
play it. (August, 1981)

It is fairly typical of the council to go around doing this sort
of thing on the quiet. (August, 1981)

The *Bulletin* Editorial

IT'S TIME TO ACT

In 1980 the *Bulletin* ran a series of articles on the affairs of the Painters and Dockers'
Union.
From the *Bulletin* (April 1, 1980).

That the union has a long and bloody record of involvement
in killings is well known.

That graft is endemic on the Australian waterfront is less
well-known publicly, having briefly been revealed by the
1975 report of the Sweeney Royal Commission and then
forgotten.

What has not been known before the *Bulletin*'s series of
articles is that the Painters and Dockers' Union has enjoyed
the *de facto* support of the Federal Government, through the
lax pay practices of the Australian National Line and the
Royal Australian Navy.

And, as this week's article establishes, the union has somehow been able to ignore the fundamental reporting obliga-
tions laid down by the Conciliation and Arbitration Act.

It is not a situation which calls for an inquiry. It is a situation which calls for a government which is prepared to act on its frequently-voiced concern for industrial law and order.

As a first step, the government should consider the immediate de-registration of the Painters and Dockers' Union for failure to comply with the provisions of the Act, and its replacement by a union comprised of more workers and fewer criminals.

The *Australian*

UNSAVORY UNION

From an article by Norman Fay, Chief of Staff, in the *Australian* (April 3, 1980).

The painters and dockers has been a most unsavory union or collection of men, which over the years has managed to extract huge excess payments from shipping companies while members of the union have died by the gun.

Malcolm Fraser

ON THE BUILDERS LABOURERS' FEDERATION

From the Melbourne *Age* (February 7, 1981).

[The Prime Minister declared that the Government would not tolerate the] predatory guerilla tactics [of] one of the most outrageous unions.

Jack 'Puttynose' Nicholls

A SUICIDE NOTE

This note was found beside the body of Jack Nicholls, Secretary of the Melbourne Painters and Dockers Union, in June 1981.
From the *National Times* (June 21–27, 1981).

I tried very hard but the rotten Fraser Government did not want me to survive. Do not think I have taken the easy way out but the rotten system has cut my life short. I had big ideas for advancement but we were chopped short . . .

From the Melbourne *Age* (April 3, 1980)

Mr Lieberman

ON THE BUILDERS LABOURERS' FEDERATION

The following extract is from an article in the Melbourne *Age* (July 16, 1981) during the dispute over the removal of the City Square sculpture, *The Vault.*

Minister for Planning and Local Government, Mr Lieberman, described the BLF as arrogant and anarchistic.

He said threats by the union to ban work on all properties sold by the Melbourne City Council were bullying. 'This is just one more example of this destructive union putting itself above the law and having the temerity to try to dictate to the legally constituted government of the city.'

Lawrence Money

WHO'S WHO?

Journalist Lawrence Money takes a satirical look at our strike-prone society. From the Melbourne *Herald* (July 27, 1981).

There was pandemonium at the headquarters of the Victorian Strike Organisers Federation — phones ringing, people shouting, staff running about.

SOF boss Mike Pugg was having a devil of a time working out the strike roster.

'Now 'ang on,' he said, 'are youse SEC blokes in or out today?'

'We're in,' said the SEC rep, 'but we're probably out again later.'

'Well who are those guys who checked in as "out" this morning?'

'That's the TWU mob, mate.'

'Struth — okay, youse wharfies are out all week, as usual, so I can slot youse power blokes in again Fridee.'

'Aw 'ang on, I wanted to go fishin' Thursdee.'

'Okay, make it Thursdee. Youse Telecom blokes can have ya walk-out Wednesday to fit in with the royal wedding — and we'll swing a postal strike Thursdee.'

'That's to stop all them slobs writin' in to complain, eh?'

262

'What about us, toots?' asked a colorful character in a tangerine satin blouse.

'Cripes, youse ballet mob wanna go out AGAIN?'

Another rep chimed in: 'Can you wangle the aircraft refuellers a 48-hour next week, Mike—they reckon they haven't had a decent break for two weeks.'

'Look,' shouted Pugg angrily, 'there's only seven days in the week, y'know, and there's still the bus drivers" walk-out, the confectioners' sit-in, the wallpaperers wildcat and seven protest marches to squeeze in—HOW ABOUT SOME COFFEE, FLOSSIE?'

'She can't, Mike—secretaries' union is having a stop-work over stocking allowances.'

'Aw, cripes, I'll make me own cuppa.'

'Can't Mike, the electric jug blew up in the last power blackout.'

'That does it,' snarled Pugg, 'I'm not workin' in these conditions—I'm callin' an indefinite stoppage of the Strike Organisers' Federation. . . .

'I'M WARNIN' YOUSE—THERE'LL BE NO STRIKES UNTIL FURTHER NOTICE!!'

Mike Pugg was as surprised as anyone when, after staying out for six months, he was awarded the Citizens' Peace Prize and topped a popularity poll taken at the Melbourne Club.

Helen Rosengren Freedman

IF YOU CAN STRIKE THE RIGHT DAY

Journalist Helen Freedman gave her impressions of Melbourne after being away for several years.
From the Melbourne *Herald* (August 22, 1981).

. . . striking has joined clock-watching and beer-drinking and 'she'll be right, mate' as a national obsession.

What's interesting right now is the way Australians have a certain tendency to justify the trade union shambles that's become a way of life, and to distract themselves from their manipulated states, by telling themselves that the situation here isn't unique, that this is what goes on everywhere else in the world.

'They may be on strike ... but they're working harder than ever!'

From the Melbourne *Herald* (October 27, 1981)

Joh Bjelke-Petersen

ON AMERICAN AIR TRAFFIC CONTROLLERS

In early September, 1981, the Federal Minister for Transport, Mr Hunt, and the Queensland Premier, Mr Bjelke-Petersen, clashed over the suggested use of American air traffic controllers to cover shortages in Australia. The Americans had been sacked.
Quoted in the Melbourne *Age* (September 2, 1981).

We have enough union troublemakers in Australia without importing more from overseas . . . We don't want Reagan rejects.

Professor Lauchlan Chipman

ON TEACHER UNIONS

Professor Lauchlan Chipman, professor of philosophy at the University of Wollongong, speaking at a Melbourne conference on education, hurled this piece of invective at the teachers' unions.
Quoted in the Melbourne *Age* (September 4, 1981).

[In reference to an ABC news report of a New South Wales industrial dispute involving teachers] Behind the television reporter, viewers saw, and heard, a foul-mouthed rabble of sloppily dressed and grubbily obese unionists, expressing contempt for the State Industrial Commission's determination and the commission itself . . .
[Chipman also referred to] the widely entrenched image of a defiant unprofessional, enthusiastically protected by teacher union goons and larrikins in the frequent industrial confrontations and tediously deceitful public campaigns which have themselves directly contributed to an erosion of public respect.

Lew Hillier

IN DEFENCE OF UNIONS

A book, *Meet The Ship Painters and Dockers*, by an ex-member of the Painters and Dockers' Union, Lew Hillier, is to be published shortly. The Melbourne *Age* (September 12, 1981) quoted two stanzas from a poem which is included in the book.

If the kid is crook, or the
    misses dies,
It's every man as one.
Chuck in fer the funeral boys,
Or a pushbike fer the son.

An' ter say these blokes is
    scoundrels mate,
Well ter me that's all tom tit
Coz I'd rather be a Dockie
Than a bloody hypocrite.

10

EXPLOSIVE EXPLORERS

Trail-Blazers at Loggerheads

Governor Darling

ON SIR THOMAS MITCHELL

Sir Thomas Livingstone Mitchell (1792–1855), Surveyor-General and explorer, led
several successful expeditions of discovery into western New South Wales and western
Victoria, the most notable being into what he called 'Australia Felix' in south-western
Victoria. Mitchell was an ambitious man, not of easy temper.
From a private letter written by Governor Sir Ralph Darling on March 28, 1831, to
R. W. Hay, Permanent Under-Secretary at the Colonial Office, London, and quoted
in J. H. L. Cumpston, *Thomas Mitchell* (1955).

You will judge of my disposition towards him by my private
letter to you of 6 June 1829. At that time I looked upon him
as a hard-working, rude, ill-tempered fellow who quarrelled
with everyone, and who, I may add, is still as much detested
as ever by those who have any business to transact with him.

Anxious to get the business of the Government done, I was
willing to make every sacrifice, and he was allowed to snarl
and growl unheeded, until at last his influence became
intolerable.

Governor Gipps

MAJOR MITCHELL AND 'AUSTRALIA FELIX'

From a despatch of Governor Sir George Gipps to Lord John Russell, Secretary of
State for War and the Colonies, September 28, 1840.

The long and expensive journeys of Sir Thomas Mitchell in
the years 1835 to 1836 though highly interesting led to no
discoveries which could be turned to profit, with the exception perhaps of the fertile valley of Australia Felix which
would surely have been reached by the ordinary advance of
our graziers even though he had never visited it.

Sir Thomas Mitchell

ON CHARLES STURT

Captain Charles Sturt (1795–1869) led several highly important exploring expeditions
into the interior of the continent. His courage and humanity endeared him to many

of his contemporaries. Major Mitchell, however, who could stomach no rival near the throne, treated him with scant respect and no courtesy.

... an officer on full pay who has never travelled anywhere.

Hovenden Hely

GREEDY LEICHHARDT

Friedrich Wilhelm Ludwig Leichhardt (1813–1848?), German-born explorer, conducted expeditions of discovery into Northern Australia before disappearing somewhere in the interior of the Australian continent in 1848. Hovenden Hely, a member of Leichhardt's Second Expedition of 1846–47, was here referring to his leader's habit of taking more than his share of the scanty rations.

The Dr is indeed the most selfish greedy man I ever saw. He sleeps by a fire by himself at night and we imagine makes tapioca. The blacks say they see him every morning making 'bull' (i.e. sugar and water) at daylight. What disgusting selfish greedings! Thank heaven we shall soon be rid of him!

Sir Thomas Mitchell

ON A BOOK OF LEICHHARDT'S TRAVELS

From a letter from the explorer, Sir Thomas Mitchell, to his son Livingstone, written in England on August 18, 1847. Quoted in J. H. L. Cumpston's *Thomas Mitchell* (1954).

Boone has sent me Leichhardt's travels and a more useless mass of rubbish never was bound up in the form of a book.

John F. Mann

LEICHHARDT: 'NO EXPLORER'

The surveyor, John F. Mann, was a member of Leichhardt's Second Expedition of 1846–47. Quoted in Alec H. Chisholm's *Strange New World* (1955).

Leichhardt! He was no explorer. He'd lose himself in George Street, Sydney.

269

Angus McMillan

ON STRZELECKI, EXPLORER

Sir Paul Edmund Strzelecki (1797–1873), Polish-born explorer and scientist, was popularly known as 'The Count'. He explored parts of south-eastern Australia and named Mount Kosciusko (1840). Angus McMillan, first explorer of the Gippsland region of eastern Victoria, claimed that Strzelecki accepted credit for discoveries in Gippsland which he himself had made. Quoted in James Bonwick, *Port Phillip Settlement* (1883).

As a foreign impostor, the Count had no claim on the discoveries of another . . .

11

RACIST RANCOURS

White, Black and Yellow

James Stephen

THE BIRTH OF RACISM

The following words by James Stephen, in 1841, anticipated the essentially racist basis of the White Australia Policy as it emerged in the 1890s.
From an article in the Melbourne *Age* (August 18, 1981).

There is not on the globe a social issue more momentous . . . than that of reserving the continent of New Holland as a place where the English race shall be spread from sea to sea unmixed with any lower caste.

Brunton Stephens

MY OTHER CHINESE COOK

An article in the Melbourne *Age* entitled 'The Birth of Racism', gave a brief history of Chinese immigration in Australia. By 1859 there were about 42000 Chinese in Victoria, comprising around one-fourteenth of the population. Europeans on the goldfields observed and resented the clannishness and solidarity of the Chinese communities. Two major anti-Chinese movements occurred in the 19th century—a riot at the Buckland River in 1857 and a more widespread movement, backed by the unions and colonial legislation, in the 1880s and 1890s.
   The following verse is an extract only from the old ballad by Stephens:

He was lazy, he was cheeky,
He was dirty, he was sly,
But he had a single virtue,
and its name was rabbit pie.

Henry Kendall

JACK, THE BLACKFELLOW

It's surprising that Kendall, a man of such great sensitivity, should have been so unfeeling in his attitude to the Aboriginal fringe-dwellers he encountered on stations and in country towns in New South Wales. Kendall's mid-Victorian smugness, his lack of sympathy for these victims of white supremacy, his nauseating comparisons between classical beauty and alleged Aboriginal ugliness, the utter shabbiness of his thinking—all these strike a chill in the modern reader who understands something of apartheid, and of the racist antipathies still existing in Australia.

Stand out you rascal! Let me take
Your measure from the top to toe,

ONLY A BLACKFELLOW!
AN EPISODE OF CIVILIZATION IN AUSTRALIA.

Far away in the remote wild West of this Continent, another of that unhappy race which the whites have dispossessed of its hunting-grounds is to pay the penalty of death for having killed a station-hand who lured away the partner of his joys and sorrows.

On this subject The Bulletin says: 'Twas ever thus:
O blackfellows, you look like men, And should be, therefore, of our kin;
We give you rum and faith. What then?
You'll surely spare us a small gin. (1882)

From the Sydney *Bulletin* (1882) and reproduced in Patricia Rolfe (Ed.)
Clotted Rot for Clots and Rotters (1980)

Including that old 'wideawake'
  Which time and you have battered so!
You're hardly handsome, and your rig
  Would scarcely suit a Fancy Ball.
In fact you are a shabby 'nig'
  Without a saving point at all.

. . .

Here, Jacky, drop the black 'dhudeen', [pipe]
  And tell me in what distant day—
You'll wash your frowsy features clean?—
  Of course, you scamp, you will not say!

'Me gib it bacca!' O, no, no—
  That little method will not do:
'Twas played out, neighbour, long ago—
  I am too old a bird for you.

. . .

In ancient days you had to trap,
  And fish, and hunt, by pool and rock;
But now you are a different chap—
  We feed you like a fighting cock.

There's not the slightest danger, friend,
  That you'll be asked to take the spade!
That game was tried; and in the end
  We hardly think the labour paid.

Much dearer than a dozen whites
  Are three of you at any toil;
You'd eat a loaf in seven bites—
  You would not earn a pint of oil!

Perhaps you're right—at all events
  You're fat enough, and pretty strong;
And, what with theft and cadging pence,
  You somehow seem to 'rub along'.

Henry Kendall

BLACK LIZZIE

I can't detect the flowing lines
　Of Grecian features in your face
Nor are there any patent signs
　That link you with the Roman race.

In short, I do not think your mould
　Resembles, with its knobs of bone,
The fair Hellenic shapes of old
　Whose perfect forms survive in stone.

Still, if the charm called Beauty lies
　In ampleness of ear and lip,
And nostrils of exceeding size,
　You are a gem, my ladyship.

.　　.　　.

You smoke a pipe—of course, you do!
　About an inch in length or less,
Which, from a sexual point of view,
　Mars somewhat your attractiveness.

But rather than resign the weed,
　You'd shock us, whites, by chewing it;
For etiquette is not indeed
　A thing that bothers you a bit.

Your people—take them as a whole—
　Are careless on the score of grace;
And hence you needn't comb your poll
　Or decorate your unctuous face.

Still, seeing that a little soap
　Would soften an excess of tint,
You'll pardon my advance, I hope,
　In giving you a gentle hint.

Brunton Stephens

TO A BLACK GIN

My comments on the previous poems by Kendall apply with equal emphasis to the following disgusting verses by the Queenslander, Brunton Stephens.

Thou art not beautiful, I tell thee plainly,
Oh, thou ungainliest of things ungainly!
Who thinks thee less than hideous dotes insanely.

Most unaesthetical of things terrestrial,
Hadst thou indeed an origin celestial: —
Thy lineaments are positively bestial!

Yet thou my sister art, the clergy tell me;
Though, truth to state, thy brutish looks compel me
To hope these parsons merely want to *sell* me.

Brunton Stephens

A PICCANINNY

Nay, my black tulip, I congratulate thee,
Thou canst not guess the troubles that await thee,
Nor carest who shall love or who shall hate thee:

Recking as little of the human passions
As of the very latest Paris fashions,
And soaring not beyond thy daily rations!

Die young, for mercy's sake! If thou grow older,
Thou shalt grow lean at calf and sharp at shoulder,
And daily greedier and daily bolder;

A pipe between thy savage grinders thrusting,
For rum and everlasting 'bacca lusting,
And altogether filthy and disgusting.

Anon

ALIEN TRIBES

This 19th century rhyme, directed against Chinese immigration, is quoted in William Linklater and Lynda Tapp, *Gather No Moss* (1968).

Two races plague Australian folks
Much more than all their monies;
The former are the Chinamen,
The latter are the bunnies.

The pig-tailed and the flop-eared tribes
Must somehow now be beaten,
For 'twixt them both the Colonists
From house and home are eaten.

Sir Henry Parkes

WITH REGARD TO CHINESE IMMIGRATION

The arrival of successive vessels containing smallpox cases amongst Chinese pas-
sengers and the discovery of a high proportion of naturalisation certificates, galvanised
Sir Henry Parkes, Premier of New South Wales, into pushing emergency measures
through the New South Wales Parliament. His speech on May 16, 1888, represents
well the state of public opinion.
Quoted in the Melbourne *Age* (August 18, 1981).

I contend that if this young nation is to maintain the fabric
of its liberties unassailed and unimpaired, it cannot admit
into its population any element that of necessity must be of
an inferior nature and character. In other words, I have
maintained at all times that we should not encourage or
admit amongst us any class of persons whatever whom we
are not prepared to advance to all our franchises, to all our
privileges as citizens, and all our social rights, including the
right of marriage.

Henry Lawson

A WORD TO TEXAS JACK

Lawson's nationalistic impulses flared into satirical verse when an American rough-
rider, one 'Texas Jack', brought a rodeo show to Australia in the late 1890s with the
idea of demonstrating the finer points of 'Wild West' horsemanship.

Texas Jack, you are amusin'. Great Lord Harry how I
    laughed
When I seen your rig and saddle with its bulwarks fore-
    and-aft;

279

Holy smoke! From such a saddle how the dickens can you
  fall?
Why, I've seen a gal ride bareback with no bridle on at all!

Gosh! so help me! strike me balmy! if a bit o' scenery
Like of you in all your rig-out on this earth I ever see!
How I'd like to see a bushman use your fixins, Texas Jack—
On the remnant of a saddle he could ride to hell and back.
Why, I've heerd a mother cheerin' when her kid went tossin'
  by,
Ridin' bareback on a bucker that had murder in his eye.

What? you've come to learn the natives how to sit a horse's
  back!
Learn the bloomin' cornstalk ridin'? W'at yer giv'n us, Texas
  Jack?
Learn the cornstalk! Flamin' jumptup! now where has my
  country gone?
Why, a cornstalk's mother often rides the day afore he's born!

You may talk about your ridin' in the city, bold an' free,
Talk o' ridin' in the city, Texas Jack; but where'd you be
When the stock-horse snorts an' bunches all 'is quarters in
  a hump,
And the saddle climbs a sapling, an' the horseshoes split a
  stump?
No, before you teach the native you must ride without a fall
Up a gum, or down a gully, nigh as steep as any wall—
You must swim the roarin' Darlin' when the flood is at its
  height
Bearin' down the stock an' stations to the great Australian
  Bight.

You can't count the bulls an' bisons that you copped with
  your lassoo—
But a stout old myall bullock p'raps ud learn you somethin'
  new;
You had better make your will an' leave your papers neat an'
  trim
Before you make arrangements for the lassooin' of *him*;
Ere your horse and you is cat's-meat—fittin' fate for sich
  galoots—

280

And your saddle's turned to laces like we put in blucher boots.

And you say you're death on Injins! We've got somethin' in
    your line—
If you think your fightin's ekal to the likes of Tommy Ryan.
Take your carcass up to Queensland where the alligators
    chew
And the carpet-snake is handy with his tail for a lassoo,
Ride across the hazy regions where the lonely emus wail
An' ye'll find the black'll track you while you're lookin' for
    his trail;
He can track you without stoppin' for a thousand miles or
    more—
Come again, and he will show you where you spat the year
    before.
But you'd best be mighty careful—you'll be sorry you kem
    here
When you're skewered to the fakements of your saddle with
    a spear;
When the boomerang is sailin' in the air, then Heaven help
    you.
It will cut your head off goin', an' come back again to scalp
    you.

P.S.—As poet and as Yankee I will greet you, Texas Jack,
For it isn't no ill-feelin' that is gettin' up my back;
But I won't see this land crowded by each Yank and British
    cuss
Who takes it in his head to come a-civilizin' us.
Though on your own great continent there's misery in the
    towns,
An' not a few untitled lords, and kings without their crowns,
I will admit your countrymen is busted big, an' free,
An' great on ekal rites of men and great on liberty:
I will admit your fathers punched the gory tyrant's head—
But then we've got our heroes, too, the diggers that is dead,
The plucky men of Ballarat, who toed the scratch so well,
And broke the nose of Tyranny and made his peepers swell,
For yankin' Lib's gold tresses in the roarin' days gone by,
An' doublin' up his dirty fist to black her bonny eye;

So when it comes to ridin' mokes, or hoistin' out the Chow,
Or stickin' up for labour's rights, we don't want showin' how.

They came to learn us cricket in the days of long ago,
An' Hanlan came from Canada to learn us how to row,
An' 'doctors' come from Frisco just to learn us how to skite,
An' pugs from all the lands on earth to learn us how to fight;
An' when they go, as like as not, we find we're taken in,
They've left behind no learnin' — but they've carried off our
    tin.

A. G. Stephens

ON THE BRITISH

Quoted in the Sydney *Bulletin* (August 6, 1900).

Britannia est insula, says the Latin primer. Britons are insular.
They are cast in a mould, and dislike to be cast out of the
mould: they run in a groove, and object to run over.

Henry Lawson

ON THE BRITISH

From Henry Lawson, 'The Ghosts of Many Christmases', in *The Romance of the Swag*
(1907).

And speaking of plum pudding, I consider it one of the most
barbarous institutions of the British. It is a childish, silly,
savage superstition; it must have been a savage inspiration,
looking at it all round, — but then it isn't so long since the
British were savages.

An American Attitude

TO THE AUSTRALIAN ARMY

In an unpublished diary recently acquired by the National Library, author and war
correspondent, George Johnston, takes several sly and angry swipes at General
MacArthur, accusing him of belittling the efforts of the Australian troops in New

Guinea. Johnston said that this attitude was widespread among American troops.
Quoted in the Melbourne *Age* (August 28, 1981).

There is a widespread tendency for many Americans to decry the Australian efforts . . . one American was asked today if the hundreds of wounded Australians coming in, had been in traffic accidents.

James Stuart MacDonald

AMERICA—A CULTURE-CONSUMING NATION

Art critic J. S. MacDonald, in an article on the perversion of modern art, hit out at America's lack of creativity.
From the Sydney *Daily Mirror* (February 5, 1945).

[America is] a culture-consuming nation, not a culture-producing one. Culture there is not a product but an acquisition. They have to take the word of other nations for the worth of something they do not create.

Len Fox

LUCKY COUNTRY

From *Gumleaves and People* (1967).

(After reading Donald Horne's book of the same name)

Australia the lucky country,
The land of beer, sport and fun,
The laughing blokes and their sheilahs
On the golden beach in the sun.

Tropics and snowfields and night-clubs,
The best of the old and the new,
And a fair go for Tom, Dick and Harry,
Provided your skin's the right hue.

Kath Walker

JUSTICE IS A CANT OF HYPOCRITES

The following poems by Aboriginal poet, Kath Walker, decry the hypocrisy of civil

law and religious faith as practised in Australia. The poems encompass the appalling attitude of the white race to the Aboriginals over the last 200 years.
From Kath Walker, *My People* (1970).

WHYNOT STREET

Officiously they hawked about
'Petition' to keep abos out,
And slavishly, without a peep,
The feeble yes-men signed like sheep.

And are we still the ousted, then,
And dare you speak for decent men?
This site was ours, you may recall,
Ages before you came at all.

'No abos here!' Why not, Whynot?
And if black-balling and boycott,
First black-ball pride and arrogance,
Boycott this vile intolerance.

INTOLERANCE

When the white glug contemptuously
Says 'nigger', it is plain to me
He is of a lower grade than we.

When the dark stockman, used to hate,
Is not accepted as a mate,
Democracy is empty prate.

When we hear from the white élite
'We won't have abos in our street,'
Their Christianity's a cheat.
When blacks are banned, as we know well,
From city café and hotel,
The stink of Little Rock we smell.

Dark children coming home in tears,
Hurt and bewildered by their jeers—
I think Christ weeps with you, my dears.

People who say, by bias driven,
That colour must not be forgiven,
Would snub the Carpenter in heaven.

We're hoping they'll move on shortly. They're nomadic you know.

From *A Decade of Pickering* (1980)

COLOUR BAR

When vile men jeer because my skin is brown,
This I live down.

But when a taunted child comes home in tears,
Fierce anger sears.

The colour bar! It shows the meaner mind
Of moron kind.

Men are but medieval yet, as long
As lives this wrong.

Could he but see, the colour-baiting clod
Is blaming God

Who made us all, and all His children He
Loves equally.

As long as brothers banned from brotherhood
You still exclude,

The Christianity you hold so high
Is but a lie,

Justice a cant of hypocrites, content
With precedent.

WE ARE GOING

For Grannie Coolwell

They came in to the little town
A semi-naked band subdued and silent,
All that remained of their tribe.
They came here to the place of their old bora ground
Where now the many white men hurry about like ants.
Notice of estate agent reads: 'Rubbish May Be Tipped Here'.
Now it half covers the traces of the old bora ring.
They sit and are confused, they cannot say their thoughts:
'We are as strangers here now, but the white tribe are the
        strangers.
We belong here, we are of the old ways.
We are the corroboree and the bora ground,

286

We are the old sacred ceremonies, the laws of the elders.
We are the wonder tales of Dream Time, the tribal legends
    told.
We are the past, the hunts and the laughing games, the
    wandering camp fires.
We are the lightning-bolt over Gaphembah Hill
Quick and terrible,
And the Thunder after him, that loud fellow.
We are the quiet daybreak paling the dark lagoon.
We are the shadow-ghosts creeping back as the camp fires
    burn low.
We are nature and the past, all the old ways
Gone now and scattered.
The scrubs are gone, the hunting and the laughter.
The eagle is gone, the emu and the kangaroo are gone from
    this place.
The bora ring is gone.
The corroboree is gone.
And we are going.'

Judith Wright

BORA RING

Australian poet, Judith Wright, expresses similar feelings to those of Kath Walker in
the following poem.
From Judith Wright, *Collected Poems* (1972).

The song is gone; the dance
is secret with the dancers in the earth,
the ritual useless, and the tribal story
lost in alien tale.

Only the grass stands up
to mark the dancing-ring; the apple-gums
posture and mime a past corroboree,
murmur a broken chant.

The hunter is gone: the spear
is splintered underground; the painted bodies
a dream the world breathed sleeping and forgot.
The nomad feet are still.

Only the rider's heart
halts at a sightless shadow, an unsaid word
that fastens in the blood the ancient curse,
the fear as old as Cain.

Michael Saclier

ON ENGLISHMEN

These words are attributed to Michael Saclier from the Research School of Social Sciences at the Australian National University, during a lecture in 1973. Quoted in Bill Hornadge, *The Australian Slanguage* (1980).

The term kipper (instead of Pom) . . . is used by many Australians and is self-explanatory. For the less observant, it derives from the statistically proven similarity between the Englishman and his favourite breakfast food—both are spineless, two-faced and smell.

Mr J. W. Bourchier

IN SOME PARLIAMENTARY NAME-CALLING

Quoted in Bill Hornadge, *The Australian Slanguage* (1980).

In the House of Representatives in 1975 Dr R. T. Gun (Labor) addressed Mr J. W. Bourchier (Liberal) as follows: 'Why don't you shut up, you great poofter?' Whereupon Mr Bourchier replied: 'Come around here, you little Wop, and I will fix you up.'

Sir Mark Oliphant

THE ABORIGINAL PERSONALITY

On the release of a biography of Sir Mark Oliphant in August, 1981, a howl of criticism greeted the publication of a letter written by Sir Mark, while Governor of South Australia (1971–1976), to the then Premier of South Australia, Mr Don Dunstan. The letter expressed concern at the intention of the Dunstan Government to appoint Aboriginal, Pastor (now Sir) Doug Nicholls, as Governor, on the retirement of Sir

288

From the Melbourne *Age* (November 9, 1977)

Mark. Sir Douglas did succeed Sir Mark in December, 1976, but retired in April, 1977, due to ill-health.

From the Melbourne *Age* (August 20, 1981).

There is something inherent in the personality of the Aborigine which makes it difficult for him to adapt fully to the ways of the white man.

[An Aboriginal as Governor could lead to Government House being] filled to overflowing [by relatives and tribesman] to whom, by custom and duty, he cannot say 'no'. The results could be chaos, inability to find or keep domestic staff, and even loss of valuables because of the 'sharing' habits of his people.

[Another problem would be] the background of the proposed incumbent . . . [He belongs to a] fundamentalist religion which is not compatible with that of most South Australians . . .

The whole education of the pastor was at his birthplace, Cummeragunja, NSW, which I cannot locate in any atlas or on any map, as it is clearly a camp or mission . . .

Does his fame as an athlete and footballer make up for this? His only publications are contributions to *Smoke Signals*, the quarterly of the Aborigines Advancement League.

Ken Tomkins

MORE EVOLUTION FOR ABORIGINALS

The following statement by Mr Ken Tomkins, Queensland Minister for Aboriginal and Island Affairs, received wide publicity in August, 1981.

Quoted in the Melbourne *Age* (August 8, 1981).

I am not satisfied that at this point in time that Aborigines can handle mortgage documents.

Mr Keane

DECENT WHITE TENANTS WANTED

This extract is from an article on Federal Parliament in the Melbourne *Age* (August 28, 1981).

Might I suggest, Your Majesty, that these people have done nothing but complain ever since we got there.

From *A Decade of Pickering* (1980)

291

Mr Keane [NSW State Labor MP] had been quoted in the *Sydney Morning Herald* as saying that Vietnamese and Aborigines would not be permitted to be tenants of proposed Housing Commission homes in the Menai area of NSW and that tenancies would be reserved for 'decent white Anglo-Saxon Australians . . .'.

Carlton Football Supporter

TO ABORIGINAL UMPIRE GLEN JAMES

Reported in the Melbourne *Age* 'Weekender' (September 4, 1981) was the fact that supporters of both sides ganged up on the originator of these words:

Go back to Arnhem Land you black bludger.

12

ACCUSING HEADSTONES

Epitaphs and Eulogies

DEADLY BREW

This epitaph of the 1820s, on a tombstone in Parramatta churchyard, was quoted by P. Cunningham in his *Two Years in New South Wales* (1828). (James Squire was a brewer in early Sydney.)

Ye who wish to lie here
Drink Squire's beer.

Anon

EPITAPH FOR DR JAMES ROSS

Dr James Ross was a prominent figure in the life of Van Diemen's Land in the 1820s and 1830s. He published the *Courier* newspaper, and was a strong supporter of Governor Arthur and of the transportation system. However, he did much for the cultural improvement of the colony. The following lines were composed by Ross's political enemies, of whom there were many. See John West, *The History of Tasmania* (1852).

Here lieth the body of James Ross, printer: formerly a negro driver: who spent the remainder of his days in advocating the cause of torture, triangles, and the gallows.

Beneath this sod, mark, reader, as you pass
The carcase buried of a great jack-ass:
Perfidious, smiling, fawning, cringing slave,
Hell holds his spirit, and his flesh this grave.
Corruption revels in a kindred soil:
A carcase fatted on an island's spoil!

Richard Henry ('Orion') Horne

'TYRANT, FOOL, SWINDLER'
(*An Epitaph for Sir Charles Hotham*)

Few colonial administrators were less popular than Sir Charles Hotham, who became Governor of Victoria in 1854. It was during his term of office that discontent among gold-diggers flared into open defiance of authority at the Eureka lead in the Ballarat field. These verses by 'Orion' Horne are quoted in Cyril Pearl's *Forever Morning* (1960).

Beneath the barrel lies a knight
Who wilfully in darkness fought,

Who never took a second sight,
Who never had a single thought.

.   .   .

He scraped, embezzled, skinn'd and saved—
Then died—from drinking bad small beer,
Leaving his character engraved
A Tyrant, Fool and Swindler here.

Charles Harpur

LINES ON A MONEY-LENDER

*A Cut-and-Dried Epitaph for T.C., Whenever it Please the
Devil to Take Him*

These lines were addressed by Charles Harpur (1813–1868) to one Tom Cullen, an
innkeeper and moneylender of Singleton (NSW). Quoted in J. Normington-Rawling,
Charles Harpur (1962).

Within this tomb lies grim and cold
He who was once the usurer C-ll-n:
Grim and cold, without the gold
He farmed so gripingly of old:
But with the worms per cent his skull in
(Or more perchance if all were told)
    Instead!
And this, though it provoke a laugh,
Is all that can of Tom be said
Even in the way of Epitaph.

Anon

SONG FOR A SCROOGE

From the Sydney *Bulletin* of 1882 and quoted in Patricia Rolfe (Ed.) *Clotted Rot for
Clots and Rotters* (1980).

There was an old man of Yass,
Many guineas did slyly amass,
    In a leaky enclosure
    He died of exposure,
And the people adjudged him an ass.

The Undertaker's Picnic

THE SILENT TOMB

(*A Dirge Specially Composed for the Melancholy Occasion*)

From the Sydney *Bulletin* and reproduced in Patricia Rolfe (Ed.) *Clotted Rot for Clots and Rotters* (1980).

There are some who sing of the young-eyed Spring,
And love and liquor — not these my toast, men.
For women and wine, though both are fine,
Are apt to pall in the end on most men.
But I shall warble of no such thing,
For the Silent Tomb is the theme I sing.
For the Silent Tomb is the theme I sing.

Oh, the silent tomb is a place of gloom
For the living, but — though they can't conceive it —
However, they swear, when they once get there,
They like it so well they never leave it.
Then let each bold grave-filler in the room
Arise and drink to the Silent Tomb!

From towns and thorpes comes the Cheerful Corpse —
The young and fair, and the old and hoary —
In a long pine chest, with a plate on his breast.

And goes to the tomb in a gloom of glory.
Then to show that your minds no malice warps,
Fill up and drink to the Cheerful Corpse!

O, the corpse has joys, though he makes no noise,
He says no word, but he thinks like thunder;
And there he lies, and he winks his eyes,
As his mother-in-law is taken under.
Then here is a toast—your glasses poise—
'May our coffins never be empty, boys.'

And the corpse he has got a gay old lot,
He has no troubles upon his mind, sirs,
And he lies in state, like a potentate,
In a rosewood coffin with satin lined, sirs.
Then charge your glasses—as who would not?—
And drink to the corpse's gay old lot.

There's one more verse for the jocund hearse;
And a line for the merry mourning-coaches
And the sombre suits, and the mirthful mutes,
Like a long procession of black cockroaches
Let us pledge them all—for the time is scarce—
The suits and the mutes and the jocund hearse.

Robert Phillips

ON THE DEFEAT OF GEELONG

Australian Rules football is believed to have been first played in 1858. Team loyalties soon developed. On the front page of the *Sportsman* in June 1888 a bookmaker, Robert Phillips, excited by South Melbourne's defeat of Geelong, declared his loyalty in the form of a tombstone inscription.
Quoted in Keith Dunstan, *Sports* (1973).

GO AHEAD
SOUTH MELBOURNE
ALAS! POOR GEELONG

Sacred to the Memory
Of Poor Geelong
In Memorium
Erected
By Their Great Admirer
Robert Phillips
The South Melbournite

Anon

AN EPITAPH FOR ROBERT LOWE

Robert Lowe (1811–1892), created Viscount Sherbrooke in 1880, was a notable figure in the politics of New South Wales between 1842 and 1850. The epitaph below, penned by a contemporary satirist of New South Wales, is quoted in John Manifold's *The Penguin Australian Song Book* (1964).

Here lies poor old Robert Lowe.
Where he's gone to I don't know:
If to the realms of peace and love,
Then farewell happiness above!
If, maybe, to the lower level,
We can't congratulate the devil.

298

Here lies the body of [say]
John Keown
Who was made up of odds
and ends:
He was nobody's enemy
but his own.
And he had no friends.

Creeve Roe

From the Sydney *Bulletin* (1890s) and reproduced in Patricia Rolfe (Ed.)
Clotted Rot for Clots and Rotters (1980)

MARCUS CLARKE

Nineteenth century novelist, Marcus Clarke (1846–1881), author of *For the Term of His Natural Life* (1874), died a bankrupt. The following notice was pinned at the Yorick Club (Melbourne), which he helped to bring into existence in 1868. Quoted in the Melbourne *Herald* (July 30, 1981).

Mr Marcus Clarke died suddenly yesterday (August 2) leaving a wife and six children — and nothing else.

OH, HENNESSEY!

Epitaph in the old cemetery at Bunnerong (NSW), long since demolished. The young lady whose death it commemorated was knocked down and killed by a horse and sulky driven by a local publican named Hennessey.

Oh, Hennessey you did me kill
And would not pay the doctor's bill.

CHILDREN FIVE

These words are said to have been carved on a tombstone in Mount Gambier (SA) cemetery.

Here lies the mother of children five,
Of whom two are dead and three alive;
Those that are dead preferring rather
To die with mother than live with father.

SAM BODIN

Mythology has it that the following epitaph was once to be seen in the Williamstown (Vic.) cemetery; but a number of other localities have also been named. If it does exist, it is an imitation of the words composed for his tombstone by Abraham Newland, one-time cashier of the Bank of England.

Beneath this stone Sam Bodin lies;
No one laughs and no one cries.
Where he's gone, and how he fares,
No one knows, and no one cares.

WRONGED

In Memory of   , who has been circumvented of his just and legal property, prosecuted by wilful and corrupt perjury, returned guilty by an infamous and bigoted jury for being a sincere patriot, and sentenced wrongfully by the laws of the land.

MAN'S BEST FRIEND

Erected in grateful remembrance of my faithful dog Fido, who died on March 28, 1904. A patient partner during 10 years of Life's journey, who had eaten the same bread with me and was to me a friend. The more I know of men the more I admire dogs. — W. Webb.

EPITAPH FOR A SETTLER

He revelled 'neath the moon,
He slept beneath the sun,
He lived a life of going-to-do,
And died with nothing done.

John Norton

ON THE DEATH OF VICTOR DALEY

There's nothing decent or dignified about a drunkard. Generally, he's a failure, a fool and a fraud. A drunkard is not an edifying spectacle either in poetry or politics. He's better dead and his death is not to be made a pretext for dropping dollops of delirious doggerel upon his coffined clay. Because a man has boozed and bummed about from bar to brothel is no reason why he should be proclaimed an immortal god. . . .

Ernest G. Moll

AT THE GRAVE OF A LAND-SHARK

From T. O'Dwyer and N. Morrison (Eds.) *The Sound of Poetry* (1968).

There was no land, they used to tell,
Old Miller couldn't trade or sell;
A clever man! I wonder how
He'll turn the lot he's stuck with now!

Bruce Dawe

AT SHAGGER'S FUNERAL

From Bruce Dawe, *Sometimes Gladness* (1978).

At Shagger's funeral there wasn't much to say
That could be said
In front of his old mum—she frightened us, the way
She shook when the Reverend read
About the resurrection and the life, as if
The words meant something to her, shook, recoiled,
And sat there, stony, stiff
As Shagger, while the rest of us, well-oiled,
Tried hard to knuckle down to solemn facts,
Like the polished box in the chapel aisle
And the clasped professional sorrow, but the acts
Were locked inside us like a guilty smile
That caught up with us later, especially when
We went round to pick up his reclaimed Ford,

ELEGY IN A COUNTRY CHURCHYARD

CASUAL VISITOR: *Who is that grave for, my good man?*
OLD SEXTON: *Old Sheepwash—owned the whole district purty nigh; died this mornin'.*
CASUAL VISITOR: *What complaint?*
OLD SEXTON: *Oh, there ain't no complaint. Everybody is puffickly satisfied.*

The old shag-wagon, and beat out the dust
From tetron cushions, poured
Oil in the hungry sump, flicked the forsaken
Kewpie doll on the dash-board,
Kicked hub-caps tubercular with rust.

The service closed with a prayer, and silence beat
Like a tongue in a closed mouth.
Of all the girls he'd loved or knocked or both,
Only Bev Whiteside showed—out in the street
She gripped her hand-bag, said, 'This is as far
As I'm going, boys, or any girl will go,
From now on.'

                        Later, standing about
The windy grave, hearing the currawongs shout
In the camphor-laurels, and his old lady cry
As if he'd really been a son and a half,
What could any of us say that wasn't a lie
Or that didn't end up in a laugh
At his expense—caught with his britches down
By death, whom he'd imagined out of town?

Hal Porter ·

THE MARRIED COUPLE

This poem is one of Hal Porter's 'Graveyard poems' (biographies of the imagined
dead) and records a marriage that never 'lived'.
From Hal Porter, *In an Australian Country Graveyard and Other Poems* (1974).

They rendered what was due, not one tithe more:
The grandee manner, the unriven mind;
Bred enough proper sons—to that resigned
More to prove usual than to hint desire.

Not tied by love but land, they aged while young
From public wearing, without smiles or frowns,
Ancestral leavings, wealth, those weighty crowns—
She queen of caution, he a wary king.

The sons, the world, admired—and ceased there
As sensing warmth's withdrawal, coolness meant

To show them free of unforeseen event,
Perfected, some hard absence at the core.

Their smiles resembled others', yet not quite:
Neither to palliate nor patronise
Theirs fell just short. Locked doors behind those eyes
Hid shut-mouth captives overspent with hate.

Alone in private night, teeth bared to wound,
They balked; like turnkeys, granted hate no pass,
Loving like mimics in a looking-glass,
From themselves severed, to each other blind.

Their statues waltzed at balls, or side by side
Spanked in a landau, letting all perceive
Her hand the seeming heart upon his sleeve —
Rift never left for rumour to intrude.

To lookers-on such warranties of love
Seemed, in their keeping, love's own monument
Whose gloss the years could never dull or dent.
He died. All wondered that she still could live.

She lived for years, elusive, duty done,
Sealed in equivocation. At the last,
Inspired to break truth's long fatiguing fast,
She cried, 'I hate him. Bury me alone.'

To this insuavity sons must sham deaf.
They buried her beside him. Someone came
To carve a stone with decades of her fame,
And in two words exposed it: *Loving Wife*.

Within a chiselled rose-wreath hand clasps hand,
Stone trapped in stone, the costly roses stone.
Below, teeth bared, they lie once more alone,
From themselves severed, to each other blind.

IN LOVING MEMORY OF MYSELF

The Melbourne *Age* asked several Australians to write their own obituaries. Here are
a few extracts from how certain of those people would like history to remember them.
Quoted in the Melbourne *Age* (April 11, 1981).

CENSORED FOR
THE LAST TIME

From the Melbourne *Age* (April 11, 1981)

Barry Humphries

WIT

[With reference to Sir Barry's last show, *Tears Before Bedtime*] Our quondam critic Ms Bronwyn Praxitiles was perhaps less than generous when she referred to Sir Barry's final offering as 'arguably, the sad, incoherent, and more often than not inaudible ramblings of a self-indulgent has-been'. It is true that Sir Barry, at that late stage in his career, and though still in robust mental health, was unable to mount the stage unassisted, and that his once popular turn 'Dame Edna' had become a repulsive hag which filled his dwindling audiences with awe and revulsion rather than mirth . . .

Barry McKenzie, Sir Les Patterson, and his other scabrous attacks on the integrity of the Australian working class ethic, however, earned him the ultimate disfavor of the authorities, and his continued reluctance to accept the title 'King of Moomba' finally forced him into permanent exile abroad . . .

When one thinks of the giant strides Australian entertainment has taken since Humphries' day, viz the Sir Norman Gallagher Omega site strikers relief massage-parlor and casino complex, it is hard to imagine what relevance old entertainers like Humphries and his ilk would have to 21st century audiences.

Sir Barry was knighted by King Charles III for his services to the British Gladiolus Society, and is survived by innumerable wives, great-grandchildren and creditors.

Phillip Adams

SOCIAL OBSERVER

Obituaries are official portraits in oily words instead of oils. A few flattering phrases that produce a stiff, academic likeness devoid of the blemishes that besmirch the best of us, let alone the Dorian Greys of politics and public life.

But there are some people who are so beyond the pale that their passing is noted with sonofabituaries, warts-and-all, boots-and-all comments on their passing. The last word on

Adams could be found within this bulging file, and it wasn't pretty reading. An account of an *ancien terrible* who held nothing sacred except cynicism, a mean-spirited misanthrope who wrote sordid articles and vulgar films. But that, of course, was hundreds of years ago, back in the 20th century.

Fred Daly

POLITICIAN

Frederick Michael Daly was one of those rare characters who although lacking the academic achievements and charisma of an Evatt or Menzies, lasted longer in the Australian Parliament than either of them.

Like his great friend, former Prime Minister Gough Whitlam, he was modest, retiring and knew his limitations. With this modesty came the realisation that, first of all, he was lucky to have ever been elected. And, secondly, while ever he lived he knew he would be looked upon as a person 'who didn't have many brains but knew how to use the few he had'. And survive he did, for more than thirty-two years.

Blessed with a rather quiet and retiring disposition, Mr Daly (known as Fred) soon realised that there was a place for humor among the rare species who inhabit the Corridors of Power. By close observation and study of that great humorist, story teller and sparkling political entrepreneur Malcolm Fraser, he developed a great sense of humor. His ability to lay his opponents in the aisles with repartee, scorn and ridicule stood out like the squire of Nareen.

Then, of course, Fred Daly was a religious man. Like Premier Bjelke-Petersen from the deep North he applied the Scriptures to his politics. He 'did unto others as they would do unto him'—only he did it earlier and more often. This approach was basic to survival and Fred Daly followed the scriptural teachings to the letter.

The immortal words of his friend, former Senator Patrick Kennelly, were indelibly recorded in his memory: 'In politics you can have the arguments but give me the numbers'. Practical and down to earth, he never forgot this logic while wiser men came and went.

308

Illustration by Melbourne artist, David Lancashire

Now that he is dead—or 'passed on' as they say in Parliament, where no one ever dies—politicians will rise in their places and intone all those pious sentiments which would have been so welcome in life but only happen in death. But perhaps one day or during a dreary night as the debates drag on in the House, and sleepy members long for the sittings to end, there will be a nostalgic murmur from some political friend or foe of long ago . . . 'Give us this day our Daly Fred.'

13

HYPOCRITICAL HUMBUG

Pharisees, Philistines and Like Phenomena

Victor Daley

A SELF-MADE MAN

It was his boast that he began
  His life in squalid ignorance,
  To learn he never had a chance
  (He seemed to think it a romance),
    This Self-Made Man.

Then when upon his chin the down
  Commenced to show, across the seas
  He came, his native land to please,
  And landed in 'the colonies'
    With half-a-crown.

And after forty years or so
  Of playing at the griping game
  A full-blown Fatman he became;
  Yet still he had the very same
    Half-crown to show.

And so he rose to wealth and power
  On that half-crown—'twas ever thus—
  While we, who have no overplus
  Of coin—it would have lasted *us*,
    Say, half-an-hour.

Vast-paunched, with pride-congested head,
  He'd rise at banquets—chiefly free—
  And tell this yarn unceasingly
  Till all who heard it wished that he
    Would drop down dead.

He walked about, as in a trance,
  Self-hypnotised by his own worth—
  His waistband girdled all on earth
  He cared for—'twas a goodly girth
    Of arrogance.

He died, as even Fatmen do
  (Thank Heaven!) and heaved a husky sigh
  As though to say, 'Poor world—good-bye!

I know that you will miss me—I
  Feel sad for you!'

And when before the Judgment Seat
  He came, no whit abashed was he,
But said to his Creator—'We,
  O Lord, I reckon, will agree—
    Our views will meet.'

'How?' said the Lord, 'presumptuous clod!'
  He answered—'Thus our cases fit—
A self-made Man am I, to wit,
And you, Lord, are, you must admit,
  A Self-Made God.'

Thomas E. Spencer

JAMES TWYCER

Thomas Edward Spencer (1845–1910) is chiefly remembered for his comic verse,
notably 'How McDougall Topped the Score'. A strain of satire, and the sardonic,
runs through much of his work.

James Twycer is a citizen
  Who leads a spotless life;
He meets his bills with promptitude,
  And never beats his wife.
He never drinks, nor smokes, nor swears,
  His clothes are spick and span;
In fact, he's an example
  Of a thorough business man.

He's known throughout the city
  As a great philanthropist;
In every public charity
  His name is on the list;
He waxes fat 'neath Fortune's smile,
  (He never felt her frown),
No p'liceman ever took him up;
  No rogue e'er took him down.

James Twycer runs a factory
  On strictly moral lines,

313

Where, if a girl forgets herself,
  She pays for it in fines;
He takes the fines reluctantly,
  But some reward they bring,
For he spends them on his typewriter [typist]
  A sweetly prim young thing!

His honesty is so pronounced,
  It makes him sad to see
Dishonesty in other folks,
  No matter who they be;
His horror for a factory girl
  He can't find words to speak,
Who fails to keep respectable
  On sixty pence a week.

If people say he sweats his 'hands',
  Or has a sordid mind,
He points unto his typewriter,
  To whom he's wondrous kind!
Or, if they say his wealth is stained,
  He says it cannot be,
Because his name is on the list
  Of every charity.

So, when he takes his walks abroad
  Folks touch their hats to him;
He's the opulent James Twycer
  (No one cares to call him Jim!)
They feel that he will, by-and-bye,
  At Heaven's portal stand,
And overawe St Peter
  With his bank-book in his hand.

Victor Daley

THE PHARISEE

He did not stand with open palm,
  Hand-feeding Charity;
He did not raise the nasal psalm
  On Sabbath-days—not he!

When he went walking down the street,
  With men of high degree,
He stopped upon his way to meet
  And greet the like of me.

He did not care for praise or pelf,
  Such meanness he despised;
He would not advertise himself—
  Yet he was advertised.

He never spoke an unctuous grace
  When friends at meals he met,
But Benediction on his face,
  Shone like an omelette.

In King Street, down below the Court,
  He used to take his stand—
This Gentleman of Good Report,
  This Man of Open Hand.

The Wreck, unshaved, unclean, unkempt—
  The brilliant man sunk low,
Would find the friend of whom he dreamt
  In Mr ——— So-and-So.

He did not care for praise or pelf,
  Nor blame that poor man's vice—
But gave him fourpence for himself—
  With half-an-hour's advice.

He did not play a solemn part,
  His style was frank and free—
And yet, somehow, I knew at heart
  He was a Pharisee.

Victor Daley

OF JAMES N. BRUNKER

From *Victor Daley* (Australian Poets series, 1963).

A pious statesman! Phoenix rare
  In any time or clime!
He makes men wish that Virtue were
  A punishable Crime.

The *Lone Hand*
OF SELF-RIGHTEOUSNESS

Quoted in the *Lone Hand* (July 1, 1907).

There are none so objectionable as the unobjectionable.

Anon
WOWSERS

From the Melbourne *Argus* (March 25, 1911).

> For six days long they lie and cheat,
>   And on the seventh at church they meet
> To render to the Lord their God
>   A threepenny bit, with a holy nod;
> And then they part with an unctuous smile
>   And a prayer to prosper the next week's guile.

F. J. Mills
ON SELF-RIGHTEOUSNESS

From 'The Twinkler' (F. J. Mills), *Square Dinkum* (1917).

Nobody is more nauseating than the self-made man who is made of self.

Vincent Buckley
NEUTRALIST

The ache of violence is not for him.
Other men may faint under the waves
of blood, or history, or self. He swims
A canting backstroke near to shore.

Only the ebb-tide makes him flap and sweat.
His great ambition: not to be swept out
from the soft uplifting swell to where the net
the bones break in the living roar.

OF UMPIRES AND SLOW HORSES

The Sporting Sphere

'Why don't you buy a safety, Bill and give that wheel away?'
'High bikes like that are out of date,' said Charley Harkaway.

'I like high wheels,' said Billy Bike, 'On Africa's sunny shore,
You're good and safe. Hark! can that be a lion's fearful roar.'

With slashing tail, a lion ran, and with terrific bound—
He caught the little safety wheel, because 'twas near the ground.

Young Billy Bike made an escape, and sadly did relate,
How Charley, on the safety wheel, was eaten up in state.

From the Sydney *Bulletin* (1890s)

Bicycling News

A WARNING TO LADIES

Keith Dunstan in *Sports* (1973) explains that when the cycling craze started in the 1870s it was thought improper for the ladies to indulge in the sport. Cycling journals lamented the desertion of wives by their husbands, as the latter took to the countryside on wheels. One alternative was the tricycle sociable, designed for two. In 1883 the following poem appeared in *Bicycling News*:

Oh! Ladies, dear ladies, be cold as an icicle,
To each man who you fancy is fond of a tricycle,
Be deaf to his tender pathetic appeals
If he cherish a weakness for riding on wheels.
For oh! if you marry, beware of the day
When he'll mount on his wheels and be off and away;
And you'll pine and you'll fret in your bower alone,
And you'll see him afar like a king on his throne.
Then take warning by me and be cold as an icicle,
To a man who is guilty of riding a tricycle,
Except—and indeed, the exception is notable—
He will sell his old 'sulky' and purchase a Sociable.

Sydney Morning Herald

ON THE MELBOURNE CUP

From the *Sydney Morning Herald* of 1885 and quoted in Keith Dunstan, *Sports* (1973).

It is the worst occasion and cause for a national gathering, that is naturally allied to more that makes directly for human degradation than any other public sport or pastime that could be named. The spirit and incentive of gambling hangs upon its skirts and penetrates to its heart. Artless and glaring extravagance fattens upon its countless forms of trickery, and knavery finds encouragement in it.

Melbourne Punch

ON THE MELBOURNE CUP

These sour remarks from *Melbourne Punch* (October 30, 1890) are quoted in Keith Dunstan, *Sports* (1973).

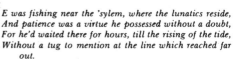

THE ANGLER
BY J·J·W

H E was fishing near the 'sylem, where the lunatics reside,
And patience was a virtue he possessed without a doubt,
For he'd waited there for hours, till the rising of the tide,
Without a tug to mention at the line which reached far
out.

And then it started raining, and the wind to blow began;
Still the angler waited calmly for the bite he couldn't get.
Then the 'sylem window opened, and a looney-looking
man

Asked politely of the angler, 'Have you got a bite, sir,
yet?'

'Not yet,' the angler answered. 'And how long have
you been there?'
Inquired the man at window, and the fisherman replied:
'Oh, just about three hours; I've got lots of time to
spare.'
And the looney promptly answered: 'Then you'd better
come inside!'

From the Sydney *Bulletin* (1880s) and reproduced in Patricia Rolfe (Ed.)
Clotted Rot for Clots and Rotters (1980)

322

A veil of gloom with RUIN painted on it in lurid letters covers the face of the land. Now with one sweep and final burst of the hook-nosed orchestra blaring out the odds, the dismal drop curtain has been drawn up and reveals—Victoria mad with delight once more at Flemington. We might say that £10 000 is a large premium for success in hippoculture. We are not absurd enough to suppose that a mere man, even if he have an immortal soul, is as good as a horse in this country.

Henry Varley

LORD CARBINE

Henry Varley, a preacher, was horrified at the public and press adulation of Donald Wallace and his horse Carbine, when the latter won the Melbourne Cup in 1890. Varley, in the name of the Anti-Gambling League, published a tract on the subject. Quoted in Keith Dunstan, *Sports* (1973).

MELBOURNE'S IDOL, LORD CARBINE.
HORSE WORSHIP AT FLEMINGTON.
'O BAAL, HEAR US!'
'O CARBINE, SAVE US!'

No time to lose. The Press hath given
    Golden applause; *Argus* and *Age*
Bend low in house of Donald Wallace
    And horseflesh passes human sage.
Go forth, ye citizens, to meet him
    Victoria's God await in line;
Ramage rides Carbine to glory
    Worship your idol horse Carbine.
O mighty crowd! expand your chests,
    In tulle and silk and race design;
Shout loud his praise, the winning horse
    Melbourne's new God, the Lord Carbine.

Edward Kinglake

ON AUSTRALIAN RULES FOOTBALL

From Edward Kinglake, *The Australian At Home* (1891).

Without wishing to give offence to anyone, I may remark

that it is a game which commends itself to semi-barbarous races.

Daniel Healey

ON CRICKET

From 'Whaks Li Kell' (Daniel Healey), *The Cornstalk, His Habits and Habitat* (1894).

Well, what is cricket after all,
    That so delights the masses?
Six bits of stick, a bat and ball,
    And two and twenty asses.

Yes, two and twenty donkey-men —
    I wish I could impound them;
Yes, asses I repeat again,
    With thousands more around them.

And then the asses bowl and bat,
    Knock down, or keep a wicket;
And run, and cheer, and shout, and that —
    Why, that's the game of cricket.

Henry Lawson

A LAND WHERE SPORT IS SACRED

From Henry Lawson, *A Son of Southern Writers*.

In a land where sport is sacred,
    Where the laborer is God,
You must pander to the people,
    Make a hero of a clod.

Mr Bill Woodfull

TO MR PELHAM WARNER

The following extract is from Keith Dunstan, *Sports* (1973).

[During the] 1932–3 'Body-line' tour of Australia tension rose so high it was almost as if a state of war existed between

A SANCTIFIED SPORT!

One English football team that visited Australia was captained by the Rev. Mullineux, an alert and enthusiastic athlete, who cannot swear, and has never been known to 'stoush' the umpire. The moral game of football was then for the first (and last) time played in Sydney somewhat as above.

Tennis among the naicest of Angledool in wayback NSW

From the Sydney *Bulletin* (1890s) and reproduced in Patricia Rolfe (Ed.)
Clotted Rot for Clots and Rotters (1980)

Australia and England . . . The real crisis came during the Third Test at Adelaide, when a ball from Larwood hit Woodfull over the heart. Oldfield was hit on the head. Later when the manager of the English team, Mr Pelham Warner, came to offer his sympathies, Mr Bill Woodfull gave his famous snub: I don't want to see you Mr Warner. There are two teams out there. One is trying to play cricket and the other is not.

C. J. Dennis

ENGLISH CRICKET

Lines by C. J. Dennis and quoted in Alec H. Chisholm, *The Making of the Sentimental Bloke* (1946).

Oh, to be in England
  Now that Summer's there!
For who plays the Game in England
  Is each morning well aware
That the cricket-pitch is water-logged,
And the in-field's wet and the out-field's bogged:
  For it's surely raining, anyhow,
  In England—now!

Jack 'Captain Blood' Dyer

ON COLLINGWOOD

Quoted in Keith Dunstan, *Sports* (1973).

I laboured the point of my hatred of Collingwood and it isn't a friendly dislike—as a club they rankle me. You couldn't like them, they think they are God's gift to football, they shun all outsiders and the only time I like to think of Collingwood is when they lose, because it hurts them so much . . . When they lose they never visit your rooms or congratulate you . . . I wouldn't drink anything they offered, you wouldn't know what they had done to it . . .

Archie Cameron

TO AN ENGLISH RUGBY CAPTAIN

Fred Daly recounts how, during the 1950s, as a matter of courtesy, he arranged for a visiting English Rugby League football team to be introduced to Archie Cameron in the Speaker's suite. Archie's opening question as he met the captain is quoted in Fred Daly, *From Curtain to Kerr* (1977).

What is a big healthy man like you doing in Australia kicking a bag of wind about instead of working in industry and helping to increase productivity and prosperity in Great Britain?

The Sydney *Daily Mirror*

TO THE ENGLISH PRESS

Keith Dunstan describes how in 1958, in the Second Test against England, Ian Meckiff took 6 wickets for 38 off 15.2 overs, and was accused by the English cricket writers of 'throwing'. The most devastating counter-attack came from Jim Mathers of Sydney's *Daily Mirror*.
Quoted in Keith Dunstan, *Sports* (1973).

You say Meckiff cheats . . . the umpire cheats . . . But that's merely cheating your English citizens back home. You should all be no-balled for squealing your pip-squeak jeremiads to your mis-informed readers, whose palates you no doubt tickle with your blubbering moan about your poor team of impoverished batsmanship being 'thrown out', 'chucked out', and 'cheated'. Why don't you be fair dinkum, as we say in Australia, and tell your English citizens your English team — a good bunch of blokes — just can't play cricket, are 'washed up', not 'thrown out', and you can't take it. Your hysterical and vile attack on Australian sportsmanship after your team was thrashed in the second Test probably arises from your peculiar but patriotic fanaticism. The English public has been served up with a highly seasoned salmagundi of excuses pretentiously presented as a reason for England's failure in the first and second Test matches.

Bruce Dawe

LIFE CYCLE

A poem by Bruce Dawe, dated 1967.
From Bruce Dawe, *Sometimes Gladness* (1978).

for Big Jim Phelan

When children are born in Victoria
they are wrapped in the club-colours, laid in beribboned cots,
having already begun a lifetime's barracking.

Carn, they cry, Carn . . . feebly at first
while parents playfully tussle with them
for possession of a rusk: Ah, he's a little Tiger! (And they
    are . . .)

Hoisted shoulder-high at their first League game
they are like innocent monsters who have been years
        swimming
towards the daylight's roaring empyrean

Until, now, hearts shrapnelled with rapture,
they break surface and are forever lost,
their minds rippling out like streamers

In the pure flood of sound, they are scarfed with light, a voice
like the voice of God booms from the stands
Ooohh you bludger and the covenant is sealed.

Hot pies and potato-crisps they will eat,
they will forswear the Demons, cling to the Saints
and behold their team going up the ladder into Heaven,

And the tides of life will be the tides of the home-team's
        fortunes
—the reckless proposal after the one-point win,
the wedding and honeymoon after the grand-final . . .

They will not grow old as those from more northern States
        grow old,
for them it will always be three-quarter-time
with the scores level and the wind advantage in the final term,

That passion persisting, like a race-memory, through the
    welter of seasons,
enabling old-timers by boundary-fences to dream of
    resurgent lions
and centaur-figures from the past to replenish continually
    the present,

So that mythology may be perpetually renewed
and Chicken Smallhorn return like the maize-god
in a thousand shapes, the dancers changing

But the dance forever the same—the elderly still
loyally crying Carn ... Carn ... (if feebly) unto the very end,
having seen in the six-foot recruit from Eaglehawk their
    hope of salvation.

Football Supporter

TO KEITH DUNSTAN

Keith Dunstan recounts that when he started an Anti-Football League in 1967 as a fun
thing to raise money for charity, he received a number of hostile letters.
From Keith Dunstan, *Sports* (1973).

If you and other fairies like you don't like Australian Rules
football then why don't you go and live in Sydney, go and
live anywhere, and leave the place to decent people who like
it.

Anon

THE SEVEN AGES OF THE AUSTRALIAN MALE

Dr A. W. Willee, Director of the Physical Education Department at the University of
Melbourne, commenced a lecture to the Eighteenth Australian Dental Congress with
the following poem.
From the *Australian Dental Journal* (August, 1967) and reproduced with the permission
of the National Heart Foundation of Australia.

(With apologies to Wm Shakespeare)

At first the youngster,
Nourished and cared for with his mother's love,
Active from dawn to dusk in thoughtless health,

'NO! DON'T TELL ME — THE INDEFATIGABLE,
UNBEATABLE, DOMINATING, FURIOUS,
INVINCIBLE HEROES GOT KNOCKED OFF...!

From the Melbourne *Herald* (September 5, 1981)

And then the youth—a surfie with his surfboard,
Or, say, a football hero, stern in training,
Eating lean steaks, eschewing wild excess,
Still vigorous and strong. And then the lover,
Wedded at last, who thinks his heart is only
The seat of his affections. Soon he merges
Into the husband, loafing around at night,
Watching his action on a TV screen.
And then the family man—his little woman
Delights in setting lavish meals before him.
And so he plays his part. The sixth age comes,
When, far from lean, this sandalled swelling goon,
Driving his car, forgetting use of legs,
Eats heartily, not well, until his waist
Is double what it should be. Last scene of all
May end his strange eventful history,
When, still not old, but far too fat, he snores,
Sans sense, sans health, sans looks, sans everything.

James Murray

ON AUSTRALIAN RULES FOOTBALL

Quoted in McArdle and Fenton, *Australian Walkabout* (1968).

Australian Rules football might best be described as a game
devised for padded cells, played in the open air.

Percy Cerutty

ON WOMEN IN SPORT

This serve against women athletes was delivered by coach, Percy Cerutty, in 1970.
Quoted in Frank Keating, *Caught By Keating* (1979).

Women in sport? Who wants straight-legged, narrow-hipped,
big-shouldered, powerful Sheilas, aggressive and ferocious
in mind and body?

George Johnston

ON FOOTBALL FEVER

Author George Johnston's summary of Australian Rules football was quoted by the late Professor Ian Turner at his 1971 Ron Barassi Memorial lecture.
From Keith Dunstan, *Sports* (1973).

In Melbourne, football is a fever disease like recurrent malaria and evidently incurable. For six or seven months of the year a mad contagion runs through the Press, TV, radio and everyday life. Melbourne has no summer — only a period of hibernation between football seasons.

Teddy Tinling

ON MARGARET COURT

This comment made in 1972 on tennis star Margaret Court, is quoted in Frank Keating, *Caught By Keating* (1979).

Margaret Court plays in such run-of-the-mill garments. I reproach her for it and decry her influence on the game and attitude to the public. The stars who don't care a damn how they look are amateurs.

Keith Dunstan

ON THE VFL TRIBUNAL

From Keith Dunstan, *Sports* (1973).

Now tribunal rights are always melodramatic affairs and the crowd turns out in the manner of the 1840s when it was the custom to pay one's respects at a public execution. The entertainment benefits to be gained from a public hanging and a football tribunal are not dissimilar. In the 1970s it is done with an all-star cast of press, radio, lights and outside broadcast vans which beam the triumphs of the innocent and the agonies of the guilty, to every home in Melbourne.

From the Melbourne *Herald* (April 13, 1981)

Football Spectator

TO AN OFFENDING PLAYER

This outburst by a football spectator at a St Kilda–Richmond match at Moorabbin was recorded by Professor Ian Turner in 1973.
Quoted in Bill Hornadge, *The Australian Slanguage* (1980).

You rotten, bloody, poofter, commo, mongrel bastard.

Peter Smark

ON MELBOURNE FOOTBALL FANATICISM

From the Melbourne *Age* (March 31, 1973).

. . . the mindless, numbing fatuity of a Melbourne football weekend, from first drooling over selection of teams to the final clutch of clichés on Monday morning.

Colin Thiele

THE OVAL BARRACKER

From Garth Boomer and Morris Hood (Eds.), *The Endless Circle* (1973).

Down at the oval, with stentorian force,
One hears his passion shout.
No compromise could ever calm that cry—
He's out! he's damn well out!

When the long sunshine sleeps across the grass
And the day's pulse-beats drag,
He slaps their noon-gold torpor with the clout
Of Get a bag! Ahhr, get a bloody bag!

And when the streaming showers lunge and dart
And football games bog into muddy farces,
He and the winter both have chilling tongues—
For God's sake, umpire, use your bloody glasses!

And though the winds rub ice across his face,
He spurns the coddling touch of coat and rug:

He needs no comfort but the heat of wrath:
For Chris' sake get a telescope, you mug!

Hawks up abuse above the crowd's wild roar,
Screws out excruciating venom through the din,
Till the red veins avow his heart's committal—
Hell's teeth, umpire, screw your eyeballs in!

Beats at the pickets with his passion's fist,
Chokes and contorts to see such wrong ignored,
Hurls in a final paroxysm his contempt—
Hellfire, ump, your eyes are up your broad!

Far down the years, the symbol of his age,
Shirt-sleeved, splenetic, wrapped in agony,
He flings his cry in Corybantic rage—
The great dumb bastard couldn't even see!

Kerry Packer

TO POTENTIAL RECRUITS FOR HIS
WORLD SERIES CRICKET

When Tony Greig introduced the world to Australian entrepreneur Kerry Packer in
1977, it was predicted that cricket was never going to be the same again!
Quoted in Frank Keating, *Caught By Keating* (1979).

Come on, we are all harlots—it is all a matter of price. How
much do you fellows want?

The London *Observer*

AUSTRALIAN PASSION!

From an article in the London *Observer* in 1978 and quoted in Frank Keating, *Caught
By Keating* (1979).

When we were living in Sydney a friend told me that one
night, while she and her husband were making love, she
suddenly noticed something sticking in his ear. When she
asked him what it was he replied 'Be quiet! I'm listening to
the cricket.'

Danny in *The Club*

TO FOOTBALL SPECTATORS

The following words are spoken by the character of Danny in David Williamson's play concerned with Australian Rules football, *The Club* (1978).

If I'm out there risking a fractured skull or a ruptured spleen for the amusement of a pack of overweight drunks in the grandstand bar then I want to get paid for it.

Jeff Stollmeyer

ON KERRY PACKER

When Kerry Packer introduced World Series Cricket he incurred the wrath of many people in the cricket world. Jeff Stollmeyer, West Indies cricket official, reportedly made this comment in 1979.
From Frank Keating, *Caught By Keating* (1979).

Kerry Packer has made lifelong friends turn into enemies.

Barry Dickins

A WIN FOR THE LIONS

This amusing football anecdote is an extract from an article by journalist Barry Dickins.
From the Melbourne *Age* (April 9, 1981).

But many was the time we watched the old Lions lose to whoever from the bridge over the North Fitzroy briquette yard at the old ground and barracked ourselves hoarse, or perhaps donkey would be a better word because we followed Fitzroy through 10 000 losses straight.

Not that they were a bad team. They were just poor, that's all. They just couldn't seem to be able to afford to win. Anyway, Carn the mighty Roys!

A grease and oil change, a million bucks and better pies, and who knows? They might beat the Combined Briquette Workers, best of three. Those were the days when Kevin Murray (Old Gummy Shark) was the indomitable captain, or was it Butch Gale? As I said, it's been a long while. Anyway.

I still love the game, and last Saturday saw a miracle. It was like meeting Christ in Frankston. The Mighty Lions won. Had done Melbourne. At VFL Park at Waverley. I was so happy I ate my pies right through the bag. Six tins and a win! Too much!

Triumphant English Cricket Follower

TO A MELBOURNE STOCKBROKER'S OFFICE

During the sound defeat of the Australians in the 1981 Cricket Test in England, a Melbourne stockbroker's office received not a wave of buying orders, but a poem, from their London agent-brokers.
Reported in the Melbourne *Age* (July 22, 1981).

> After many weeks of stick,
> During which we've felt quite sick,
> At last, today, your justly dues—
> A total thrashing for Kim Hughes.
> For now it comes our turn to scoff
> At all you strines who wrote us off.
> When next you think of bashing poms,
> Please don't forget our Willis bombs.
> So, colonial cousins all
> Do in future watch the ball.
> With three more matches yet to play,
> You'll have to sharpen up—or pray.

Lawrence Money

AND SO IT CAME TO A SHORT PASS

Journalist Lawrence Money takes a satirical look at football.
From the Melbourne *Herald* (August 3, 1981).

And it came to pass that the worshippers of Foo Tee congregated on the seventh day to offer up praise to the leather icon.

And they gathered at a sacred site where their ancestors

338

had gathered before them—but never before for a trial seventh-day service.

And the umpire said: 'Let there be play.' And there was play. And the worshippers gave thanks.

Then the icon soared into the heavens and the Crusaders from the Hill of Wind and the Park Victoria lifted up their arms and took unto themselves many screamers.

And the umpire said: 'Thou shalt not infringe' and gave the frees to certain Crusaders among them.

And lo, the worshippers spake unto the umpire with words of wrath, saying: 'MUG! GALAH! WHITE MONGREL!'

Full thirty minutes the battle raged then the two high priests came forth, one to each team, and spake unto them, saying:

'Go out and shark ye the packs, picketh thee up the crumbs and create thine own opportunities up forward.

'For whosoever among thee that does not do these things, then shall he suffer on the track of tan.'

Thus it was that the Crusaders from the Hill of Wind heeded these words—the brothers Madden, Terry of Daniher and the rest—and really put in and won the hard icon.

And the icon was elevated through the tall timbers to bring up the twin calicos.

And it was 67 plays 64 on the Mocopan scoreboard.

And when the horn finally sounded, the black and white walls came tumbling down.

And the red and black Crusaders threw up their arms in joy and ascended another rung up the ladder to Celestial Bliss.

Robert Coleman

TO THE JOGGERS

From an article by journalist Robert Coleman in the Melbourne *Herald* (August 8, 1981).

Of all the hackneyed clichés that have found their way into the language, 'fun run' must be one of the worst—and also the most contradictory.

How anybody can regard running as fun is beyond my comprehension.

I always thought the great compensation for reaching mature age was that you didn't have to run anywhere any more.

Barry Oakley

AUSSIE RULES

From an article in the Melbourne *Herald* (August 20, 1981).

You can watch Australian Rules in total comfort in Sydney ... Ten feet from the toilet, six feet from the fridge and beer, and you have it in front of you on television.

Robert Coleman

AUSTRALIAN BATSMEN

Journalist Robert Coleman made the following comments with regard to the Australian batting collapse in the 1981 Test against England.
From the Melbourne *Herald* (August 22, 1981).

You can say what you like about our Test batsmen—but at least they're improving.

Just look at the results: 111 at Headingley, 121 at Edgbaston and 130 at Old Trafford.

See? Getting better all the time!

With a run-inflation rate like that, in a few seasons they'll be able to put together a score that Bradman, on a good day, would have belted up by himself.

Tony Jewell

PRE-MATCH CONFIDENCE

In an interview with the Melbourne *Herald* Richmond coach, Tony Jewell, spoke of his team's determination to beat Carlton.
Reported in the Melbourne *Herald* (August 28, 1981).

If beating Carlton means getting in (to the five), I'd stake my

'...AND DELIVER US FROM VFL SUNDAY FOOTBALL, AMEN...!'

From the Melbourne *Herald* (October 31, 1981)

341

life on that one. It won't matter if we break legs, arms, heads, anything to get there . . .

Garrie Hutchinson

PARK THE FINAL STRAW

The intention of moving the Grand Final away from the MCG to VFL Park in 1984, has come in for considerable criticism from all sides of the football spectrum. Garrie Hutchinson made this comment in the Melbourne *Age* (September 1, 1981):

The Orwellian threat to move the Grand Final away from the MCG is fairly typical of things Victorian—we are, after all, a State rich in tradition and history, a tradition and history of wrecking it, of those in power being blissfully unaware of what makes the place worth living in.

The *Australian*

WHARFIES SNOOKERED BEHIND THE AMBER

When the Australian Snooker Championships were held at the Waterside Workers Club in Brisbane a somewhat incongruous scene ensued.
From a report in the *Australian* (September 12, 1981).

Sinking shot took on a different meaning for Brisbane's wharfies this week.

Instead of knocking back Johnny **Walkers**, the city's waterside workers intricately lined up **snooker** shots and sank coloured balls, as opposed to amber pots.

And despite this distaste for what they wryly called 'culture', the wharfies admitted they'd have to 'put up with the "bloody pansy game"'.

Queensland has been hosting the Australian Snooker Championships, being held, of all places, at the Waterside Workers Club in Brisbane.

So at the trial run before the first competition, it was stubbies, blue singlets and thongs, versus three-piece suits, polished leather shoes and bow ties.

For the elegant snooker players it was a pleasant change, for the wharfies 'just a chance to perve at pansies' and 'a bloody waste of serious drinking time'.

From the Melbourne *Herald* (September 2, 1981)

But the blue-singlet set, led by Ted the Pole, willingly offered some unqualified approval as well as much advice.

'Line up the shot properly, ya fool,' was a common cry from Ted as he spilled beer on the deep green felt.

'Give it a good whack,' was Ted's second favorite cry.

The Melbourne *Herald*

OF JOHN McENROE AND HIS ILK

These lines on American tennis star, John McEnroe, are from the Melbourne *Herald* (October 26, 1981).

Thousands of kids looking to tennis as a career are worshipping heroes who are Pied Pipers of Poison.

Abuse the umpires, smash your racquet, scowl, swear, and forget that it is only a game.

Superbrat John McEnroe is the most embarrassing thing and the worst influence to hit top tennis in the history of the game.

He makes Ilie Nastase look like a choirboy.

Vitas Gerulaitis

ON AUSTRALIAN TENNIS UMPIRES

In the final of the Miracle Indoor Tennis Championship at Frankston (Vic.) American player, Vitas Gerulaitis, walked off the court after a dispute over the umpiring, and thereby forfeited the match to Australian, Peter McNamara. These comments by Gerulaitis were reported in the Melbourne *Age* (October 26, 1981), on the day following the incident.

I'd rather get hit on the head with rocks thrown by the fans in Rome than go through this.

The officials are not biased, they're just bad. I've seen Australian players get the shaft here as well. I've got nothing against Australia. I love the people and the place, it's just the officials.

These are the worst conditions I've ever played under. I don't care about being beaten, but I don't want to be beaten by the umpires. That's not fair.

From the Melbourne *Herald* (October 22, 1981)

From the Melbourne *Herald* (October 26, 1981)

John Kiely

OH, FOR THE PACE OF THOSE GOOD OLD DAYS

From the Melbourne *Age* (October 29, 1981).

Joggers? Oscar Wilde would have called them the ineffable in pursuit of the unattainable.

Once, decent people came to beaches in Sunday best, with hampers, parasols and slim volumes of poetry. Now the denuded foreshores are mere training tracks for elephantine herds of joggers; footballers, cricketers, blubbery middle-aged executives, tubby housewives dragging near-choked, flailing terriers in their wake. All jogging, jogging, jogging.

One goes on to the balcony in March hoping to see a school of frolicking dolphin, or gannets slicing into the sea in search of dinner: instead there is this heaving sea of breasts, bellies and buttocks, an appalling pulsation of pyknics.

Why do they do it? A fifty-year-old neighbor every morning staggers by across his personal Sahara, short of breath, leaden of limb, grey of face. Perhaps he has been told that he has a ricketty heart, and has decided to go out heroically, a Pheidippides of Marathon, 2 500 years too late.

Bud Collins

AN EXTINCT RACE

This comment by Bud Collins, United States tennis writer, was quoted in the Melbourne *Age* (October 31, 1981).

In this era of higher pressure, highest stakes and highly-blown tempers, we could use the resurrection of an extinct species called the Aussies.

The Melbourne *Herald*

ON JOHN McENROE

This comment from journalist Barry Dickins comes from an article, 'Tennis! It just isn't cricket', in the Melbourne *Herald* (November 14, 1981).

Someone ought to use [McEnroe] as a net for the Croatian army mixed doubles. That'd sort The Brat out.

SOME OTHER MALICIOUS MOMENTS

From R. Barassi, *Australian Football Stories* (1981).

There was the dour, dry coach who was told just after his side had been thrashed that he had to meet the Queen. 'Why do I need to meet another one,' he snarled, 'I've just been with eighteen of them.'

.   .   .

Little Carlton rover Syd Jackson, one of the finest Aboriginal players to grace the turf, was a master of the smart reply. When he was walking from the ground one day a Collingwood player snarled at him, 'You yellow little mongrel.' Syd replied, 'You're colour blind, aren't you?' and received a swift punch in the eye for his trouble. Still not lost for a word, Syd put on his injury report that he was suffering from a 'white eye'!

Laurie Nash, South's super player, had a traditional rival in Melbourne's star forward Jack Mueller. After one torrid game Mueller, who had had four quarters of frustration, spat out at Nash. 'You kicked me out there today, Nash.' Laurie, never at a loss, shot back, 'And that was the only kick you got all day.'

.   .   .

Brownlow Medal winner Alan Ruthven once hit a bad spell with Fitzroy when he seemed to be taking very few kicks and hardly any marks. One day, he managed to take a mark in front of the stand and even the Fitzroy supporters shouted in derision as he held the ball aloft. It had been a clear, uncontested mark, so the Baron was more than a little surprised when the umpire came over and took the ball for a bounce up. When he challenged the umpire, he said cheerfully, 'You wouldn't want to spoil a good mark by kicking it, would you?'

. . .

Coach to his players after a particularly badly-played first half: 'Once upon a time,' he said mildly, 'when I was a very young boy, my mother bought me eighteen red and blue wooden soldiers. I learned to love and know each and every one of them. I used to play with them for hours on end. I really loved them, even though all they did was to stand in the same spot looking woodenly ahead without doing anything. Finally the sad day came when I lost them. I searched for them everywhere without ever seeing them again. Until today,' he thundered, 'WHEN I'VE GOT THE WHOLE BLOODY PACK OF YOU BACK AGAIN.'

. . .

Murray 'The Weed' Weideman was having a hard time with one of his supposedly fabulous players.
    'If you go on like this I'm going to give you an open clearance,' snarled Weed.
    'You can't, you haven't anybody to fill my vacancy,' snapped the player.
    'You wouldn't leave one,' fired back Weideman.

. . .

When Alex Jesaulenko took over as coach of businessman Lindsay Fox's St Kilda, a wag in the crowd yelled out to Alex, 'If it doesn't work out, you'll spend summer driving a truck with a sign "You are passing another Jezza".'

. . .

Player to another who made a habit of belting him over the head every time they went for the ball: 'Why don't you knock it right off? I certainly don't need it to play on a stupid bum like you!'

348

From Frank Keating, *Caught By Keating* (1979).

If the ILTF and the WCT were the Russians and the Americans we'd all be dead by now. (John Newcombe, 1971)

.   .   .

What is it, being a footballer? If you take away Match of the Day and the Press and the fans and the hangers-on, it's all very empty and lonely. (Rodney Marsh, 1971)

From the Melbourne *Herald* (August 10, 1981).

Melbourne would only have to have six accidents to put six goals on the board. (Jack Dyer)

From the Melbourne *Herald* (August 28, 1981).

Cloke has been back for two weeks after knee surgery, but I wouldn't back him to complete the course in a fun run. (Mike Sheahan on Richmond centre half-forward.)

ACKNOWLEDGEMENTS

My grateful thanks go to the following authors, owners of copyrights and publishers who have given permission to reproduce poetry, prose and illustrations in this book. Every effort has been made to trace the owners of copyrights and if any such have been inadvertently overlooked I ask their indulgence.

MR PHILLIP ADAMS for the extracts from his articles in the Melbourne *Age*.

ANGUS & ROBERTSON PUBLISHERS LTD for the poem 'The Australian Dream' from *Selected Poems* by David Campbell; the poems 'The Pleasure of Princes', 'The Kings' and 'Australia' from *Collected Poems 1930-1970* by A. D. Hope; the extract from 'Confessions of a Zombie' by A. D. Hope from *Native Companions*; the poem 'The Commercial Traveller's Wife' from *Bloodthirsty Bessie and Other Poems* by Ronald McCuaig; the poem 'At the Grave of a Land-Shark' from *Poems 1940-1955* by Ernest G. Moll; the poem 'The Utopia of Lord Mayor Howard' from *A Counterfeit Silence: Selected Poems of Randolph Stow*; the poem 'Bora Ring' from *Collected Poems 1942-1970* by Judith Wright.

AUSTRALIAN CONSOLIDATED PRESS for the two cartoons from the *Bulletin* issue of 20 October 1981, and the cartoons from the early Sydney *Bulletin*, reproduced from Patricia Rolfe (Ed.) *Clotted Rot For Clots and Rotters* (Wildcat Press 1980).

MS S. BAKER for the extract from *The Drum* by Sidney Baker.

PROFESSOR VINCENT BUCKLEY for his poems 'Secret Policeman' and 'Neutralist'.

MR NOEL COUNIHAN for his linocut *Parson 1932*, reproduced from Roger Butler, *Melbourne Woodcuts and Linocuts of the 1920s and 1930s*.

CURTIS BROWN (AUST) PTY LTD SYDNEY for the poem 'Full As A Boot' by A. D. Hope.

THE HON. FRED DALY A.O. for the extracts from his book *From Curtin to Kerr*.

MR JIM DAVIDSON for the extract from the article in *Meanjin Papers* (Vol. 3, No. 2, 1944).

MR GEOFFREY DUTTON for his poem 'Thoughts, Home From Abroad 1966'.

MR MAX HARRIS for the extract from his article 'Rhubarb Royalty' in the *Australian*.

The Melbourne HERALD for the cartoons, reproduced from the newspaper.

MR BILL HORNADGE for the poetry and prose extracts from *The Australian Slanguage*.

MR BARRY HUMPHRIES for his statements quoted in the Australian Press.

THE JACARANDA PRESS for the poems 'No More Boomerang', 'Dark Unmarried Mothers', 'Whynot Street', 'Intolerance', 'Colour Bar' and 'We Are Going' from *My People* by Kath Walker.

LARRY PICKERING ENTERPRISES PTY LTD for the cartoons by Larry Pickering from *A Decade Of Pickering*.

MR MIKE McCOLL JONES for the extracts from *My Funny Friends*.

MR DAVID LANCASHIRE for his illustration.

MR PETER LINDSAY for the extracts from *Addled Art* by Lionel Lindsay.

LONGMAN CHESHIRE PTY LTD for the poems 'A plea on behalf of a newly elected Politician', 'Life Cycle' and 'At Shagger's Funeral' by Bruce Dawe from *Sometimes Gladness* and the poem 'The Decay of Preaching' by Bruce Dawe from *Condolences of the Season*.

MR RANAN LURIE and ALAN FOLEY PTY LTD for Mr Lurie's cartoon.

MR MUNGO MacCALLUM for the extracts from his column, 'The Legislators', in the Melbourne *Age*.

THE MACMILLAN CO. OF AUSTRALIA PTY LTD for the extracts from *Sports* by Keith Dunstan.

MELBOURNE UNIVERSITY PRESS for the poems 'O'Flaherty to his Mistress', 'O'Flaherty Passing Through' and 'O'Flaherty

351

is asked to be Politically Active' by B. A. Breen from *Behind My Eyes*.

THE NATIONAL HEART FOUNDATION OF AUSTRALIA for the poem 'The Seven Ages of the Australian Male'.

MR PETER NICHOLSON for his cartoon from the Melbourne *Age*.

MR HAL PORTER for the poems 'Behind that Sun-splashed Tourist Poster' and 'The Married Couple'.

MR T. W. SHAPCOTT for his poem 'Three Kings Came'.

MR RON TANDBERG for his cartoons, reproduced from the Melbourne *Age*.

TAYLOR-TYPE PUBLICATIONS (AUSTRALIA) PTY LTD for the extracts from *Australian Football Stories* by Ron Barassi.

MR COLIN THIELE for the poems 'The Oval Barracker' and 'Bird in the Classroom'.

THOMAS NELSON AUSTRALIA for the extracts from *More Unspeakable Adams* by Phillip Adams.

UNIVERSITY OF QUEENSLAND PRESS for the extract from the poem 'A Hat in the Ring' from *Collected Verse* by J. S. Manifold.

UNIVERSITY OF WESTERN AUSTRALIA PRESS for the extract from the poem 'Bailiff' by Lee Knowles.

MR CHRIS WALLACE-CRABBE for the poems 'A Wife's Story' and 'Melbourne'.

352

INDEX

INDEX

354